Praise for *RatSnakes*

"Cefalu bares all and lays out the gritty and true life of an undercover agent and the workings of the ATF. A must-read for law enforcement and the public."
—Joe Pistone, former undercover FBI agent, alias "Donnie Brasco"

"The law enforcement undercover community is limited to those who are born with the ability to take on some of the most dangerous, 'up close and personal' assignments. In that select group, Vince Cefalu is one who stands out because of his bravery and his ability to walk undetected among the most hardened criminals."
—Joaquin "Jack" Garcia, former undercover FBI agent and New York Times bestselling author of *Making Jack Falcone*

"Vincent Cefalu is the real deal. In *RatSnakes*, he takes us on a wild ride through his dark world of paranoia, danger, fear, hard living, hard drinking, and the chase. In the end, it's a gripping story revealing how some of our most effective federal undercover agents earn their chops, make their living, and work to protect their fellow Americans in ways that usually go unrecognized."
—Sharyl Attkisson, host of *Full Measure* and former CBS investigative correspondent

"Retired ATF undercover agent Vince Cefalu has created a read that's going to leave readers with their mouths open. If you've never used the terms, 'oh my god,' 'holy shit,' or 'what the f*&%$,' *Ratsnakes* is going to introduce you to a new emotional feeling. It's not just about real world undercover operations; it's about the people and the agencies willing to operate behind enemy lines."
—William Queen, ATF special agent (retired) and *New York Times* bestselling author of *Under and Alone*

"With each page, Vincent Cefalu brings the heart-pounding reality of the street and tough undercover work to life. If you're looking for a read you won't be able to put down, this is it."
—Katie Pavlich, *New York Times* bestselling author of *Fast and Furious*, journalist, and editor of Townhall.com

RATSNAKES

RATSNAKES

Cheating Death by Living a Lie: Inside the
Explosive World of ATF's Undercover Agents
and How We Changed the Game

VINCENT A. CEFALU

BenBella Books, Inc.
Dallas, Texas

BenBella Books, Inc.
10440 N. Central Expressway, Suite 800
Dallas, TX 75231
www.benbellabooks.com
Send feedback to feedback@benbellabooks.com

Printed in the United States of America
10 9 8 7 6 5 4 3 2 1

Library of Congress Cataloging-in-Publication Data
Names: Cefalu, Vincent A., author.
Title: Ratsnakes : cheating death by living a lie . . . inside the explosive
world of ATF's undercover agents and how we changed the game / Vincent A.
Cefalu.
Description: Dallas, TX : BenBella Books, Inc., [2019] | Includes
bibliographical references and index.
Identifiers: LCCN 2018058142 (print) | LCCN 2019001375 (ebook) | ISBN
9781948836258 (electronic) | ISBN 9781946885968 (trade cloth : alk. paper)
Subjects: LCSH: Cefalu, Vincent A. | United States. Bureau of Alcohol,
Tobacco, and Firearms—Officials and employees—Biography. | Law
enforcement—United States—Biography.
Classification: LCC HV8144.B87 (ebook) | LCC HV8144.B87 C44 2019 (print) |
DDC 363.2092 [B] —dc23
LC record available at https://lccn.loc.gov/2018058142

Editing by Laurel Leigh
Copyediting by Scott Calamar
Proofreading by Lisa Story and Cape Cod Compositors, Inc.
Text design by Katie Hollister
Text composition by PerfecType, Nashville, TN
Cover design by Brian Barth
Printed by Lake Book Manufacturing

Distributed to the trade by Two Rivers Distribution, an Ingram brand
www.tworiversdistribution.com

Special discounts for bulk sales (minimum of 25 copies) are available. Please contact
bulkorders@benbellabooks.com.

A true dedication for this book would require fifty or more pages. To say I have been blessed to serve with the best our country has to offer would be an understatement.
To my mom and dad, who never left my side,
I love you and miss you.
To my wife, my ex-wives, and my children, who willingly backed the life I chose, I love you.
To every state, local, and federal cop I've ever served with,
Semper Fi, *this book is about and for you.*
Finally, to the country that allowed a seemingly average kid to rise from his youthful foolishness
to live his dream, I LOVE YOU. God bless America.

CONTENTS

CONTENTS

FOREWORD

If you believe what you see on television, undercover police work seems to be a glamorous occupation: pretty girls, plenty to drink, top-end cars, and lots of glitzy living. Written by one of the nation's premier undercover operatives, *RatSnakes* obliterates that Hollywood myth by taking you into the real world of undercover! You will learn what it takes to volunteer and be a member of this exclusive club of RatSnakes.

The Bureau of Alcohol, Tobacco, Firearms and Explosives (BATFE, most commonly referred to as ATF) is charged with the enforcement of our nation's firearm, alcohol, and explosives laws. While the alcohol side of ATF is mostly regulatory in operation, the firearms and explosives agents deal with the worst of the worst criminals. Where you find guns and explosives, you find drugs—a lethal combination!

In order to root out the vilest of the criminal element, unfortunately, good men and women must enter that dirty, grimy, underground world. Obviously, this is extremely dangerous work, and it also takes a toll on the agents and their families. Undercover work puts a strain on family relations that is unmatched, even in the military.

Vincent A. Cefalu pulls back the curtain on this profane, vulgar, and violent ecosphere. In this book, you will meet some of the top undercover agents in the United States, probably even in the world. Vince shares many of their stories with you. He also shares the ineptness of some of the, as he calls them, "empty suits" within the management chain at ATF: bosses more interested in their own selfish self-promotion than the reputations or the safety of the undercover agents who do the dirty work and make the arrests.

For example, you would think an agent who has been unlawfully ordered to install a wiretap has two choices. One, they can implement the wiretap and subject themselves to the laws governing the misuse of wiretaps; or, two, they can go up the chain of command to make their superiors aware of the unlawfulness of the tap. A normal person would expect upper management to discipline the commander making the order and, at the least, shake the agent's hand and say "thank you." That didn't happen! In one instance, the agent received direct discipline, a bad report was put in his file, and, worst of all, he was taken off the streets and condemned to a small office with nothing to do. This is but one sample of the corruptness of many in the middle-management levels at ATF.

Please do not interpret this as a condemnation of ATF, as the organization contains thousands of top-notch street agents and good management people. To the contrary, ATF is charged with the most difficult laws in our land to enforce. Overall, they do a good job. However, Congress has neglected its oversight duties and allowed bad practices to establish themselves.

A good example, familiar to the public, of Congress gone wrong was Operation Fast and Furious. Over 2,500 high-powered rifles were allowed to "walk" across the border from the United States into Mexico around 2009–10. This ill-devised plot was the brainchild of the management team in the Phoenix ATF office. In a series of televised hearings, Congressman Issa of California and Senator Grassley of Iowa spent many thousands, if not millions, of your tax dollars to determine who was at fault. They properly and accurately identified who was to blame. Some of these men had broken the law.

But when the TV lights were turned off and the cameras were gone, absolutely nothing happened to anyone. Those guilty were allowed to retire with their full pensions and benefits; one even secured a job as a consultant to ATF.

So what message does that send to the agency? In the country school that I come from, it says just go ahead and thumb your nose at Congress because they are not going to do anything to punish you.

In the interest of full disclosure, Vince and I are brothers-in-arms and great friends. A time long ago, back when we were called "police officers," and the term "cops" was considered demeaning and totally inappropriate, I served as a police officer in Tulsa, Oklahoma. Later, during my tenure in the US Congress, I was chairman of the Appropriations Subcommittee with jurisdiction over the Treasury Department. At the time, nearly 40 percent of federal law enforcement was under Treasury, including the United States Secret Service, Customs, and the Internal Revenue Service as well as the department's enforcement wings, the Federal Law Enforcement Training Center, Financial Crimes Network, and ATF. My tenure covered the time of the 1993 Waco, Texas, incident and the subsequent rebuilding of ATF.

When you finish reading *RatSnakes* you will, I hope, have an appreciation that you did not have before for the dedication to your safety of these unsung heroes of the dark alleys, smoke-filled biker bars, and run-down motels. I believe you will understand that these are people of high intelligence, many with advanced academic degrees, who prefer to fight criminals head-on rather than sit in nice, safe offices. They are people who have dedicated their lives to making a safer world for the rest of us.

Now it is time to turn the pages and get an up-close and personal view into a world that wants to destroy us, and the exceptional men and women who protect us from that fate. You are about to meet heroes that you never knew existed and who will continue their shadowy role in the world of undercover to protect you and your family.

A toast to the RatSnakes!

—Jim Lightfoot
Former six-term congressman,
US House of Representatives, from Iowa

DISCLAIMER

This book is based on notes and recollections of Vincent A. Cefalu. Some names and locations have been changed or omitted to protect the privacy of individuals. In passages containing dialogue, quotation marks are used when the author was reasonably sure that the speaker's words were close to verbatim and/or that the intended meaning of the speaker was accurately reflected.

· ·

TO KNOW THEM IS TO LOVE THEM. OR NOT.

The original rat snake is just that, a snake. It squeezes its prey to death, easily can be tamed, and eats vermin and other targets of opportunity. In the Wild West days, rat snakes were kept in jars, and, when circumstances dictated, these starving predators were released indoors. They would find and kill the enemy—in other words, eliminate rodents that had infested frontier homes. Once their purpose was served, they were recaptured and put out of sight in jars—until the next infestation.

This is much the same way ATF covert operatives are used. They are dispatched to infiltrate a sordid, blood-spattered, degraded world, dominated by characters accustomed to vulgarity and violence. Only those mentally resilient and clever enough can navigate their way inside this dangerously clandestine setting, and then survive in its confines while doing their jobs.

1

I should know. I spent twenty-eight years as an ATF undercover operative. During that period, I was formally assigned to field offices in San Francisco, Sacramento, Stockton, and Atlanta. However, assignments took me to cities large and small across the country. I would wake up one day in Las Vegas and the next in Tulsa. I might be asked to work an armed career criminal in New York, a gun trafficker in Miami, or a biker gang in Biloxi. To be completely honest, there were so many gigs I can't remember them all.

In this book, I deliver an eyewitness and transparent view of the organization and the operatives with whom I regularly risked my life. For decades, we were a dirty little secret within ATF, hidden from public view while various empty suits took credit for our work. Now it's time to recognize a team of heroes who've rarely been introduced to the public for whom they've given years of their lives to protect and serve.

Forming an elite brother- and sisterhood, our mission, and sometimes our daily existence, was very much like that of the nineteenth-century housecleaning snakes. We were (and many of us still are) the quintessential human rodent hunters, released from our jars when an unsavory task needed attention. Within the deadly world of covert crime investigation, we are called "Undercovers," "UCs," or "Operators." Within our own circles, we call ourselves the "Core" or "RatSnakes."

Allow me to introduce the RatSnakes.

VINCE (YOURS TRULY)

I was running hard through a dry creek bed that I had traversed a thousand times—only this time it was pitch-dark. My heart felt like it was pounding up into my throat. We'd done it! My buddy and I had just pulled off our first real heist. We'd busted into cars and gone on shoplifting sprees, but this time we'd broken into the local junior high school, pilfered anything that looked valuable, and then scrammed. We would have immediate street cred. The tough kids would idolize us.

We were both thirteen years old.

"Freeze, motherfucker, or I'll blow your fucking head off!"

The voice shouting at us in a thick Italian accent was one I would later come to know all too well. The creek bed lit up like a stadium, and I stared down the barrel of a shotgun wielded by Novato, California, police officer Yugo Innocenti.

I thought to myself, "I am so fucked. My parents are gonna kill me."

Note to self: Schools have alarms.

I was the only child of a bartender and a nurse. Both of my parents worked evenings and nights, making a normal nine-to-five schedule impossible, and they ultimately divorced. But even without that disruption, I was a naturally high-strung kid, mostly unsupervised. My personality, combined with too much freedom, resulted in a whole host of bad decisions by me. These included but were not limited to alcohol and drug consumption, stealing, burglarizing, and a multitude of run-ins with police departments throughout Marin County, California.

Another friend—I'll call him Mike—and I were best buddies in junior high school. He was the quiet one and I was the loud one. We spent a lot of time smoking weed and doing generally not good stuff. We cut school together. Shoplifted together. In fact, our parents forbade us from hanging out together. Our close friendship found us locked up together at Marin County Juvenile Hall on several occasions. Although we were repeat customers, it was always for nonviolent, less serious stuff. Because of our age and low-end violations, we were not placed in the senior unit with the big boys in two-men lockdown rooms. That would change based on one really stupid but very cool idea.

Because we were in a dorm atmosphere, at night, at lights out, there was only one counselor, a.k.a. guard, on duty. Mike had the idea to stash a set of clothes and a pair of shoes so we could go over the fence. I didn't think it was a very good idea, but at that time in my life, I had a hard time saying no. The fences were about twenty feet tall, and the upper eight or so feet had very coarse, tightly woven wire—so you couldn't get your fingers through the mesh—with razor wire along the top.

During head count and bed check, the counselor found the shoes we'd stashed, but we still had a set of uniform clothes and socks. We had no idea where we would go, how we would eat, or what would happen if we got caught. As with most of our bad decisions, we said, "Fuck it," and headed for the yard. The nearest fence was twenty feet away. Lucky for us, it butted up to the cafeteria roof. I boosted Mike, he grabbed onto the gutter to pull himself up and around the fence wire, and then he reached down and helped me up. It was dark and cold, and we were about ten miles from the closest town.

We ran like hell and dodged every pair of headlights that came our way. My girlfriend at the time was the only one we knew to reach out to. She got us cigarettes, food, and street clothes. For a few hours, we felt like Butch Cassidy and the Sundance Kid. The very next morning, as I met my girlfriend on her way to school, boom, I was grabbed by the cops. In all honesty, I was so relieved. I was cold, hungry, and knew my parents were probably freaking out.

Mike stayed on the run for another week. I was sent back to juvenile hall, straight to the senior unit, and placed on three days Temporary Removal from Group (TRG), which meant twenty-three hours a day in lockdown, with meals in the cell. If there was anything funny about this, and there wasn't, it was that Mike ended up with my girlfriend.

I tell this story not to glorify or boast about my behavior. I was and am truly ashamed of how I conducted myself in those days. I am merely attempting to explain how and why I may have migrated to a gritty agency like ATF, and then became a fairly successful undercover agent. My experience as a juvenile lawbreaker helped me to think like a criminal when it became my job to chase them.

The net result of my unlawfulness was that at age seventeen—after I was involved in an auto theft wherein a police chase concluded with my buddy and me dumping a stolen convertible into the San Francisco Bay—a judge gave me a choice. It was the same damn judge I'd appeared before numerous times, and this time my luck had run out.

"Mr. Cefalu," he said, as I stood before him in the courtroom. "I have had enough of your foolish behavior and have spent enough of the court's time and resources over the years trying to get you on track."

"Yes, sir," I said, not knowing what else to say.

"Here's your choice. If you provide the court with proof you have enlisted in the US military within the next thirty days, I'll suspend your sentence."

"Shit."

"I beg your pardon?"

"Nothing, sir."

"If not," he continued, "bring your suitcase, because you're going to jail for a year."

Upon hearing this, my mom gasped and my dad smiled. Later that day, the last words I heard from my father's mouth were, "I never thought my son would be a pussy." Then he hit me upside my head with a three-pack of frozen pork chops.

When I came to, my mother was sobbing and my father was gone.

"I'll show that son of a bitch," I said as I stomped out the door. Thirty days later, I stepped off a bus at the US Marine Corps recruit depot and onto the yellow footprints (painted on the asphalt to show new recruits where to stand, assuming we were too stupid to get into formation otherwise).

While a pain in my ass at the time, that judge and my six years in the military built the foundation for what would become a lifelong career in law enforcement and probably saved my sorry butt from a long stint in some penitentiary.

JAY (A.K.A. BIRD)

 Jay Dobyns grew up in the quintessential middle-class family: mom, dad, brother, sister. Jay's parents lived in the same house and stayed married their entire lives. His dad was a veteran and hard as nails, but also a soft-spoken construction contractor. His mom was salt of the earth and what bound the family together. While I was in and out of juvenile detention, the most diabolical event in Jay's high school years was accidentally egging a police car, which landed him and his buddy a stint washing the police car with toothbrushes. Wow, total gangsta.

At the University of Arizona, Tucson, Jay was a standout wide receiver. He was tall, clean-cut, handsome, and tough.

So, how did a shitbag like me and a pretty boy like Jaybird end up best friends and UC partners for over twenty years? It began around 1988, when I had been with ATF for about a year. I was a teaching a class, and Jay was attending a different one at the Federal Law Enforcement Training Center (FLETC) in Brunswick, Georgia. While there, most of us frequented a local watering hole named Brogan's, just over the causeway on St. Simons Island.

Brogan's was an understated workingman's bar where the blue-collar element of ATF felt at home. From blocks away, you could hear shuffleboard players shouting and jukebox music blasting. On many occasions, I used that auditory signal to vector in on Brogan's while whiskey-blind from some other island tavern. My favorite table at Brogan's was just inside the second-story balcony. It provided a beautiful view of the beach and the beach bunnies sporting the latest Victoria's Secret–style bikinis. More important to me was the handy X factor that no other island bar offered: you could take a piss right off the deck into the needles and cones of two-hundred-foot-tall Georgia pines.

As undercover operators, we early on mastered the study of our surroundings. It was imperative to become experts at examining and identifying escape routes, to know who was with whom, and to recognize potential threats. Over time it became instinct—a skill necessary to stay alive in our world. Missing any signal and not being ready to adapt got you dead.

Enter Jay Dobyns. This is where Jay's and my recollections differ. My version is the truth.

I first saw him from my balcony perch as he approached the bar through the parking lot. I thought, "That fucker is huge. Look at the guns on him." I made a mental note to track his location and then went back to my boys. We were drinking and planning training scenarios for first-time undercover prospects. A short time later, I was distracted—no doubt by one of the many hard beach bodies prancing in and out of the bar—when I felt a hand on my shoulder. I turned to see Jay offering my weapon of choice: Jack Daniels on the rocks. I was caught off guard. He was not only massive and daunting, but he was that guy you knew all the women were going flock to. I already hated him.

As Jay handed me the whiskey, he said, "Nothin' from nothin'. I've heard you do some serious street work, and I just wanted to buy you a cocktail."

My strongest suit always has been my weakest suit: my big mouth. Out of instinct and because he had entered without an invite what I perceived to be my world and personal space, I blurted out, "And who the fuck are you?"

"ATF agent Jay Dobyns. Have a good night."

I turned my back to him and faced my buddies.

"Who is that fag? I thought he was going to groupie-grab my dick," I said.

Jay disappeared inside the bar, taking my insult in what I would later learn was his normal, casual stride. One of the boys said, "That's the dude who got shot in Arizona, first day on the job. Motherfucker got taken hostage, shot, and came right back to work."

I thought to myself, "Ain't I the fuckin' asshole."

Another buddy chimed in that they had heard good shit about Jay, and he was some kind of college football star. Every time I looked over, he was laughing and so were the people around him, most of them hot chicks.

A few hours went by, and Jay meandered out onto the balcony to get some air. I called the waitress over and ordered two shots of JD. I didn't know if he drank and didn't care. He was gonna drink my drink, or that would be the end of our friendship before it started.

I joined him on the balcony, handed him the shot, and said, "So you're the dumb fuck that walks into bullets."

He graciously took the cocktail and said, "That's me. Thanks for the drink."

We slammed back the shots and laughed as the booze trickled down our throats. Then, as if channeling the same wavelength, we both whipped out our junk and pissed off the balcony.

MICHELLE (A.K.A. BAMBI)

The product of a "normal" East Coast family, Michelle was anything but stereotypically normal. She drank most of the boys under the table a time or two and could take a lot of ribbing, but if a line got crossed, and you never knew exactly where that line was, you would find yourself being challenged to a fistfight. Michelle was not tiny, nor was she shy. She was known for her signature greeting, "Waaasssuup?" She had an infectious laugh and a smile made for movies. She was tall and, to put it gently, STACKED. Our female UCs had to fight the predictable stigma of being thought of as just arm candy. And what were they going to do if it broke bad?

The guys who thought that or said that hadn't met Bambi.

First of all, Bambi would beat a motherfucker with another motherfucker. Yes, female UCs can create some issues, such as having to deal with sexual advances by a criminal. But they solve way more challenges than their presence creates. A female partner can more easily conceal electronics. Violators who are planning harm or a rip-off may not view the female of the team as a threat, which means that female may very well be the one to save your ass. Don't get me wrong, many females do solo UC work and do it as well as any male. But if a violator says, "Come alone," you probably can get away with bringing your "ol' lady" to a deal. Bring another guy and things can go to shit rapidly, whereas you almost always can explain away your girlfriend.

It's much easier for cover teams to recognize a female voice in a room of men talking on a wire. A female can excuse herself to the ladies' room and call the cover team without anybody following her into the bathroom. And, juries tend to love female cops.

All that aside, Bambi melded seamlessly into the UC cop world and did not consider herself too good for any task. She was smart and a total team player. I'd go through any door with her any day.

GUNDO

 Gundo was a strange cat. It was like he made it to the 1970s and got stuck. He was a hyperintelligent investigator and always seemed to see that one angle the rest of us didn't see or had missed. Gundo came to ATF by way of local law enforcement, and to say he was a likeable guy would be a massive understatement. If someone didn't like Gundo, they were an asshole. Gundo only spoke when he had something to say, so consequently everybody listened when he did. He had the love and respect of both the agents and the bosses. He was the clear head when the rest of us were in chaos. He did a few years as a boss and decided it was not his flavor, so he returned to fieldwork. Whether appearing as a neat and clean-cut boss type or the grizzled, white-bearded, hair-down-to-his-ass street agent most of us came to recognize, Gundo always brought his A game.

Gundo was a tall, good-looking, wiry, Midwestern guy—and the consummate chameleon. You got a sense he didn't like the big city but endured it to put bad guys in jail. In the 1980s, he had been the old man of his academy class. Much like the other cops ATF had hired, Gundo got in under the wire. In those days, you had to be employed by your thirty-fifth birthday in order to be able to accumulate twenty years of service to retire by the then mandatory age-fifty-five retirement date. Gundo just made it. I asked why he waited so long to get on with the feds, and he just said he wasn't sure a law enforcement career was for him. He'd finished college, done an internship with the Missoula, Montana, sheriff's department, and had been "intrigued but not sold." He looked around at probation department jobs and juvenile probation jobs, and accepted an offer from the Missoula County Sheriff's Office before ultimately joining ATF.

Gundo told me he knew exactly when he had found a home at ATF. Sitting in his academy classroom, the instructor put on a prerecorded video of then ATF assistant director Phil McGuire. After doing the whole welcome-aboard speech, McGuire simply said if you're going to be an ATF agent, remember first and foremost "we work harder than the others, and we play harder than the others." Gundo said he looked around the classroom, and everybody was smiling. Mr. McGuire got that part right.

BOX

 Now here was an operator's operator. Having fled Cuba as a child with his parents, Carlos Baixauli, a.k.a. Box, grew up with a hard-fought work ethic. He loved this country and wanted to be part of its security. He graduated college—no minor task since his family had been dispossessed of all personal wealth before fleeing Castro's Cuba—and joined law enforcement at the state level in Miami, Florida, working with the Division of Alcoholic Beverages & Tobacco. This made him a natural selection for ATF. That and being fluent in Spanish during the height of what would become known as the Miami drug/cocaine wars, an intensive series of conflicts between the US government and multiple drug cartels during the late 1970s and early 1980s.

Box easily melded into ATF undercover culture, and after a decade or more of undercover work (and with a beautiful wife and children), he migrated to the ATF National Academy where he ultimately ran the entire undercover training program.

JIMM

Which brings us to Jimm Langley, one of my oldest friends in ATF. Jimm joined from the US Customs Service, where he operated fast boats and chased bad guys (and girls) all over the Atlantic. I know this because on more than one occasion I was right there next to him. Jimm hailed from Kentucky and was assigned to the Marathon, Florida, customs office. We were "bunkies" on an international cooperative smuggling interdiction operation in the Bahamas. After that detail, Jimm, Bernie, who was our US Customs boat captain on that trip, and I all hired on with ATF.

DINO

Short, round, and Puerto Rican, Dino was a former US Army paratrooper and a commissioned officer. He ultimately would partner up with Bambi. Dino was the opposite of Gundo in terms of having a calming effect on the team. There wasn't a damn thing about Dino that could have been described as calming. You didn't even have to try to wind him up for him to be ready to explode. And once wound up, there was no shutting him down. Who knows why he was this way. Maybe because he was short and had to be loud to be heard—sorry, Dino.

He came to us by way of the Federal Bureau of Prisons. After surviving the Atlanta Cuban prison riots of 1987, he was looking for higher ground. When I was transferred to Atlanta in the early 1990s, Dino was one of the first to call and welcome me aboard. When I finally met him in person, he was hyper and motivated, and I knew we would end up doing some good things together.

PAT

Wow, where to begin? Pat Kelly (RIP, our brother) is affectionately referred to as the Godfather of undercover. After serving his time as a frogman for the US Navy Underwater Demolition Teams (the genesis of the modern Navy SEAL teams), Pat entered local law enforcement in the Midwest. He eventually gravitated to the Treasury Department and got pulled into ATF during the moonshine hiring push. He didn't have a college degree, but that would prove to be a nonissue.

Pat was gruff, no bullshit, and had no tolerance for laziness or whining. He was an old-school man's man. When it was business, it was all business. When it was time to play, well, that's when he took the gloves off for real. He sported his thick, slightly graying, bushy mustache for as long as I knew him.

Pat took over the undercover program pre-Box, pre-Jimm, and pre-Charlie. His classes were long, sometimes all day and into the night, because you didn't go home until the work was done. Everybody has a Pat Kelly story to tell.

CHARLIE

Charlie Fuller was another byproduct of the Miami cocaine wars of the 1970s and '80s, and he was just a damned natural when it came to undercover work. This guy had more hustle in him than baseballer Pete Rose, except Charlie's hustle was of the street variety. He talked more shit than Wolfman Jack and two wartime radio stations. Charlie had worked a long-term undercover early in his career that admittedly "fucked him up." This would be the catalyst for his transfer to the ATF Academy, where he worked with Pat Kelly and eventually took over the undercover program at FLETC. Charlie took a liking to me, and, unexpectedly, we later became partners for the final year of his career in Atlanta.

MILTON (A.K.A. THE RAGIN' CAJUN)

No one ever asked Milton, "Where are you from?" With his exceedingly thick southern Louisiana accent, you just knew. His crawfish low-country boil was legendary during the course of an undercover school or RatSnakes reunion. He was what we called a big ol' boy, and he had a hard side, probably from his days as a criminal investigator for the Louisiana Department of Justice or from wrestling alligators in the bayous (pure speculation). He was big, he was strong, and he had a bullshit tolerance level of zero. When the shit broke bad, he was the guy you wanted on your six.

This is how he and I met. I was invited to help teach a three-week undercover block of instruction for a new-agent class. At this point, I knew only a few of the players, but my name was out there in the field as a worker. I arrived at the academy a couple days early, per instructions, and checked into my rented townhouse on St. Simons Island, where the instructors stayed as a perk. Not knowing anybody yet, and having nowhere to be, I decided to stop in at Pam's #1 cop bar, a staple of anyone passing through the training center. Since my trainee days, Pam's had been our home away from home.

As always, Bob, the co-owner, was stationed at the front door like a sentry, not for security but to greet old friends. Behind the bar was Bob's wife, Pam, and both immediately greeted me with a handshake and a hug.

It was early in the day, and everybody was still in class, so I meandered over to the bar. I sat a couple stools down from a guy I thought was some local greasy, unkempt fisherman. We were the only two at the bar, and there was an elderly couple having lunch at one of the tables. Without a word, Pam slid over a JD on the rocks. I thought to myself, "I have spent way too much time in here."

The dude sitting two stools down reached over with his drink to toast. We tapped glasses, and he said, "Right on, JD."

I remember thinking, "Fuck, I am such a shit magnet."

Bob walked over and asked, "You two degenerates know each other?"

We both stared straight ahead into the bar mirror and simultaneously said, "Nope."

"Vince Cefalu, ATF–San Francisco," said Bob, "meet Milton Bonaventure, ATF–Baton Rouge."

Both our heads snapped around.

"That's funny as shit," I said. "I figured you'd just been released on parole."

"I thought the same about you, too, motherfucker," he said.

We slid our stools together and started what would become one of my most cherished friendships for the rest of my career.

. . . .

In these pages, I will tell you the famous, not so famous, and infamous stories of life within the world's greatest undercover agency, the Bureau of Alcohol, Tobacco and Firearms. If you are shocked, I am sorry. If you laugh, you are welcome. If it makes you sad, it's the truth.

My sole purpose in writing this book is to identify and glorify the heroes I was privileged to serve with. This book represents *my* crew of "Untouchables." It is not my intent to suggest that it is all-inclusive or even begins to represent all of the talented, hard-working agents in the bureau. I believe that ATF has the most dedicated and focused employees in the country. There are ATF special agents who have never done one undercover operation and yet have solved some of the most heinous crimes and incarcerated some of the most violent offenders in the nation. There are support staff, compliance investigators, analysts, and ATF National Laboratory folks who help to make this all work. Without them, there would be no RatSnakes. There are many who have sacrificed much to protect the United States. They did it without regret, and with a smile on their faces. I wasn't the best UC operator ATF ever had, and I wasn't the worst. But I knew and loved the best, and on occasion they would let me in their circles.

CHAPTER 1

··

WIRED FOR SPEED

On my first solo undercover meet, I was wearing so much electronics, I was afraid I was going to shut down the city's electrical grid. It was 1987 in San Francisco, and my job was to be introduced by a confidential informant (CI) to a violator. I was going to meet the bad guy at his house to buy a small amount of cocaine and a stolen pistol—a quick in-and-out deal. I had a one-watt transmitter with a range of about two city blocks, on a good day, and if there weren't too many structures between me and the agents monitoring the wire. I had the transmitter taped to my inner thigh. I had a repeater in place to boost the signal. I was wearing a Nagra recorder taped to the small of my back.

This was before the days of microrecorders and computer chips, and we had limited equipment options. The Nagra recorder was our best solution in the day. These reel-to-reel tape machines dated back to the 1950s and were revered for their stereo-quality recording. When I first saw this thing, I couldn't believe it was the best the feds had, but it was. You didn't just slap a tape in it and hit Record. Nor could you play it back without a playback unit. It was large and bulky—roughly the size of a big handheld calculator—with two microphones at the end of two eighteen-inch wires. There were several preferred ways to carry this device. You could place the recorder on your back and wrap surgical tape around and around to hold it in place. You then ran the wires up your back and over your shoulders and taped the microphones to your chest. This made it impossible to wear the Nagra with just a T-shirt or light clothing. The other way to carry the device was to wear a medical wrap around your ribs that was specially designed to hold it. Neither scenario was easy for me because I only weighed about 175 pounds.

I was also carrying a panic—a.k.a. "oh, shit"—button. This was a simple battery-operated pressure switch that would send a unique squelch over our police radios, signaling distress by the UC, i.e., my rookie ass. The panic button was about half the size of a pack of cigarettes and really couldn't be concealed too carefully or it would be hard to use. Most UCs who did carry it just stuck it in their pocket, which ran the risk of accidentally depressing the button due to the device's rudimentary design.

With the electronics loaded on, the next dilemma was to figure out where to carry my handgun. A bad guy carrying a gun to a meet isn't too worried about who sees it. But our duty weapons back then had serial numbers—starting with the letters *US*—and some even had a Treasury badge on the side of the pistol. In other words, you couldn't let the violator see or handle your pistol. That first time, I had my gun stuck in my belt on my hip toward the back. Nothing says cop like a leather holster, so I never used one. For those who have seen the 1992 Tarantino movie *Reservoir Dogs*, where the undercover cop practices his role in front of a mirror before the meet, that was me on my first deal.

The average civilian has seen shows where the cool undercover cop walks in, buys the dope or guns, and busts the bad guy. We wish it were that simple. In reality, a simple fifteen-minute undercover meeting can be the most stressful time in a man or woman's life. There are no rules. Anything can happen. On more than one occasion, agents have gotten ripped off. It's not like you can break out a test kit for a twenty-dollar crack rock buy. Those test kits cost money, plus when you are buying only a small amount of drugs, it would look silly to be wasting some of the crack to test it. It was not uncommon on larger-scale buys to test the drugs before exchanging money.

Agents are often "flexed" (sold fake dope). It looks like dope, but it isn't. Although most states and the federal government have laws prohibiting the sale of counterfeit substances, most jurisdictions won't prosecute these cases. They lack jury appeal and, after all, it's not even dope. Some of the larger rip-off cases would be prosecuted. It also depended on who the violator was and the extent of their criminal history.

Now, when it comes to agents purchasing guns on the street, you might think that is an easy one. It's not so easy in a dark alley with your heart threatening to pound out of your chest. Not to mention that street thugs call practically every firearm an Uzi. In fact, an Uzi is an Israeli-made submachine gun first designed in the late 1940s. It's known as one of the first weapons to employ a telescoping bolt design, meaning the magazine or clip is in the pistol grip, allowing for a shorter weapon, which is an obvious advantage. But most street thugs don't have a clue about the firearms they sell. Sometimes the guns don't work, or they are broken. Sometimes they are purported to be "machine guns," and they are not. There are field test procedures to determine if a firearm is fully automatic, but sometimes it's impossible to tell until the gun is actually fired at a range. It's the agent's job to examine the product closely. Unfortunately, some UCs have been duped into purchasing toy guns. It looks like a gun, acts like a gun, but when you get back to the office, you realize you have spent five hundred dollars on an air pistol. This never happened to me, but it could have. Try living that one down in your group.

Undercover work is scary—every time. But nothing is as scary as your first significant UC assignment. Everything is on the line: the respect of your fellow UCs, the confidence of your bosses, and ultimately your life. Will you choke? Will you be compromised? Will you remember the bust signal? Will you talk too much? The goal of undercover work is to develop evidence and capture a recording of the violator talking, not a recording of the undercover talking.

That first time for me was not all that stellar. The deal went fine, but I learned a lot from the debriefing with the cover agents. Apparently, the wire was cutting in and out after I left the vehicle and entered the residence. When the wire did work, the only person the cover team could hear talking was me. After I had seen the dope and guns, I just handed the violator the money and left. I never counted the cash for the recording or described the merchandise for the recorder. Live and learn.

. . . .

You might be wondering why anybody would want to be an undercover operator. Few normal jobs result in death if you are not good at them, and undercover work entails tiptoeing on the edge of a cliff in a storm every minute of every day. Frankly, not everybody possesses the skill set, the personality, or the balls to be an undercover agent. Although ATF is one of the premier agencies when it comes to undercover investigations, not all agents are expected to do undercover work, despite the fact they all have received the necessary training. Within ATF, undercover work is voluntary, and no agent can be forced to do undercover.

There are many reasons—some good, some not so good—for crossing into the undercover world. The textbook answers, which are all true, are to protect our communities, make a difference, stand up for the law.

However, hidden within those reasons is the juice, a.k.a. adrenaline rush, the recognition/fame/glory, personal challenge, and—full disclosure— pussy. Some girls love Good Bad Boys and Bad Good Boys.

You know from meeting Bambi that, of course, there are female undercover agents. They are some of the finest operators this bureau has ever produced. I initially thought about dedicating a chapter to our female UCs and calling it "SheSnakes," but that would suggest they were different, and that their contributions were less heroic or somehow different. In short, we can be country girls or boys, kids from wealthy families, inner-city youths, or the girl next door. We come from New York, California, Texas farms, Detroit suburbs, and the beaches of South Florida. Some are model gorgeous and many of us are just stone-cold ugly. Some are physically huge, others are small and nondescript looking. Some barely graduated from college, others possess advanced degrees from Ivy League schools. But the dynamic we all have in common is the *need for speed*.

For me, that need for speed started in my youth and ultimately led me to ATF, although after getting an honorable discharge from the military at age twenty-three, I initially envisioned my career would be as a detective or some kind of agent with the US Customs Service. When I attended basic investigators' school, in the class of forty-eight students there were approximately thirty US Customs agents, a couple ATF agents, a Secret Service agent or two, and the rest were recruits from the Office of Inspector General, or OIG agents, who investigated fraud and other crime for the US Department of Commerce. The Criminal Investigator Training Program (CITP), as it was called in the 1980s, was a generic investigators' academy that most federal agents had to attend before moving on to another academy for agency-specific training. Suffice to say, I didn't leave that school knowing much of anything about ATF. Although I had applied to almost every federal law enforcement agency out there, Customs was the first to offer me a job. My foot was in the door.

Once I finished my advanced training and boat school, I was supposed to report to Key Largo, but at the last minute my assignment was switched to Key West. It didn't matter to me because I didn't know where either one was. When I arrived in Key West and got settled, it was interesting to find out that my supervisor was a former ATF agent, as were four of the senior agents in my office. Eight of the nine drug task force Customs agents in Key West were former ATF agents. I remember thinking: "I sure am glad I didn't go to that apparently fucking train wreck of an agency"— especially the Philly office, which had the worst reputation. As time went on, I learned why ATF had such a bad rep.

During the drug wars of the 1970s and '80s, the United States built up its drug interdiction capabilities using the US Customs Service. They were hiring busloads of agents, buying airplanes, blimps, fast boats, helicopters. It looked like they would take over the world. Around the same time, in the early 1980s, rumors began circulating that the Bureau of ATF might be abolished. WTF? The ATF had only been a bureau for approximately ten years. Hell, it hadn't had enough time to fuck shit up good, and they already wanted to abolish it. When I say "they," I mean then US president Ronald Reagan (and some others). Case in point, ATF agent Ariel Rios, a member of the presidential anti-drug task force in South Florida, was allegedly in possession of a reduction in force (RIF) notice at the time of his tragic murder during an undercover deal in 1982.

The word was out—you'd better start looking for somewhere to go in another agency, because there wasn't going to be an ATF in the near future. That was why agents were jumping ship en masse and heading to Customs. Plus the fact that, due to regulations and the small size of ATF back in those days, the bureau was promoting at a much slower rate than at Customs. The ATF agents who came over to Customs were superstars and rose through the ranks at lightning speed. I didn't give a fuck about climbing that ladder. After working a big smuggling case with one token ATF agent sent down from Miami, I realized these ATF guys could investigate circles around the other agencies. Besides, I didn't like bobbing around in a boat on the ocean all that much.

By the time I considered going to ATF, the bureau had fought off attempts to abolish the agency—with the incidental help of the insurance industry, which benefited from ATF's expertise in arson investigations, as well as the National Rifle Association (NRA), which hated us but also was horrified at the thought of the Federal Bureau of Investigation (FBI), a.k.a. Big Brother, taking over the enforcement of gun laws.

After they heard I was going to ATF, the guys in the Key West office took every opportunity to bust my balls. One agent, whom I later found out had been a no-shit ATF legend, handed me a knife one day when we all were at lunch. I asked him: What's this for? He replied, "If I was going to ATF, I'd slit my wrists." However, to a man, one by one they came up to me at my going-away party and whispered, "You're going to love ATF. It was the best job I ever had."

They were right, although another one of my early undercover experiences was a study in what *not* to do. Generally speaking, the UC designates a distress or bust signal he or she will use. That signal will determine the actions of the cover team—the group of agents monitoring the operation, who are ready to move in when it's time to make arrests or extract the UC from an operation gone bad. The bust signal should be something the UC would not generally say by mistake but easy enough to remember. My youth and inexperience, and maybe a little too much bravado, caused me to pick the absolute worst verbal signal I ever could have come up with.

I chose "motherfucker" or something like that as my signal. I recall the senior agents questioning my choice, but they let me make my own mistakes. The problem with using that particular term as my bust signal was that after six years in the US Marine Corps, I was very familiar and loose with that little epithet.

With the cover team in place, I called the violator, in this case a street methamphetamine dealer in Sonoma County, California. I was going to buy a small amount of meth, and the deal was set to happen at his house in a shitty, white-trash neighborhood. He said, "Come on, let's do this." I proceeded to the house and shook hands with the dealer, and he invited me inside. Literally, within thirty seconds of entering the residence, you guessed it, the first of many "motherfuckers" passed my lips—well before the dope had exchanged hands. I heard engines rev and doors slam down the block—*shit, I just gave the bust signal.* As luck would have it, the violator was in another room, and I was able to call off the dogs by telling them over the wire it was a mistake.

Not two minutes later, I motherfucked somebody again. This time the violator was standing right next to me. I said, "I'm going to step out and get a smoke." I went out on the front porch and waved off the vehicles slowly rolling my way. I made my way back into the house and closed that deal as fast as I could. Then I used the bust signal—on purpose—and the cavalry came. Needless to say, I *never* used that bust signal again.

Chapter 2

....

T-MEN

By the time I came on, ATF was moving away from investigating the illegal liquor business and focusing more on the illegal firearms trade and other violent crime. I did, however, have one occasion to be present in court as a uniformed police officer sitting in on a magistrate's hearing regarding bootlegged liquor. All officers who had issued citations or made misdemeanor arrests would sit in the jury box and wait for their case to be called. This was in Georgia around 1983, and one of the long-time barbers in Athens had a nice shop in the town square. He was an old African American guy, and many of us would have him cut our hair. His shop was a meeting place right out of a Norman Rockwell painting. So, I was surprised to see him in court that morning.

When they called his case, he was charged with selling moonshine out of his shop. As he was answering the magistrate's questions regarding the violation, he stated his defense, something along these lines: "Judge, I didn't know it was illegal to sell shine, because I've been selling gallons of it over the years to those fellas over there."

I had a good chuckle watching several of the old-timers in our group awkwardly avert their eyes as the barber pointed straight to the jury box where we police officers sat.

To be honest, I came to ATF with exactly zero experience or knowledge about moonshine. I didn't understand the bootleg liquor trade or its culture. From my perspective, it was old news. And yet, as I learned to respect and appreciate, long before modern-day ATF agents arrived on the scene, or, for that matter, before we were born, a group of brave agents established a tradition of heroism that serves as a model and reminder of what an ATF agent should strive to achieve. These law enforcement agents of days gone by were the ones who ran toward the sound of gunfire. They repeatedly answered the nation's call to service in the most dangerous and unfavorable law enforcement operations in the history of the United States. They did so because that's what dedicated agents do. "They" were the special agents working under the auspices of the US Treasury Department, charged with enforcing US Prohibition laws in the 1920s and early 1930s.

Viewed as progressive in its time, the temperance movement already had gained widespread traction when the US government, via the Eighteenth Amendment of the Constitution, put a nationwide ban on alcohol production, transportation, and sales. The actions of those who saw a profit to be made through illicit alcohol sales, coupled with the violence that protected their activities, put them on a collision course with the US Treasury Department and those who enforced its laws, the Alcohol Tax Unit of the IRS.

I had been a US Treasury agent for almost a year before I heard the term "T-man." On my first visit home after completing training, I was at the house of my childhood best friend's parents. We were having cocktails, and her dad, Jack, called me a T-man. Jack was my idol. Jack was the man everybody wanted to be. He was a no-shit World War II hero, gravely injured months before Germany surrendered. He had a history degree from UC Berkeley and was a wealth of knowledge. That being said, I still felt I had to correct him. He went on to explain how, back in the day, Treasury agents were called T-men. He was right, of course.

The T-men chose to set any personal feelings aside and enforce the most unpopular laws in our land. They fanned out across the country—sometimes working solo and enlisting the help and support of local law enforcement agencies—and brought the battle to the gangsters and moonshiners. Since most of the glory and public attention was directed at the FBI and J. Edgar Hoover's media machine, the T-men were able to do their jobs without undue congressional or governmental oversight (or interference). The practice of recruiting local help would ultimately carry over decades and become the greatest tool in ATF's arsenal.

Unfortunately, when Prohibition was repealed in 1933, violence and illegal untaxed liquor sales did not stop. In fact, bootleg sales and moonshine wars continued, and what resulted was death. As more moonshine stills popped up across the country, the duties of the Prohibition agents took them to the streets of Chicago, the sunny beaches of Florida, and the mountains of Kentucky in pursuit of the daring and Wild West–like moonshiners. While other federal agents were conducting conventional investigations, ATF agents were lying in tick-infested woods waiting for the operators of a still to arrive. Agents also could be found dressing and acting in a manner that allowed them to mingle unnoticed with their quarry, the illegal liquor purchasers, and entering the bowels of the inner city or rural brothels and smoke-filled shot houses to make undercover purchases of liquor.

The stories of the FBI's diligent pursuit of bank robbers and dissident political groups are legend. Many of us can rattle off names like Baby Face

Nelson, Machine Gun Kelly, and the like as linked to famous FBI chase-and-capture stories. But unless you chose to distill illegal liquor—in other words, "run moonshine"—or in other ways participate in the shady side of Prohibition, you likely would not have encountered those shadowy figures known as T-men or "revenuers." While Chicago-based Prohibition agent Eliot Ness and his team of Untouchables gained well-deserved fame, there are countless other agents who carried out their duties without thanks or recognition. We all have heard about high-speed, backroad pursuits to make the arrests of major tax-evading criminals back in the day. These weren't sexy headlines. And, sadly, many good men and women lost their lives battling these criminals, most of the time receiving only a mention in the local newspaper when struck down in the line of duty. At the time of this writing, 188 ATF/Alcohol Tax Unit agents have lost their lives in the line of duty.

. . . .

The 1960s changed everything. Little did I know at four years old, sitting in front of the television watching the news of John F. Kennedy's assassination, that I would one day be on a presidential protection detail. The Vietnam War, and even more specifically, US entry into combat after the Gulf of Tonkin incident in 1964, marked a time of social unrest, criminal chaos, and a divided country. One glaring sign of our country's troubled times was the emergence of fanatical and sometimes violent quasi-political radical groups, such as the left-wing revolutionary Symbionese Liberation Army (SLA), the Weather Underground that sought to overthrow "US imperialism," and the controversial Black Panther Party (BPP). Growing up in the San Francisco Bay Area, I had a front-row seat to the craziness. The one common thread among these groups was that they all were out for self-interest, and many relied on violence and criminal activity to support their "cause." They were known to possess and use exotic and extremely powerful firearms and explosives.

These and other groups—such as the Hells Angels motorcycle gang, which notoriously became part of the decade's counterculture movement in San Francisco and beyond—relied on crime to finance their operations. They used firearms to violently protect themselves and advance their agendas. ATF was a major source of aggravation to these groups, evidenced by several bombings and attempted bombings directed at ATF's San Francisco office. Unlike other federal agencies, ATF's success gauge (litmus test, if you will) was often the level of violence the agency incurred.

In the era of the shooting assassinations of President John F. Kennedy (1963 in Dallas, Texas), civil rights leader Martin Luther King Jr. (1968 in Memphis, Tennessee), and presidential candidate Robert F. Kennedy (1968 in Los Angeles), Congress again turned its attention to addressing firearms violence in America. The Gun Control Act was signed into law by President Lyndon B. Johnson in October of 1968. Congress had therein armed the federal government with a set of laws and regulatory guidelines that finally would make it possible to significantly impact armed criminals in this country. However, in doing so, they initially left out one important feature: Who would enforce these laws?

With such dynamic and unpopular laws, there was a need for an agency with a history of taking on monumental initiatives, and it had to be placed within the Treasury Department, because so many aspects of the new laws were tied to taxation as well as regulation. Once again, Congress turned to the revenuers, with their unique and aggressive well-documented can-do approaches and previous successes. On July 1, 1972, the US government created the Bureau of Alcohol, Tobacco and Firearms.

ATF was initially staffed with former IRS agents. Many migrated over from the ATTU, the Alcohol Tobacco Tax Unit of the IRS, and the rest came from Treasury Department sister agencies, such as the US Secret Service (USSS), US Customs Service, and other IRS divisions. Slowly, new hires were brought into the ranks. The infrastructure for training new agents was already in place through the Treasury Law Enforcement Officers Training facility in Washington, DC. The Federal Law Enforcement Training Center (FLETC), where I ultimately would do all of my training, had not yet opened its doors in Brunswick.

The old Treasury guys brought a wealth of investigative experience to the fledgling agency, but the gun laws were new, and they incorporated the nation's explosives laws as well as federal arson statutes. In other words, the arson and explosive statutes were tied to the gun laws. Federal fucking arson laws? Hell, even when I came on with ATF fifteen years later, I didn't know there were such laws or that I would be expected to enforce them.

Those hired in ATF's early days still were primarily concerned with the illegal liquor trade. The majority of the original six to eight hundred agents were assigned throughout the southeastern United States, where the bulk of moonshining occurred. In those days, the first "modern" ATF agents still wore a green uniform like their T-men predecessors, and they spent most of their days and nights surveilling stills and shot houses. The newly formed ATF had to reach out to fire science and military explosive experts to develop training in those areas for its agents, and it had to do that quickly. The inherited laws made ATF responsible for investigating any arson, or destruction by explosive, of any federal property or building that affected interstate commerce. Simply stated, if it blew up or was intentionally set ablaze, ATF had jurisdiction. That fact alone set the tone for the now decades-long confrontations over control between ATF and the FBI.

While all this was going on, gun violence had gone even crazier in America. Drug sales and use were on the rise, and violence was breaking out everywhere. But ATF's agents were basically confined to six or eight states. The bureau reacted and scattered agents across the country, gradually pulling away from illegal liquor cases and putting manpower toward halting the sale and use of illegal firearms and related violent crime.

As they jumped into the fray, it didn't take the field agents or management long to realize that if agents were to be effective, they would need to find a way to get close to the bad guys. The logical approach was to utilize undercover operatives. In the legal world, the best evidence is an eyewitness who is party to a crime. So, if our guys (in those early days, there weren't very many female agents) were present when the crime was committed, it was considered a slam-dunk case.

Lucky for us, several of the old IRS guys who came over had some undercover experience. The undercover tactic had been around since the cowboy days in some form or fashion, but in the early 1970s, there was no formal training beyond a couple short classes at the academy. Traditional investigation just didn't require that level of direct contact with the criminals. ATF had no other choice than to create an undercover program. There was no known formalized and comprehensive training offered by other agencies. ATF needed training suited to its new and uncharted jurisdictions. Because of the aggressiveness of its agents, the bureau already had compiled many case studies on what to do and, more importantly, what not to do.

Meanwhile, to complicate these processes, the US Supreme Court was handing down decisions in favor of the accused like Halloween candy. The landmark Miranda decision (*Miranda v. Arizona*, 1966) resulted in the well-known "Miranda warning," allowing a detainee not to make self-incriminating statements; the Escobedo ruling (*Escobedo v. Illinois*, 1964) assured criminal suspects a right to counsel during police interrogations; the Mapp case (*Mapp v. Ohio*, 1961) deemed that evidence obtained during "unreasonable searches and seizures" could not be used in criminal prosecutions. In our favor, the John W. Terry decision (*Terry v. Ohio*, 1968) allowed law enforcement officers to frisk a suspect if there was reasonable suspicion of the individual committing a crime—hence, the term "Terry frisk." These and a whole other slew of court decisions would directly impact the way we could and would do undercover work going forward.

CHAPTER 3

....

ACTING SCHOOL WITH SAND GNATS

I recall hearing the singer-songwriter Stevie Nicks once say something like: "If you ever have a chance to be a rock 'n' roll star, do it! It's the best job you'll ever have." With due respect to Ms. Nicks, she's never lived the life of a UC. Take the rock 'n' roll lifestyle, mix in homemade explosives, exotic automatic weapons, cop-sick groupies, high-stakes narcotics deals, militant subversive organizations, and sadistic suspects intent on mayhem, and you have a typical ATF undercover operation.

One of Bambi's first undercover deals was executed with a senior agent named Steve Brady. Bambi keeps the violator's picture on her bulletin board to this day as a trophy and as a reminder of how quickly things can change in a UC environment. Bambi became a special agent in 1989. Before that, she worked as a secretary at ATF headquarters in Washington,

DC. Some of us had cut our teeth in violent or dangerous environments, but she had no prior law enforcement experience, so making the leap to UC was especially challenging for her.

On this particular day, Steve and Bambi were returning to the house of a crack dealer, from whom they previously had made several low-level buys. Upon entering the house, they saw the violator parked on his couch, one leg partially covering the sawed-off shotgun he was sitting on. It was clear he wanted them to see the weapon. This was not consistent with past meetings. Bambi recalls: "I thought I was going to shit my pants, literally."

They pretended to ignore the shotgun and began to engage the guy. While Steve was talking, the violator waved his hand and interrupted. He said, "I had a really shitty dream last night. I dreamed you two were cops, and I had to kill you."

In this type of situation, an agent might react involuntarily with body language or stuttering that would confirm, or at least validate, the violator's fears. Or, the agent can purposefully respond. Bambi's training and her wits kicked in. Without any noticeable hesitation, she blurted out, "Dude, if you aren't gonna tell us about some kinky shit you did in your dreams, why are we even talking about them?"

The violator's wife in the next room busted out laughing, and the situation was defused. Bambi didn't ramble on about not being cops or ask the guy why he would say that. She merely redirected the conversation with humor, and all was well. The violator got so relaxed that he went on in-depth about the drug trade, even offering advice to Steve and Bambi. The buy went down, and the violator went to prison. More importantly, Bambi came away thinking, "I can do this."

. . . .

Back in the 1960s and '70s, UC work was definitely a fly-by-the-seat-of-your-pants kind of tool. Before ATF got in the game, undercover techniques were primarily directed at quick-hit buy busts* and really didn't lend themselves to long-term or ongoing investigations. By later standards, the early techniques were extremely unsafe and sometimes reckless. In true American innovative fashion, when you don't have what you need, you build it. And that's exactly what ATF did.

In 1974, ATF Headquarters (HQ) and the seven regional directors (or the seven Chinese Warlords, as they affectionately were referred to because of the power they wielded) concurred about the need to create a UC school that would develop a specialized program to increase the safety and effectiveness of our agents. This became the first formal undercover training program anywhere in the US law enforcement community. The first class was held in Virginia Beach, in southeastern Virginia. It was designed as a two-week program, and all students and staff had to attend every class. The syllabus was put together by a couple senior ex-IRS guys who had worked organized crime back in the day. ATF agents from the southeast who had a fair amount of undercover experience also contributed to the original class content. They used actual case studies and events to address real-world scenarios that new agents might be confronted with. They created lesson plans from scratch and developed accompanying role-play scenarios, many of which are still used today and formed part of my own training when I came on to ATF. The lessons had to address techniques and protocols for cover stories (also known as backstopping), invitations to partake in drug use, sidestepping entrapment, agent misconduct, handling sexual advances, and using technology.

As a prerequisite for attending, each agent needed to have worked at least one long-term undercover operation. That first class in 1974

---

* An undercover operation intended to culminate in the immediate arrest of the violator(s).

comprised all male students.* The first half of the day consisted of class-room presentations. During the latter part of the day, one half of the class did practical exercises and the other part dispersed to assigned locations to gather intelligence for mock UC scenarios. The next day, they would swap. The staff role-played as violators, and then they would critique each student on his performance. Before the end of the first week, two students had their hotel room raided by Virginia Beach Police. Apparently, the students had been overheard in public talking about a kilo of cocaine. They were participating in a field training scenario but, of course, no one had tipped off the local cops about the unique lesson plan.

On Thursday afternoon of the first week, the director of Internal Affairs was scheduled to teach for three or four hours. The story goes that as he was starting his presentation, someone asked how many of his staff had worked undercover. The IA director answered that he and most of his staff had done so. Another student followed up with a question that was similar to this: "We don't mean buying shots or small purchases of whiskey. How many of you IA guys have worked on the streets buying guns, narcotics, or explosives?" The director responded that none had. The students then told him only experienced undercover agents should instruct other undercover agents about situations related to UC work. After a few more minutes, the students as well as the staff turned their chairs around so their backs were to the guest instructor. That was the end of that block of instruction and probably helped to set the tone for the bad blood between street guys and IA that carried over for years.

ATF continued to refine and further develop its techniques and policies related to undercover, while constantly adjusting to the changing

---

* I have it on good authority that in the back of the classroom were half gallons of gin, bourbon, scotch, and vodka, and several coolers of beer. There was one rule: Be on time. It didn't matter how you were dressed or whether or not you were completely sober, but you'd better be on time. There had to be standards, right?

times and events in the country. Classes were expanded and mock scenarios added and subtracted to remain relevant for field agents. By the mid-1970s, female participation in undercover operations needed to be addressed practically and procedurally. Agent techniques were refined. Policies were put in place to protect the agency (and the bosses' asses). Most agents and everyone else realized at the very early stages that undercover work brought with it all sorts of possible bad juju.

After the Virginia Beach example, several more advanced undercover schools were conducted at off sites. In 1975, most federal law enforcement agencies permanently migrated undercover training to the FLETC site in Brunswick. It formerly had been a US Navy base, so many of the facilities were already built and just needed to be adapted for UC training purposes. FLETC was administered by the US Treasury Department, although it serviced agencies throughout the federal law enforcement community and ultimately became the home of the ATF National Academy and its advanced training programs.

. . . .

While all this was going on in ATF, I was bouncing my ass in and out of juvenile halls and running from the cops. Jay was playing college football in Arizona. Milton was just entering high school and doing whatever Cajuns do in the swamp. Bambi was running around some military base with her hair in pigtails. Gundo was riding around in pickup trucks in Central Montana, shooting at stop signs with a shotgun. Jimm was deer hunting in Kentucky, and Box was digging living in Florida. Pat Kelly and Charlie Fuller were learning how to be rookie ATF agents, but the rest of us didn't yet have a clue what we were going to be when we grew up.

When I found my way to ATF and entered the academy in 1987, it was way more relaxed than any of my previous training. I liked it. They treated us like adults and federal agents, not like college freshmen. My entire class was made up of male agents, which was an anomaly because by that time most of the classes had a fairly large female contingent. It also allowed for a little more male silliness than if the classes had been coed. Early in my ATF training I established myself as a problem child, although I was not the only miscreant in the class.

I'd first encountered Pat Kelly while attending the basic criminal investigator school for the US Customs Service. His wife, Gina, was working at Pam's #1 cop bar. Therefore, it was Pat's and every other ATF agent's favorite watering hole. I only knew Pat from a distance in those days. I'd see him drinking with a bunch of questionable-looking characters and think that I needed to stay far away from that guy. I had no idea he was a fed, much less an ATF instructor. I had just entered federal service and had a high and tight haircut and was still fully enamored with the fed coat-and-tie thing. I'd see Pat at the bar night and day. Sometimes he'd walk around behind the bar and carry kegs out. He would look at me, and I tried to avoid eye contact just due to his ominous appearance. I never thought to ask who he was and simply gave him a wide berth. I would laugh to myself in the years to come at how wrong my impressions of him were, and even more so at the fact that all those unsavory people he was always hanging out with were actually ATF agents before my time.

Even when, as a new ATF agent, I was introduced to Pat, he wasn't immediately all warm and fuzzy. He took his job seriously and until you proved you did, too, it was strictly instructor/student. During our orientation for ATF New Agent Training (NAT), we met most of our regular instructors. Pat had the least to say, and it went along the lines of, "If you're still here at the end of your training, I'm the one who will teach you how to stay alive."

One day, he was teaching from a lesson plan directed at being prepared to deal with unexpected yet common issues that could arise during undercover operations. Things like if your cover team is spotted or you are confronted about being a cop. Or you accidently forgot to take a government pen out of your pocket and it's noticed. Or if you should or shouldn't conceal your badge on your person during an undercover job. That last decision was a tricky one. If you were confronted as a cop or thought you were going to be killed during a rip-off, it could be nice to discourage the violators by letting them know they would be killing a law enforcement agent. On the other hand, knowing your identity could be exactly what caused the violator to panic and act violently.

ATF policy required undercover operators to be armed while working. The rare exception had to be approved by the boss, most of whom generally didn't want that liability. I know plenty of UCs who have done a deal unarmed. I never did, but I considered it a couple times. It always seemed a little bit crazy to ask permission *not* to be armed. But there were times when a violator would say something like, "Don't come here strapped."

As Pat and the class were round tabling the possible responses to some of these issues, someone raised their hand to ask a question. Pat called on the trainee, and this was the gist of the exchange that followed:

TRAINEE: What if a bad guy points a gun at me and tells me to do something I'm not supposed to do?

AGENT PATRICK KELLY (CALMLY): Look, your only job is to go home at the end of every day. If a violator puts a gun in your face and says, "Suck my dick," I suggest you learn how to suck a dick real fast.

The entire class went silent. I think we all got the point.

As the weeks passed, Pat would show up unannounced in various classes, sit at the back of the room, and watch. He'd sit through an hour here or an hour there. He wasn't watching the instructors, he was watching us. Seeing who did and did not participate. Who did and didn't show their asses. Being an overachiever in those days, I decided I would be one of the first to piss the instructors off.

By the time I had entered the ATF Academy, I had about ten years of fairly good police experience. I had been through four training academies already, and could pretty much have skated through this one—I didn't, but I could have. Being a fed will inflate a cop's ego for sure, but being an ATF agent expands even the biggest of egos.

One class on traditional and electronic surveillance was being taught by a boss from HQ. A boss who eventually would run the entire ATF internal affairs unit. That would have been good information for me to have had before running my mouth. As he was covering some fairly technical issues regarding radio and transmitter frequencies and atmospheric impact on undercover transmitters, our group had quite a few questions. Most of us hadn't used any high-speed (super-secret, highly advanced) equipment up to this point. But that didn't matter to Hankinson; this seemed to be just a forum to impress all of us with how much smarter he was than we were. Each question from a student elicited a sigh from him, as if to say, "Are you people just stupid?" Then he begrudgingly would answer the question.

After a couple hours of this, I could tell I had arrested more bad guys, bought more contraband, and gotten more pussy in my short career than he would over his entire career. Plus, I didn't like the way he was embarrassing my classmates. We were only four weeks in, and this was painful to endure.

So, when he opened a door, I stomped through it. He turned around from the whiteboard and asked if any of us had the slightest idea how to conduct an aerial surveillance. I raised my hand and said as loudly as I could, without yelling, "I am guessing with a fucking airplane."

I'm fairly sure the world stopped rotating at that very moment. Hankinson's neck bulged, his face turned red, and I knew I probably had fucked up. Before he could respond, the class erupted. Amid the laughter, I heard a few muttered "oh, shits" from my classmates.

Pat Kelly's voice boomed from the back of the room.

"Cefalu, out-fucking-side, *now!*"

I couldn't get out of the room fast enough. In the hallway, Agent Kelly grabbed me by the back of my neck and said, "Walk with me." We exited the building at a rapid pace. I figured he was going to kick me out of the center and that we were headed to the dorm to clear out my shit. Instead, he told me to get in his truck. He gave me a smoke, and then just stared at me in silence. Finally, he said, "Son, you wanna complete this fuckin' academy, or you got another job waiting on you back home?"

I said, "Yes, sir, I do, and no, sir, I don't."

He barked, "*Stop* calling me sir! My name's Pat, and I'm an agent just like you. Now, when you go back in there after lunch, you better be damn convincing and convince your fellow students I ripped you a new asshole. Number two, when Hankinson takes the stage after lunch, you raise your hand and wait for him to call on you. Then you're going to stand up and apologize for your disrespectful comments. You getting all of this?"

"Yessir," I said.

"Don't fucking call me sir. Call that fucking asshole Hankinson sir, and be convincing." He ended with, "I was wondering who was gonna finally call that arrogant cocksucker out. Yah done good."

. . . .

During my time in ATF basic school, Charlie Fuller had been shadowing Pat and taught some of the classes. Charlie was going to take over the undercover program due to Pat's upcoming retirement. They were best buds from the old days. Their personalities couldn't have been more different. Charlie was gregarious and always cutting up with everybody. He was far easier to approach than Pat. However, he was equally passionate and serious about undercover work. If he thought you probably would suck at it, he would tell you, nicely. Charlie had come straight out of the field as an agent. He wasn't going to be a boss and never wanted to be one. He was a cops' cop.

Luckily, Charlie took an early liking to me. That would prove valuable one particular day in training. Apparently, I had underestimated how much I drank the night before. We were scheduled to train on the firing range around 8 AM. That basically meant we would get to take the whole day to fuck off and shoot machine guns and exotic firearms like suitcase guns, cane guns, and pen guns. For whatever reason, I didn't make the bell that morning, and sometime around 10 AM all hell broke loose. I thought my dorm-room door was going to come off the hinges. On the other side of my door was Charlie, and he was pissed.

"What the fuck, Cefalu?" he screamed.

Still a little groggy, I asked what time it was.

"Ten-oh-fucking-clock in the morning," came the answer. "I ain't got time for this shit from you."

He said I had five minutes to be outside. He gave me a ride to the range, and when we got there, he smoothed things over for me with the other instructors. Despite my tardiness, I was allowed to continue the day with the rest of my class.

Many rookie agents possess favorable character traits, such as mental stamina and "the look," but undercover work is not an innate skill. Weeks, months, and sometimes years of training on and off the books is necessary to build the skills required to survive life as an undercover ATF agent. For most of us, the ATF training academy was where it all began. It was there that I refined the thuggish Vinny D. character I used for the better part of my career with very few exceptions, and where clean-cut kids like Jay and Bambi developed their not-so-squeaky-clean personas. It's where Box morphed his state cop personality into that of a full-blown street thug. Jimm had to dirty up his traditional law enforcement mind-set to become a covert operator. Gundo let his hair and beard grow. It's where the women learned to drink with the boys and occasionally show their tits to a group of men. (Settle down. Not all UC females showed their tits and it usually was done to gain credibility or blend in to an environment.) We all learned to lie and do it well. In short, this was RatSnake basic school.

Here the Core was forming, and events occurred during school that were not talked about again, except in some cases in this book. Appropriate or not, these sorts of antics built a strong trust between us all. In the UC world, it's a lot easier to trust someone when you have dirt on them and they have dirt on you.

Pat and Charlie fully won me over during my basic and advanced training, and not just by overlooking when I missed classes due to hangovers. They introduced me to the legends in the business, and they personally mentored me, eventually sweet-talking me into the undercover world where I would spend most of my ATF years. I truly don't know whether to thank them or beat their fucking asses. But they groomed me, and for that I owe both of them my life. Because of them, I was able to survive countless undercover operations and dodge IA for most of my career.

In an attempt to salvage my reputation before it is totally destroyed by the end of this book, I will share a few redeeming facts about my academy days. I was chosen by the academy staff to be the main UC operator during the final exercise. This was deemed an honor, as it identified that agent as one of the best performers. I had the second-highest grade point average in my academy class, and I also received the Ariel Rios award for leadership. Named after slain ATF Special Agent Ariel Rios, this award was voted on by one's fellow classmates, so it was unique that way. I can't help but mention that the agent with the second-highest number of votes would rise to number two in the bureau while I remained a street agent. If you've heard of me before, then you know I was a whistle-blower within the ATF later in my career. This other agent was ensconced in ATF upper management during the first of two attempts to fire me for participating in blowing the whistle on corruption within ATF and events related to what became known as the Fast and Furious scandal. He eventually was run off the job due to his complicity in that scandal and other executive abuses.

Shit, Billy, if I'd known you were going hold a grudge, I'd have let you have the award.

. . . .

Two or three weeks of any type of training might be sufficient for entry-level skill sets. But with the vastly changing landscape of criminal activity and enforcement strategies, techniques, and technology, ATF went on to create an advanced undercover school. Like so many other things in government, politics played into the student selection process, meaning the decision was left to the respective Special Agents in Charge (SACs). Most of the time, the choices were appropriate, and the students appreciated the extra training, but sometimes the participants hadn't done even one undercover operation since leaving the basic academy. Sometimes the SACs sent their golden boys or girls as a reward. Occasionally, they sent an agent solely to help pad that individual's résumé. When I became an instructor, we had a saying among ourselves: If we haven't heard your name before you came to the advanced UC school, you probably shouldn't be here.

My first assignment as an instructor in an advanced undercover school was back at FLETC in 1988, after I'd been a field UC agent for a year. It would be my most memorable teaching experience. See, I hadn't yet attended the advanced undercover school. My assigned teaching partner for the class was my old friend and former partner from San Francisco, Darren Gil. He had transferred to Las Vegas, and we hadn't seen each other for a couple of years. We had literally helped raise each other's kids in the early days. The instructor teams got an authorized rental car and were assigned to a two- or three-bedroom condo on the island. When you checked in, the rental office would tell you which unit or house you were assigned to. You also would be given your assignments for the school and told where to be for the first day's meeting with the academy bosses.

Darren and I went together. When the rental lady gave us our condo assignment, it didn't have some amenities that we would have liked. It was a nice unit but didn't include a hot tub or a stereo. We asked if there were any other condos available. The lady said she only had one other unit assigned to our group and showed us the check-in package for that one. It had a hot tub, a barbeque grill, and two stereos. The unit had been assigned to Alex D'Atri and another agent.

Darren smiled, and I knew what he was thinking. We started lobbying for Alex's unit. The poor lady didn't know what to do. We lied our asses off and told her it would be okay. She caved in and swapped the units. This would begin the two-week train wreck.

See, Alex was a big boss and a legend, and the guy assigned to room with him also was some big shot. They were down from HQ on business and to monitor this class. After checking in, Darren and I made the drive across the causeway to Pam's #1, where we met up with Milton and Bambi and the rest of our crew. We didn't mention what we had done and figured our little scam would go unnoticed.

After a couple hours, Jimm came storming into the bar and headed straight for us, and he was breathing fire. The place was full, but he didn't give even one fuck who heard him.

"Cefalu, who the fuck do you think you are?"

I started to respond, and he kept going.

"Motherfucker, you think that shit is funny?" and blah, blah, blah.

I started laughing and so did Darren. I guess we answered his question.

Alex and the other guy showed up. Jimm ordered us to drive back to the island and swap the units back. I was surprised he didn't bust us in the mouth when Darren said, "We can do that, but I already spanked one off on my pillow." I quickly followed that up with, "Yeah, and I already wiped my ass with my towel."

Luckily, Alex was a regular guy, and he and I had met before. He waved Jimm off and let us keep the unit. Jimm stayed pissed for the rest of the night, but only that night. Mostly because he would have done the same damn thing. We were constantly submerged in a world where gaming the next guy was how it worked. Practicing on each other kept our skills sharpened.

. . . .

As with most advanced training in ATF, the majority of the students were senior and experienced agents, and the advanced school was far less formal and far more relaxed than basic school, albeit incorporating much more complex training scenarios. The classes regarding new technology were far more advanced, and the students often would be the first to see and field-test some of the equipment.

Certain scenarios took the students off base to real-world environments, such as bars and restaurants. The school was approximately three weeks long, and it was a group endeavor. Unlike in basic school, there were no predefined outcomes; the results were driven by the students' performance. In basic school, there were eight or ten separate scenarios aimed at addressing only one aspect of a potential hazard an agent might face doing undercover work. The advanced school ran one scenario for the entire three weeks, taking twists and turns en route. This required the students to adjust along the way. They were required to be in role at all times. That meant that even after class time, they could be called in or confronted out in the town—just like in the real world. A role player might confront a student on a Saturday morning while they lounged at the beach. A role player might walk up to a student at a restaurant and challenge them on their undercover story or identity. Because of the fluid nature of the class, students and instructors sometimes had time off during the day and did not report to the classroom until six or seven at night.

We might be at the beach all day or just running around the island, and it wasn't out of the question for students or instructors to show up for class after having had a few cocktails. For one thing, there was a new bar in town and all rumors pointed to Charlie Fuller as being the owner. But, of course, those rumors couldn't have been true, because Charlie was an ATF agent and would have been prohibited from owning such an establishment since ATF regulates the liquor industry. The fact was, his sister or some other relative's name was on the license. That didn't quell the rumors, nor did it keep Charlie out from behind the bar while most of us were in the bar, often during daylight hours. Most of the instructors were really good friends and hadn't seen each other for quite some time—we are talking gunpowder and a match. There were so many moving parts to this school that things naturally got out of hand from time to time. That first class Darren and I taught always will be affectionately referred to as the "class from hell."

The point is that these schools, no matter how well conceived and executed, couldn't fully prepare agents for the real UC world. In fact, you couldn't run a yearlong UC school that could prepare agents for what they would be walking into. But the schools were helpful and far better than nothing—and a few weeks of intensive UC training is how it started for most of us. Walking out of the academy, an agent might feel confident, but out in the field, he or she quickly realized they only had part of the picture. Working undercover could be described as walking on a high wire without a net. Blindfolded. An agent has to make that walk—and survive it—again and again and again to begin to fill in the rest of that picture.

CHAPTER 4

....

CRÈME DE LA CRÈME

I said that everyone has a story about Pat Kelly. Here's one I heard from Pat's old trainee/partner, Bob Harper. The two of them met when Bob was a small-town detective in Missouri. One day in 1969, Pat walked into Bob's local police department on some business. Pat was unshaven, sporting his telltale bushy mustache, and wearing a shitty tweed sports coat and blue jeans. Having seen this dirty-looking dude drive up in a red convertible Cadillac, Bob already was suspicious. Pat's firearm was visible, and that put Bob on full alert until the seasoned agent flashed his badge and credentials.

Over the next few months, Pat tried hard to recruit Bob to the ATF division of the IRS. When Bob finished his college work, he did join; in 1970 he attended the academy and was assigned to Kansas City as Pat's trainee. Bob couldn't wait to get his big, fancy Cadillac, shiny Treasury badge, and credentials.

The boss welcomed him to the Kansas City Office, and he and Pat sat the new agent down.

The boss said, "Son, do you have a gun?" Bob said, "Yes, I do," and pulled out a two-inch snub-nosed .38 revolver.

The boss said, "Good, you can carry that. We are out of guns right now."

At the time, a standard-issue weapon for an ATF agent was a Smith & Wesson Model 10 or a Model 66 .38-caliber revolver with a four-inch barrel. Needless to say, Bob's little snubbie had significantly less power and accuracy. And, of course, he no longer had his police service pistol.

Then the boss said, "Pat, give him your badge." Pat handed it over.

The boss sat at his desk and typed out a letter that authorized Bob to carry a gun and make arrests, signed it, and handed it to the new recruit. He told Bob, "This will have to do for now. We are out of badges too."

When it came to his duty vehicle, Bob was handed the keys to an old, hand-me-down Chrysler still painted Border Patrol green. The boss drove the Cadillac. That is, unless an agent needed it for an undercover operation—or, I suppose, to go impress and recruit a small-town detective.

. . . .

On day two of Bob Harper's tenure at the Kansas City office, it was time to hit the streets with his training officer, Pat Kelly. When Bob asked where they were headed, he learned that Pat was going to meet a guy to buy a gun at some bar out of town. "Plan on spending the night," Pat said.

They checked into a new Holiday Inn for six dollars a night. Bob thought this was big-time; he rarely had left his hometown. He did think it was odd when Pat told the desk clerk they only needed one room, and Bob spoke up when Pat suggested to the lady that if she didn't have a room with two beds available, one bed would be fine. After settling on a single room with two beds, they went out, made the buy, and had a couple beers.

When they got back to the hotel room, Pat took a shower—and left the bathroom door wide open. He came out of the bathroom undressed and asked if Bob was going to take a shower before bed. Bob said no. He was feeling a little uncomfortable at this point and put his gun under his pillow. This was 1970, for chrissake, and he was from Missouri.

When Pat walked over, sat down on Bob's bed, and pulled the covers back, Bob freaked out. He pointed his gun at Pat and asked what the hell he was doing. Pat calmly said he thought they would share a bed. Bob said, "Well, you are wrong." Pat climbed into his own bed, and there was no more conversation about what had occurred that night, until they returned to the office, whereupon Bob went straight into the boss's office and demanded to talk to him.

The boss shut the door and said, "I heard you did okay last night." Bob couldn't focus and blurted out, "That agent is gay, and I ain't working with him." The boss asked if he was sure, and Bob told him the story. The boss said he would get to the bottom of it; they were about to have a group meeting and could talk about it further after the meeting. He led Bob down the hall to the conference room. They walked into the room to see all of the agents from the office seated around the conference table. Standing next to the table was a butt-ass naked Pat Kelly.

The boss patted Bob on the back. Pat Kelly said, "Welcome to ATF!"*

. . . .

By the time Darren and I were running around St. Simons Island with our class from hell, ATF had grown considerably—everyone got their own badge—although even in the late 1980s, a lot of the time agents flew by the seat of their pants and fixed whatever got broken along the way. Or at least we tried to. En route, ATF developed a whole bunch of written rules and policies. Headquarters didn't just randomly make up these policies.

---

* As the bureau progressed, so did its attitudes and policies.

Many of the guidelines for work in the field were clearly the result of botched operations or incidents of the past. One area of learning experience for ATF and its agents was improving the practices and technology for long-term undercover operations. Undertaking such operations has never been easy. The logistics alone are mind-numbing. It involves real people leaving real friends and family behind for an indeterminate period of time. Today, ATF has an entire branch in headquarters dedicated to the undercover effort. There is a small army of support personnel to smooth out the process. Jimm Langley and three of his colleagues at the time—Steve, Turbo, and Tim—didn't have any of that infrastructure to rely on when they took on one of the first and one of the largest infiltration cases of the day, maybe in history. These were four highly motivated but diverse personalities. Steve had come to ATF by way of the US Army. Like Jimm and me, Turbo hailed from US Customs. Timmy came to us from the US Marshals. I met him when we both were assigned to the San Francisco field division. After my first time working with him, I was convinced of two things: One, I wasn't the craziest agent in the field division. Two, he scared the shit out of me.

There is nothing like riding a motorcycle down the highway at one hundred miles an hour and knowing that absolutely nothing is going to happen to you. No ticket, no fine, and no annoying and costly court date. This was the situation for this intrepid quartet of agents—it literally was their job. The foursome had made great strides infiltrating an outlaw biker gang known as the Warlocks. Founded in the late 1960s, by the early 1990s the notorious club had claimed South Florida as its own. Our guys had gotten so deep in the organization that they were being given ever-increasing responsibility in the club's business.

A fledgling member of a motorcycle gang gets to do the real shit jobs. This prospect or probate period usually lasts one year, depending on the new guy's loyalty and performance in the club. During that year, he can expect to be the grunt for every scumbag who is a patched member. The new guy is lower than whale shit. He will fetch beers. He will clean motorcycles. He will be expected to stand guard duty over clubhouses and/or parties. He will be expected to throw down with the patched members if there is a fight with rivals, often referred to as a "mud check." All this is intended to test the new member's loyalty to the club. At the end of his prospect period, he receives his "cut," the three-piece patch worn on the back of a biker's vest, and becomes a full patched member. It doesn't take much imagination to understand how harrowing this can be for undercover agents, who are guided by volumes of "manual orders" they must comply with while pretending to be thugs.

Most biker clubs have mandatory runs, usually to put on a show of force at big gatherings. During one particular "Bike Week" in Daytona, Tim was designated to drive one of the "crash" or follow vehicles. These are vans or trucks that follow the club at a safe distance and carry the group's narcotics and weapons, and they also are used to transport broken-down bikes. Yes, it's an FNG's* job, but one that does impart some trust and responsibility. In this case, the van Tim would drive was in fact an ATF undercover vehicle, registered to a fictitious person. A week or so before the run, one of the club's officers freaked out because the van's registration had expired.

Since various states have different rules regarding undercover vehicles, it's a bureaucratic nightmare to renew the registrations for these vehicles. The Warlocks chapter officer insisted that Tim's van have a legal appearance before the run. The agents contacted the Miami field division operations officer and raised hell with him. "We need that fucking registration sticker ASAP," they said, or something along those lines.

They were advised it was going to take a while.

---

* Fucking new guy.

RatSnakes think fast and act fast. Jimm took the license plate off his vehicle and photocopied it. He then cut out the sticker portion of the tag and used a marker to color it yellow to correspond with the current year's designation. He taped the fake sticker to the UC van's license plate. Problem solved, or so the agents thought.

As wave after wave of bikes left two by two from the Warlocks' clubhouse, followed by a couple crash vehicles, the boys were feeling pretty good about themselves. An official run with a major criminal club is quite the accomplishment, and they would be included in all the festivities and meet other club members. The weekend would be filled with guns, bombs, and drugs. It was the perfect place for the UC agents to advance the criminal investigation. They practically had stars in their eyes.

It was a dark, rainy morning when the club left for Daytona. They all knew that virtually every mile from Miami to Daytona would be covered by police. Any time a major Outlaw Motorcycle Organization (OMO) event comes to the attention of law enforcement, all resources are directed at surveillance and fugitive arrests. Roadblocks and tactical teams always are on hand just in case something breaks out between rival clubs. That is why the club officer insisted that the van's registration be up to date. The Warlocks knew that their every action was being scrutinized, and the cops were waiting for an opportunity to pounce.

About thirty miles outside Daytona and about ten miles behind the main pack of bikes, Tim was cruising up I-95, cranking the music and wondering how much evidence he and the guys would be bringing back with them. He glanced in the rearview mirror to see not one but three police cruisers behind him with their lights flashing. One of the club's "ol' ladies" had been designated to keep Tim company on the ride. Playing the role of a biker thug, he turned to her and said, "Let me handle this. You just sit there and shut the fuck up."

This is where it went from bad to worse. Tim figured he would walk to the back of the van, away from the club's "girl," and smooth things over. He couldn't come out of role. That would have been disastrous. But he would smooth talk the cops and be on his way.

Not so fast, Two Dogs.

When the officers approached the vehicle, they ordered both Tim and the ol' lady out of the van at the same time. They searched Tim and the girl, and then walked them back to the front of the police car. At this point, the officer doing all the talking pointed to the rear of the van and asked, "So what the fuck do you think happened here?" Tim looked and saw a long yellow stream of water running down the back of the van. The rain had caused the ink from the marker to run down the license plate. With the biker chick standing right there, Tim couldn't explain his sub-terfuge to the officers. He was arrested and handcuffed. Worse, the police towed the vehicle containing much of the club's supplies. They also placed the young lady in the back of the squad car to give her a ride to the police department where she could call someone to come and pick her up.

The issues arising from this unanticipated arrest of an undercover, which were many, caused Tim to make a decision. For one thing, when he returned to the club after making bail, he would need to have a defensi-ble story about how he got the van and most of the club's property back. Meticulously ironing out these details would require involvement from a much higher level in the chain of command within ATF.

When Tim got an opportunity to be alone with the arresting officer, he said, "You have to call this number, and do it right now." The officer was hesitant. He wasn't going to be told what to do by some biker scum-bag. Eventually, Tim's demeanor and insistence gave the officer pause, and he made the call. Once the ATF supervisor was contacted at the number Tim gave the cop, things moved quickly. Arrest records were created for completely fictitious persons, with corresponding fingerprints. There was hoax bail. In other words, preserving the agents' undercover status became a real nightmare. Fortunately, that is what ATF does, and they worked the problem. This did not, however, save Tim and Jimm from taking a beating for putting the club's run in peril.

This Warlocks case not only was legendary, it provided critical lessons that served as building blocks for future similar operations. The case culminated when several South Florida SWAT teams and the Miami ATF Special Response Team (SRT) descended upon the entire club when they were leaving a patched member's funeral. Dozens were arrested, and many were sent to prison. Many years later, ATF would again set their sights on the Warlocks, but that's a story for another day.

. . . .

While the Warlocks case was advancing, I was teaching new operators at the academy. By this time, I had taught dozens of basic academy classes and several advanced UC schools. One of my classes was loaded with some pretty good operators in their own right. Many would go on to be legendary undercovers, others not so much. Unlike the early days, this class had many female agents as well.

One of the instructors happened to be a longtime buddy of mine. Carlos S. (not Box) and I went way back. He recently had gotten divorced and was on the prowl. One of the women in this class was very attractive, not coming with very many cases under her belt and, as I recall, she was, like others, sent to pad her résumé. She was prissy, with perfectly painted nails and high-end clothes, and would show up for surveillance practical exercises wearing high heels. She seemed to think she was too good to do undercover work. All that didn't sit well with the instructors, male or female. Hell, the females disliked her even more than the males because women had a hard time being taken seriously in the beginning, and this chick just furthered the stereotypes.

Yep, she was a real bitch. She went so far as to say she only dated doctors and lawyers and would never date a cop. That didn't win her any friends, for sure. She completed the school, and to this day, she is the only student to ever give me a bad evaluation. What makes that hilarious is what happened next.

After the class had ended, I was sitting at my desk one day and the phone rang. It was Carlos calling to shoot the shit and talk about what a debacle that whole class had been. Well, of course, I turned the conversation to this female agent—I'd caught him chatting her up a couple times. I even had asked him once, while at the school, if he was going to try and hook up with her. He hinted that he might, and it didn't come up again. I was curious how that all turned out, so I did what Vince does. I blurted out, "Dude, did you ever close on that crazy bitch?" It got quiet, and he let on that he had. I laughed and said something like, "Well, at least you don't have to talk to her ass now that you're back home."

Carlos was in Miami and that agent was from somewhere up north. It got real quiet again, and he said, "Well, yeah, I probably still have to talk to her." I asked, "Why would you do that?" He said, "Because we are getting married." I thought he was joking and I started laughing my ass off. When I finally realized he wasn't joking, I said, "Well, I guess I won't be getting an invite to the wedding." He said, "Naw, probably not, brother." I am happy that I was wrong, because they stayed married to this day. She remained true to her original attitude about undercover work but did rise through the ranks.

· ·

For all my trash talking, make no mistake: Being an undercover agent is damn hard. Being a female undercover agent is six times as hard. Being the *first ever* female ATF undercover agent brought unimaginable stress and pressure to perform.

In 1972, Jo Ann Kocher made history as the first female ATF agent to be sworn in. She has told me over the years that it was the best day of her life. She successfully completed training and entered the field. Her fellow agents were cordial and welcoming, but she could tell all eyes were on her. They all had seen the press release with Jo Ann being sworn in at the main Treasury office. None of them had been flown to the main Treasury to be sworn in. None of them had been featured in a press release. Jo Ann reported to her new office dressed exactly as she had when she was sworn in: professional dress, pumps, and that hideous 1970s beehive hairdo. Her revolver in her purse.

Jo Ann knew she eventually would be asked to do undercover work. She always wondered if she could. Hell, we all did, but none of us ever were going to be the first of our gender to do it. She would be—on one hot and humid day in August 1974, barely two years on the job. Jo Ann was sitting at her desk when her supervisor came over to her and said, "Call Bill, the boss of the White Plains office. He needs you for an undercover operation this afternoon." That day, Jo Ann was wearing a short blue-and-white dress with a matching ribbon that tied into a bow at the back of the waist. Pantsuits were her usual attire, except for raid and arrest situations, when she wore jeans and a T-shirt. She didn't have time to go home and change.

Bill told her she would be playing the part of a girlfriend at a motel where another ATF agent was to meet someone who was selling guns illegally. Her attire wasn't a problem at all, except she had nowhere to conceal her gun. (Because she was the first, ATF had not yet begun to address simple but unique situations related to female UCs, such as where they would keep their gun.) Jo Ann remembers deciding that she would have to keep her purse near her at all times.*

---

* Even today, it's less common for female violators to wear guns, so a female UC potentially can attract more attention if she's seen carrying a weapon.

She drove to White Plains with visions of Peggy Lipton's *Mod Squad* escapades flittering in her head. When she got there, she met with the boss and Kelly, the case agent who would be making the buy. She remembered meeting Kelly from her first week as an agent. Back then he had short brown hair and was clean-cut. He now had a full beard and nearly shoulder-length locks. It didn't surprise her. Many undercover agents looked and acted like "bad guys," but she wondered how she would fit in this clandestine part of law enforcement. Would she need to change her personality and act tough? She always had prided herself on her femininity and didn't want to change, even for the sake of a role. Playing a girlfriend might just be the ticket she needed, at least to get a start.

She joined several other ATF agents and local police officers at the briefing. Agent Kelly told them he'd been dealing with a violator named Perry for several weeks now. Perry was a businessman who'd been collecting and selling guns for some time and was now into weapons prohibited by ATF laws.

"I bought a sawed-off shotgun from him a few weeks ago," said Kelly. "He wants to sell me another gun this afternoon."

Jo Ann sat there, wide-eyed, as Kelly explained they would be meeting at a motel in Westchester County. Instructions were in the agents' briefing packages. Kelly's team had done surveillance on the area and were confident it was a place where they could meet safely, transfer the gun, and arrest Perry with minimal risk.

"I've told Perry that I'm meeting my chick at the motel and invited him to come over with the gun. Jo Ann will be playing my girlfriend," Kelly said.

Jo Ann was trying to remember everything she learned in training as Kelly said that the signal for the bust would be when he closed the trunk after transferring the gun to his car.

"Don't mess this up," she remembered thinking.

In school she'd been taught that the undercover agent always gave a predetermined signal to the covering team when it was time to make the arrest. In this case, Kelly would not be wired, so the signal would have to be visual rather than spoken.

She got up the nerve to ask a question. "What kind of gun will you be buying?"

"A bazooka," came the answer.

A bazooka is a portable shoulder-fired missile weapon, in other words, a military-style anti-tank rocket launcher.

Jo Ann's mind raced. "A damn *bazooka*?" she thought.

This was not going to be a typical first undercover buy. When they got to the bland, two-story concrete motel, they checked into a room on the first floor and parked the undercover government car right in front. Kelly took the covers off one of the queen-sized beds and rumpled the sheets to make it look like it had been used. He also took out a half-full bottle of scotch, placing it and several glasses on the dresser. He poured the liquor and water over ice in two of the glasses. Jo Ann could have used a drink to calm her nerves.

She knew her role as Kelly's girlfriend was mainly for show and backup, if needed. But she didn't want to do anything that would ruin the investigation. Perhaps naively, she wasn't at all concerned for their safety. Several other ATF agents and local police officers were secreted around the motel complex.

When Perry knocked on the door, shortly after they got there, she froze for a few seconds. Kelly looked at her briefly before opening the door. She wondered if he could tell she was nervous.

Perry was not what she expected. A man in his late twenties, he had long sideburns and a receding hairline. He was well dressed and polite. He and Kelly exchanged a few pleasantries, and then Kelly pointed to Jo Ann. "That's my chick, Jo Ann." Perry glanced at her, and the two men immediately started to talk about the price of the bazooka. They agreed on the price and they all went outside to Perry's car. Jo Ann kept her white purse close to her side, slung over her right shoulder, in case she needed to get to her gun quickly.

Perry opened the trunk of his car, and she saw her first bazooka.* The weapon was more menacing than she thought it would be. It was longer and thicker than the pictures she had seen. Kelly inspected it, found it to his satisfaction, and gave Perry the money. Together they lifted the weapon out of Perry's car and carried it to Kelly's government vehicle.

At that moment, Kelly closed his trunk and shouted, "Federal agents. You're under arrest." Jo Ann reached for and produced her small revolver from her handbag. She didn't need it. Agents and officers came from everywhere. One was standing on the second-floor landing of the motel, pointing a shotgun at them. Perry instantly realized what was happening and gave up without a struggle. He seemed stunned. They went back to the office, where Perry was processed and interviewed. Bill, the boss, and Kelly thanked Jo Ann for her participation and told her she did a good job. Basking in the praise, she headed back to her office.

Jo Ann's career with ATF continued for another twenty-four years, including numerous surveillances, arrests, search warrants, and undercover assignments in New York and around the country as well as supervisory roles in Hawaii and San Francisco, where she became the Assistant Special Agent in Charge (ASAC) of the San Francisco Field Division from 1996 to her retirement from ATF in 1999.†

. . . .

While Jo Ann was blazing trails on the East Coast, Bonnie would be the

---

* I spent twenty-seven years doing this shit and *never* bought a bazooka.

† I was excited to hear that Jo Ann is planning to write a book in the future chronicling her exploits as ATF's first female special agent.

first female hired on the West Coast. Bonnie came to ATF directly out of college with no prior police experience. Having women in the ranks was such a new thing to ATF that they were freaking out, according to Bonnie. She later would find out that prior to her arrival, the San Francisco SAC held an all-hands meeting. "If any of you try to get in her pants, just leave your gun and badge on my desk," the male agents were told. Bonnie remembers that at first the other agents would barely say hello to her out of fear for how it would be perceived.

Her first UC was with Bill Bertoloni, an ATF legend. He said it would be an easy job for her to cut her teeth on. She would play the girlfriend and just watch how it was done. Bonnie was pretty excited. When they met up the morning of the deal, Bill had lost his voice, completely. With his laryngitis, Bonnie figured they would cancel the deal. Instead, Bill told her that she would take the lead. Bonne was scared shitless, but she sucked it up. They met the violator, bought the gun, and she had instant credibility with other agents from then on.

Bonnie would go on to distinguish herself with more demanding UC operations, further solidifying the worthiness of female agents in a historically all-male agency. She was called upon when San Jose State University experienced a bomb attack in the mid-1970s. Investigations had developed a suspect but no clear-cut way to approach him to garner proof. Bonnie looked at the problem from a new and different perspective. The suspect had a girlfriend who was renting out her studio apartment. Bonnie befriended the girlfriend and rented the studio. The girlfriend said Bonnie should make herself at home and feel free to use anything in the apartment. While digging around the apartment one day, Bonnie scored. The bomber had sent a typed letter to the university, claiming responsibility. Bonnie found a typewriter in the small attic. It was sent to the ATF laboratory for forensic examination, and bingo, it was the typewriter used by the bomber. Case solved.

After proving herself for over five years, Bonnie was tasked with a job that had her going home in tears. Having grown up in Sacramento, California, she was of course familiar with the reputation of the Hells Angels club. Bill Bertoloni was one of the undercovers on a racketeering and conspiracy case against the club in 1979. The groundbreaking RICO case (so-called for the Racketeer Influenced and Corrupt Organizations Act of 1970) included two waves of prosecution conducted out of the San Francisco US Attorney's Office. The first phase was the prosecution of club members with direct evidence against them in the form of firearms, explosives, and narcotics buys. This phase took over two years. The undercover agents worked out of the US Attorney's Office and lived in hotels. This stretched the ATF budget for lodging and per diem, and Bill and the other agent eventually were sent home.

The second phase involved prosecuting historical cases that had developed out of the original case. However, that part wasn't explained to Bonnie clearly. When she formally was assigned to the new Hells Angels task force and appointed to lead the second phase, she went home thinking she was going to be expected to work undercover with the Angels. For days, she was scared at the thought of being raped by a bunch of drug-crazed bikers. Eventually, her role was clarified; her sole job was to assist in the prosecution efforts through follow-up investigations and evidence presentation that did not include undercover work. She served in that capacity for two years before leaving ATF for the US Customs service. When I asked her why she left, her answer was simple: She thought ATF had the best agents but the worst managers.

Bonnie went on to use her ATF experience to help develop and enhance the US Customs undercover program. But before leaving ATF, Bonnie made her mark. It was the 1970s, when radical groups were popping up all over the country, including in San Francisco and Berkeley. A San Francisco police substation had been blown up, and there was a failed attempted bombing of the ATF office. Having jurisdiction in explosives cases, ATF jumped into the fray.

Members of the counterculture Weather Underground, including prominent member William Charles "Bill" Ayers, were fugitives and believed to be operating in the San Francisco Bay Area. FBI intelligence suggested that some of the women in the group might be lesbians and hiding within the gay community in San Francisco. Bonnie and another female agent were given government investigative funds and told to mingle in the gay community, at the time still considered a radical group. The agents were looking for specific women who were on the run. Their operation was not successful, but Bonnie will forever remember hanging out and dancing in the rowdy "no boys allowed" bars of that past decade.

Bonnie, Jo Ann, and many other female agents would take the reins over the years that followed those early days. They actively participated in advancing the undercover programs within ATF, both for the females who followed as well as their male counterparts. This was uncharted territory for everyone. You are only as good as your partner, and with the growth of the bureau, there would be more and more scenarios requiring a larger role for females. When ATF agents starting dipping their toes into the narcotics world, female UCs again proved their worth and equal willingness to confront evil.

. . . .

By this time, I hope it's clear that undercover work is not math or chemistry; it is an art. There can be wrong answers. But almost any answer could be right depending on the scenario facing a UC, the experience level of a UC, and, hell, even the mind-set of the bad guy. In this chapter, I've tried to describe what it was like to be an agent during the bureau's early years and how certain mentalities about undercover work advanced over time. Then and now, being the UC on a case involves another layer of responsibility. For example, our reports had to be precise and exact. The case agent or surveillance agents could write less-detailed reports, for example: *I saw the violator show up and walk into a hotel room, and then I saw the violator leave. He was carrying a package.* This type of generalization normally was sufficient because multiple agents saw the same thing, and it was undisputed.

However, the UC was often the *only* person to see the violation of law, hear the dialogue, and be able to testify to exact details that established the elements of the crime and therefore guilt. Sometimes, and I stress sometimes, we were lucky enough to have audio and video recordings. But more often than not, the equipment failed, we lost battery life, or we were able to record only intermittent parts of a transaction. When that happened, it opened a Pandora's box for the defense attorneys. The case agent and the UCs were generally the ones to get beat up the most on the witness stand.

> **A DEFENSE ATTORNEY MIGHT ASK SOMETHING LIKE THIS:** Isn't it true, Agent Cefalu, that you lie for a living? How is it possible that at the very moment you say my client admitted whatever, that the wire cut out?

> **OR THIS:** Agent Cefalu, I see in your report you had a telephone conversation with my client, but you didn't record it. Is that because you were trying to entrap my client and didn't want the jury to hear my client decline your offer?

If there were multiple defendants being tried together, the defense attorneys would come one after another, with no other goal than to discredit the UC. Experienced UCs already would have addressed the answers to such questions in their notes, reports, or trial preparation. But it can be very draining to be attacked for hours during a public hearing.

As the bureau grew in stature and budget, it began to undertake larger and more intricate infiltration-type cases. This required much more manpower, much more money, and a buttload more exposure for its agents. Staying in a long-term role created a host of potential problems both personally and professionally. The field divisions had to commit their UC and cover team agents to an open-ended commitment. That meant that if a field division gave up five agents to a UC operation, that division was down five agents for the duration of the case. Those agents weren't working cases for their bosses; they were working them for somebody else's boss. Historically, ATF has been a statistic-based agency. That is to say, everyone from the lowest agent to the SAC is judged and evaluated on the number of cases taken on and the number of bad guys that go to jail. Taking away the number of cases those five agents could have produced at home significantly dropped that field division's numbers.

As ATF took on larger, more complex inter-field division cases, the bureau needed to address some pitfalls. One of the biggest issues that began to occur was agent long-term exposure and potential burnout or compromise. In response, ATF expanded on the "undercover pool" concept that had been initiated in the 1980s. Mental health/welfare protocols were developed to address the effects of long-term exposure on agents and their families.

After the independent Treasury report on the ATF investigation of Vernon Wayne Howell (a.k.a. David Koresh) and the sect known as the Branch Davidians, a "control agent" scenario was devised and became a required protocol for any long-term undercover operation.

In the early 1990s, ATF undercovers infiltrated the Branch Davidians group, who were based at the so-called Mount Carmel Center outside Waco, Texas. The investigation of the notorious Seventh-day Adventist splinter group led by Koresh (preceded by his rival, George Roden) for illegal manufacture and possessions of firearms and explosives occurred over nine months prior to ATF serving arrest and search warrants that led to a planned raid on the Branch Davidian compound on February 28, 1993. After sect members were tipped off about the raid, a shoot-out ensued, resulting in the deaths of four ATF agents, with seventeen other agents wounded. Six Branch Davidian members were killed during the shoot-out. The Department of Justice tasked the FBI with attempting to resolve the standoff to avoid the appearance that ATF wanted revenge. The subsequent fifty-one-day standoff led by the FBI culminated in dozens more deaths when sect members who were barricaded inside set fire to the compound.

After the failed raid and loss of life, there were demands for congressional hearings. The US Treasury Department commissioned a comprehensive study of the investigation and operation related to the Branch Davidians. Experts from all fields related to each portion of the investigation weighed in. Although some of the findings are subjective and have been challenged, it was a well-done report, albeit the consummate Monday-morning quarterbacking. The report specifically challenged portions of ATF's ongoing undercover planning and execution. Although the Waco operation had been approved at the highest levels, the panel found certain aspects of the UC plan insufficient. They did *not* find fault on behalf of any of the undercover operators, only in some of the assumptions the plan relied on.

Reports aside, the emotional toll of the Waco case on agents was incredibly high. Prior to the seven-week standoff, ATF undercover agents already had spent months away from their families, working on an investigation that ended violently and tragically. The control agent protocol was implemented to recognize and help compensate for collateral damage to agents' well-being during long-term investigations. Basically it meant that if an agent spent a particular length of time of uninterrupted UC or suffered a traumatic incident during a UC, there would be an independent set of eyes on him or her to ensure the agent's and their family's well-being. It was a tricky prospect to be a control agent. Imagine suspecting some sort of meltdown of your assigned UC agent and having to be the one to make the call to shut it down and pull the agent out. What if you were wrong, and the agent and his wife were just having typical marital problems, and you shut down a case that the agent had been successfully working for months?

I intentionally never worked as a control agent; however, one source of pride for me and many was having a role in developing a peer support program. ATF didn't create the concept, but I think we perfected it. As ATF agents, we suffered an inordinate number of lethal encounters. ATF recognized the damage and potential byproduct of leaving its agents out there to figure it out and fend for themselves after such an encounter. Through the peer support program, experienced agents who had survived such encounters were trained and available 24/7 to respond to agents after such incidents. The program was so successful that ATF received funding to offer its peer support agents to outside agencies. The program was adapted to be used in the undercover pool, and a clinical psychologist was hired to train and support the peer support agents. I could grumble about ATF management doing what bureaucrats do and creating more policies than anyone needed, but I was privileged to be part of the peer support team and saw its value on many occasions.

CHAPTER 5

SNAKE CODE

There is no such thing as a real RatSnake code—at least not one you'll ever be able to prove or show in writing. Snake code is an implied set of expectations for loyalty and dedication built on deep-rooted feelings for your fellow agents. The notion of coworker loyalty isn't new, but if someone from another profession, let's say an insurance agent, turns on a coworker or drops the ball, it's unlikely that either of them will be killed as a result. Within specialized law enforcement and investigative units, the loyalty mentality is amplified. I won't go all psychobabble on why this is. I think anybody reading this book recognizes the need for an unshakable devotion to your team. Snake code, and its close relation the "thin blue line," is a real and vital part of the job.

Much about the UC world is unwritten. But if I were going to write a field guide, the section on Snake code would include some real-world examples, a.k.a. practical suggestions for how not to fuck it up when your and everybody else's asses are on the line.

EXERCISE DISCRETION.

During my first day on the job at the Organized Crime Drug Enforcement Task Force (OCDETF) in San Francisco, most of the guys came over and welcomed me. Larry Williams did so from sitting behind his desk. He was one of the most senior agents in the OCDETF group and in San Francisco. All the new guys and even some of the old guys gave him a wide berth. He looked like the classic Marlboro man, had a reputation of being a badass, and had little use for new guys or management. He was also the first one to call me on my first day in ATF and welcome me aboard. He liked that I was an ex-cop and former Marine, so he took me under his wing. Even with that, I tried to stay out of his way.

Larry was a legendary investigator with a photographic memory. I literally have seen someone ask him for a specific report dating back six or eight years and watched him open a drawer filled with files and barely look down to pull out the report. On that first day, after shooting the breeze for a couple minutes, he asked if I was any relation to Bob Cefalu. He was asking about my father, and I didn't know what to say. I actually was somewhat surprised that my dad's questionable associations hadn't hindered my background investigation as an ATF candidate. Growing up on the Milwaukee, Wisconsin, waterfront, my father held several bartending jobs for Frankie Ballistreri, a notorious Mafia boss. Frankie lined up my dad's job in San Francisco when my parents decided to move to California. But that had been almost thirty years earlier. I didn't think Larry was privy to that information since he hadn't been the one to do my background investigation, but little did I know that Larry became aware of my dad by other means.

I answered Larry's question in the affirmative and asked why. He got up and walked into a big storage room filled with old files and notes on past investigations. He moved a couple boxes and pulled out an over-sized poster board showing a link chart (a visual chart used to track groups of violators during ongoing investigations) and knocked the dust off of it. Right there in the middle of the chart was my dad's name and picture. WTF?

When I saw that the chart was titled "The Finetti Murder," I relaxed.

Ten years earlier, there had been a particularly heinous murder of one of my dad's friends in front of his daughter. It all stemmed from some dispute between my dad's bosses, who were local gangster types, and a man named Finetti, who apparently had a connection to the under-world. My dad's employers brought in a hit man from Hawaii. They obviously didn't say that was their purpose, just that the visitor was a friend. This "friend" asked to borrow my dad's Cadillac to take a trip to Lake Tahoe with some of the bosses. Of course, my dad let them use the car. Sometime over the next couple days, this Hawaiian cat killed Finetti at his house and was driving my dad's car. Since interstate crimes had been committed, ATF had gotten involved in the case, and my father's name appeared on the link chart. The loan of the Cadillac to the so-called friend was proven to be the sole extent of my father's knowledge of and involvement in this crime.

As a bartender over the years, my father had opportunities to boost his income. He would refer to himself as a sports analyst. I called him a bookie. A little-known fact about ATF is that in the early 1970s, the investigation and enforcement of gambling laws was delegated to ATF. It only lasted about six months, but my father again showed up on ATF's radar.

The lesson for me was that Larry kept all of this under his hat. He was old-school and knew that we all have skeletons in our closets. This skeleton didn't affect anyone else on the team or my ability to do my job. Over the years, I've kept in mind Larry's example for how to behave when it was my turn to live out that part of the code.

DON'T ASK. DON'T TELL.

The way a UC sees it is that he or she knows things others do not, and we like it that way. We didn't want the bosses knowing all of our shortcuts and ways to skirt policy. For example, it was against ATF regulations to use your own personal funds to pay an informant. However, when you were standing in a dark alley with your snitch, who was doing great work for you, and he asked for a hundred bucks to pay his rent, you had two options. You could tell him to call you later, after you had gone back to the office, filled out the proper paperwork, and had it approved. Or, you could take a hundred dollars outta your pocket, give it to him, and later replace it after ATF had approved the funds.

The only way bosses would find out about these measures was if they had been for-real, no-shit UC operators earlier in their careers. Or, if somebody told them. Bosses who had been no-shit UCs knew about these policy sidesteps and understood they were sometimes necessary to get the job done. They would turn a blind eye, preserving our code, or simply rely on the guideline of "don't ask, don't tell." If we got caught, the consequences would fall upon us. To be very clear, sidestepping or loosely interpreting policy does not mean breaking the law, which is *never* tolerated by a RatSnake.

MANAGE UP.

An agent named Louis "Louie" Quinonez had been Bird's local partner in Arizona for many years. As such, Louis and I had become friends. Louis was hyperintelligent, intellectual, and admittedly a quirky guy. He had a long family history of law enforcement. I always liked Louis—liked working with him and partying with him. I just didn't ever want to work *for* him. We had such different personalities. Well, I must have jinxed myself, because while I was working in Georgia, that is exactly what happened. Louis was announced as my new group supervisor in Atlanta. I am, and always have been, crystal clear about my character flaws and personal shortcomings. Hell, I wouldn't want to supervise me. It was an ongoing joke among the RatSnakes that Louie was being punished by being made my supervisor. I was actually fine with it. I trusted Louis implicitly. He had lived the Snake code.

His promotion came at a time when I was assigned to the drug task force run by the Athens PD, and we were extremely busy. He gave me his total support, and I did my best to keep it between the lines and keep him out of hot water. He was very nervous as a first-time supervisor, since he had a one-year probationary period, and his bosses were micromanaging control freaks. I told him many times, "Louis, whatever you do now will set the stage for the rest of your time here." What I was trying to impart to him was that you couldn't cower to the SAC and ASAC for a year, and then change and start standing up to them. It was best to set the tone early. For the most part, he did that, and also he and I navigated our new work relationship fairly well. Although our time together wasn't without its trials. One Saturday morning, while I was at my son's football game, Louie called me, and that call would test our friendship.

When I say Louie was quirky, it is not a criticism or a slam. The RatSnakes always had agreed that he would just think too hard and too much about stuff. The gist of his phone call was that he wanted me to consider leaving the group he supervised and transferring to another group in Atlanta. He felt that our being so personally close was not good for him or me. I was perplexed. I had worked in this group for years, and these were my people. And I was basically making Louie's group the hardest-hitting one in Atlanta. I thought, "Why do I have to be the one to leave, why doesn't Louis just move to another group?"

If Louie was anything, he was fair. We discussed, and he listened to my side. He ultimately agreed with me and dropped the matter. We remained friends and comrades throughout the whole time he remained in Atlanta. I think at the end of my pitch that day, I offered him a Midol.

BE STAND-UP.

Among our crew it often was said that ATF agents were the worst cock blocks ever. That is to say, the male agents and sometimes the female agents would disrupt a fellow agent's progress at a romantic endeavor just for the fun of it. Kind of: "If I ain't getting laid tonight, neither are you." But we also would go to great strides to pump up one of our folks. In my personal experience, the best example of this aspect of the code in play occurred in Stockholm, Sweden.

Jay Dobyns and I had been tapped to teach in Budapest, Hungary. About forty-five days before the assignment came out, I was ordered to conduct some UC training for a group of Swedish federal police who were touring US law enforcement facilities. I fought it tooth and nail because I was up to my ass in ongoing investigations, but an order is an order. The relevant part of that story is that there were six male police officers and one six-foot-tall beautiful female officer in the group. After a week together, the female officer, Lotta, spent a couple extra weeks in the United States. At my house. When she left, we both thought that probably would be the last time we would see each other. Then the Budapest gig came up. I sent Lotta an email, and she invited me to come stay with her on the trip. My travel agent told me, "You have to fly right over Sweden to get to Budapest." I asked the agent to book a stopover in Stockholm the week before I was due in Hungary.

Jay and I had planned to fly together. When I called to break the bad news that I would just meet him there, he asked why, and I told him of my plans. His response was, "Fuck you, I'm going with you." Since he was my best friend, I said okay. Lotta said she would love to show the both of us around. So, we changed our flights, and we were off to Sweden. Having upheld my end of the code, Bird owed me one.

We landed in Stockholm about 7 AM and stepped off the plane into Minnesota-like winter weather. Lotta met us at the airport, and then we made the short drive to downtown Stockholm, where her apartment was located. Her place was situated amid cafés up and down the block, with old fixtures and flickering lights that gave it a charming European World War II–era ambience. And it was tiny. A very small, one-bedroom upstairs studio.

It was snowing outside and minus who-the-fuck-knows-how-many degrees. Like me, Jay was still dressed for California weather. He had on cowboy boots, ripped jeans, a wife-beater tank top, and a leather motorcycle jacket. Without any prompting, he said, "Hey, guys, I'm going to go find a cup of coffee and check out some of the area." It was clear he wanted to give Lotta and me a little time to get reacquainted. We took full advantage of his generosity for the next hour or so. Then we heard a knock. I opened the door to see a visibly frozen Jay Bird. His lips were chattering, his knees were shaking, and there literally was a three-inch-long icicle hanging off his goatee. I busted out laughing, asked, "How'd ya like the architecture?" and invited him in. I guess we were even. Now that's how a RatSnake does it.

BE LOYAL.

The basics:

- You don't rat out a fellow operator unless said operator goes criminally rogue.
- You don't fuck another operator's spouse.
- You don't ask a fellow RatSnake to break the law.
- What happens in our circle stays in our circle.

I'll never forget walking into Pam's #1 upon my arrival for the start of a new undercover school. As I approached a table where most of the crew had already assembled, Jimm Langley came up and kissed me square on the mouth. Before that very moment, my father and my sons were the only men I had ever kissed on the lips. I choked it down, hoping for a handshake from Box and the rest. Not so lucky. Next came a sloppy kiss from Box, then Bambi, then Carmen, who was Box's wife, and then Bird, and so on. I'd say I was freaked out, but I really wasn't. Shit, I had escaped from a medium-security juvenile detention facility at age fifteen; I could survive some slobber from my friends.

This also was the first time I was exposed to another tradition. Not one agent, old or young, can tell me how this came about or when. At the end of each of our gatherings, someone would put Don McLean's "American Pie" on the jukebox. Every RatSnake present would sing—at the top of their voices—the song that never seems to end. This tradition among the RatSnake world continues to this day. I guess it was just some cool shit to do.

We began eating and drinking to excess, preparing for the long classroom days to come. I remember standing around listening to everyone's stories, and one thing stood out. They weren't bragging about their own accomplishments, they were bragging about each other's. They were pumping each other up, and they even included me. Someone chimed in about a good case I'd made out in California. I liked this RatSnake shit.

WHILE I'M ON THE TOPIC, DON'T BE A SHOWBOAT.

That night at Pam's #1, every time there was a break in the conversation, there was one guy who would say, "Let me tell you about this case I'm working now," or "I did this undercover that nobody else could do." He took any chance he could to interject how cool he was. That was my first exposure to this particular agent. Unfortunately, it wasn't my last.

He was later involved in the OMO infiltration case of the Warlocks I told you about in the last chapter. The team of RatSnakes working the Warlocks case started out very close and tight-knit. That didn't last long. As the infiltration got underway, the agent who thought he was God's gift to ATF began to showboat, thinking he could do it better than the others.* He started railing against Tim's drinking with the bikers, while doing the exact same thing. He set up buys or deals to garner his own fame without properly informing the other UCs. As the relationship was deteriorating between this agent and the other UCs, he became

---

* To be somewhat clear, this agent's name was not Jimm, Turbo, or Tim.

more critical of their performance. One such occasion brought things to near blows. The group of UCs was approaching an intersection on their bikes. Tim looked away, and then looked back just in time to slam into the rear of the self-serving agent's bike. No one got hurt, no major damage. Shit like that happens when you are running hard. But this agent didn't see it that way. He saw an opportunity to cut Tim out of the case. The others UCs had to talk him out of ratting Tim out. That event further built his reputation as a one-way son of a bitch not worthy of RatSnake status.

After all of his criticisms and perceived disloyalties during this investigation, karma caught up with his ass. The case was successfully executed and brought awesome prosecutions. But as news of the case was unsealed, so were this agent's own misgivings. Apparently, he wasn't the stout law enforcement loyalist he wanted everybody to think he was. After the arrests, he was overheard in US Marshals' lockup apologizing to one of the defendants he had befriended. That was it for the other UCs on the case. The team spent over a year trying to put these assholes in prison, and this agent apologizes for doing his fucking job? Oh, it gets better. During the period preceding the massive takedowns, he was riding around with the sister of one of the outlaw gang members—a huge Operational Security (OPSEC) violation. It was said that Internal Affairs didn't get involved until somebody made it public that this agent had personally purchased a motorcycle from a close associate of the Warlocks for well below market price. Somebody fairly high up the food chain must have stepped in and saved his ass, because the agent got minimal discipline for these infractions. His path, though, was clear. He was definitely heading for management, because none of the guys from the Warlocks case—nor most of the rest of us—would work with him ever again by choice.

TRUST AND HONOR.

In our day-to-day interactions, RatSnakes may have seemed nonchalant, as if not taking the job seriously. That couldn't have been further from the truth. In fact, most of us were scared shitless most of the time when we were undercover. We took our jobs very seriously—sometimes to the point of paranoia. We simply had to be able to trust one another beyond normal levels. If you partnered up with another UC, you expected to be in agreement on how to proceed. You had to discuss options and agree on a response before it happened. For example, giving two different answers to a question from a violator could be fatal. Your reaction to an action should not come as a surprise to your partner.

In one case, Jimm and another agent were not full members of an OMO they were investigating. Therefore, they were not allowed to be involved in club business or attend "Church"—what bikers called their weekly or monthly club business meetings. Jimm and his partner were in the clubhouse but not in the room where the meeting was being held. But they could hear a heated debate. Jimm's partner became convinced that the bikers were plotting their murder. Jimm heard nothing that led him to the same conclusion, but his partner started to come unglued. He tried to convince Jimm they should leave before the meeting let out. Jimm wanted to stay. When they heard the meeting start to break up, without warning, the agent pulled the wire he was carrying out of his pocket and handed it to Jimm. Moments before the door opened, Jimm had to stash the wire quickly so the bikers wouldn't walk out to see him holding a recording device. Jimm never worked with that agent again. There were other events that caused concern about this agent's ability to maintain his composure under pressure, and many besides Jimm also ended their contact with this agent.

PROTECT ALL LIVES.

On and off the job, we would constantly say and do things to desensitize ourselves to the danger we would be walking into. A non-UC might not get our sense of humor, but that was okay. We did. Jokes aside, no agent ever wanted to break his or her word. We tried to maintain the highest level of honor. This also applied to working with confidential informants. UCs probably took a slightly different view of CIs (confidential informants) than did the average field agent. We all were trained to keep a snitch down. Control their every action and never let them believe they were equal. But when you were working UC with an informant, if he died, you probably died too. So we tried to maintain some sort of working relationship with informants who were active. Sometimes we would become fond of and get closer to a CI than was prudent. But if you asked someone to betray their own, you often were the only friend they had left. A CI's life during and even after the case often was your responsibility.

UCs lent themselves to a variety of details and services. We could get into areas other agents or cops couldn't. We might be asked to do particularly tricky surveillance on foot in areas of high crime. We often were asked to get pre-raid eyes on areas that were too hard for our teams to recon because they wouldn't blend into the type of environment. One such occasion required our UCs to secure and protect a high-level government witness, since UCs could come and go from safe houses without drawing attention. This female witness had ratted out her husband, Blair Guthrie, a very close associate and "meth cook" for the Hells Angels. She did so for domestic reasons, just so she could get away from him. We did our job, round the clock, 24/7 for weeks on end. Her husband was charged with manufacturing machine guns and silencers. He was ultimately convicted and sent to prison. We were directed to highly encourage her, in fact, to convince her that she needed to go into the US Marshals' witness protection program. We were not to take no for an answer. But you can only help those who want to be helped. Just when I thought I had convinced her to go, she flip-flopped and decided not to. She came from a wealthy family and thought their money could protect her.

While protecting her, we agreed to let her call Sonny Barger—one of the founding members of the Oakland, California, chapter of the Hells Angels—and try to get a read on his attitude toward her for snitching on a close associate. The call was recorded, of course. She and Sonny had a brief conversation, during which she told him her actions were only directed at Blair and not the club. Sonny told her that was good enough.

When the detail was over, the FBI arranged for her safe travel back to her family's home in Texas. They provided her a local contact agent should anything arise that might be suspicious. I understood why she didn't want to go into hiding for the rest of her life, but I wish she had. Blair served about four years in prison. Within days of his release, there came a knock at the door of his ex-wife's parents' house in Texas. When she opened the door, the flower deliveryman opened fire and killed her in her parents' foyer.*

Any loss of life is tragic, but this one hit home more than most. I was young and wanted to save the entire world from bullies. I always will remember that protection detail as a failure.

DON'T BREAK THE CODE.

A fitting example of what happens when the code is broken is a story that involved the infamous Jay Dobyns bikini episode, which basically

---

* I am not saying Blair's release had anything to do with this young lady's murder. I'm merely telling a story. You decide.

went like this. During the training session known as the "class from hell," a bunch of us were partying at the condo assigned to one of the female instructors for the class duration. Bird went to the bathroom and saw her bikini hanging in the shower and thought it would be funny if he came out wearing it, and, trust me, it was. It was funny as shit. Here's this six-foot-two, former college wide receiver wearing a skimpy bikini, with—wait for it—a banana stuffed in the bottoms.

This female agent was liked and well trusted. She was a good operator and a loyal friend. At the time, she was dating a train wreck of a new agent back home. Speaking from personal experience, the guy was a tool. He also was the only probationary agent I ever recommended for termination. Professionally, I stand by my recommendation that he should have been fired. Lucky for him, our boss at the time, Lou Bristol, was old-school and asked me to tone down my recommendation. He said it was my job as his training agent to unfuck this kid. I respected Lou more than almost any boss I had ever had, so I tried.

When the female agent told her then boyfriend about the bathing suit incident, he apparently became infuriated (more likely, jealous) and insisted she report this horrible act to management. To be clear, the definition of sexual harassment or discrimination is predicated on *unwanted* behavior. For years, this female agent either had participated in or hung around us when our off-duty antics got out of hand. She was definitely in the inner circle and knew all of our secrets. And, she laughed her ass off when Bird walked out of the bathroom in that bikini.

Being a gambler, I would have bet my house that she would never file a complaint. Especially since most of the grief would fall on Box (he was in charge of the class and was present during the incident), who had welcomed her into his home many times.

She did report the incident, and the entire episode was devastating on both sides. Box took some time on the beach, slang for a suspension. The ensuing investigation that sucked many of us in quickly showed that she had repeatedly and regularly engaged in similar activity, and she withdrew her complaint. Unfortunately, she couldn't take back the fact that she had intentionally broken the trust of her brothers and sisters. The other female UCs in our group took her actions particularly hard. They saw it as fucking up their hard-fought standing in this circle. After it all went down, a sign on the front door of a prominent local PD crime squad had this agent's name printed inside a circle with a line through it. She would never recover with our collective crew.

. . . .

In closing, let me break it down. You never heard the above stories. Snake code. You will *never* hear some other stories. Snake code. We all lived through this together, the good, the bad, and the ugly. Repeat after me. Snake code.

CHAPTER 6

....

OUT OF THE CAGE

In addition to undercover work, agents perform a wide variety of investigative duties that can give rise to some crazy shit. My second-favorite duty was "executing search and/or arrest warrants." We called it "kicking in doors," because that's exactly what we did. In the 1980s, we probably had one battering ram for all eleven San Francisco ATF offices. So, we kicked the doors open. Or tried to.

Back then, we served most search warrants under the cover of darkness, using stealth approaches. You had to stack up a team at the door, breach (break down) the door, and make entry quickly to surprise the violator(s). Kicking in a door is an art. Failing on your first try would definitely get your balls busted when you got back to the office. Failing on a second or third try brought serious ridicule. My first attempt at kicking a door didn't go so well. With everybody stacked at the door, literally lined up nut to butt, I gave the go signal, drew back, and with all my strength, I kicked it.

Effectively kicking a door requires you to target the lock and physically break it away from the door frame. What you *don't* want to do is kick at the dead middle of the door. Yes, that's the weakest part, but kicking the center generally doesn't defeat the lock. I learned that the hard way. My foot went all the way through the door up to my knee. The violator started screaming and ran toward the door. The team all crashed into me, thinking the door was going to be broken open. I didn't know what else to do, so standing there on one foot, the other still firmly stuck in the door, I pushed my revolver through the hole I'd made and ordered the violator to get on the floor. Thankfully, he complied. My team helped me extract my foot from the door and proceeded to execute the search warrant. I heard about that one for a *long* time.

My skills improved over time, but even that didn't ensure smooth sailing. The very next time I was the breaching agent, I nailed it, first try. I hit it so perfectly that the door flew open with a crash. The crash was the result of the inside doorknob smashing through a one-hundred-gallon glass tank, spilling exotic tropical fish all over the entranceway. Due to agent safety, we couldn't stop, and about nine agents flowed into the house, with no choice but to stomp over very expensive fish as we went. I'm sorry about the fish, but you really can't make this shit up.

. . . .

Every undercover assignment could be equated to kicking in a door and not knowing what awaited on the other side. All the training and planning in the world can get you only so far before that door eventually has to be flung open and you have milliseconds to react to an unforeseen scenario. You probably won't be surprised when I say that the greatest day in a UC operator's life is when he or she is turned loose to do just that: kick open the door and get out of the cage to show the UC world what they've got.

It's potentially also the worst day in a UC operator's life. All the talking is over; time to produce.

Imagine, if you will, being twenty-something years old, having a butt-load of authority, and then given the freedom to go out and hunt down bad guys. When she became an instructor, Bambi was famous for encouraging students to be scared to death. She felt that was a healthy way to approach undercover. Bambi was attracted to UC work early on. It helped that her ATF partner, Randy Beach, was a high-strung ex-cop who loved putting bad guys in jail. Bambi had confided in me that whenever she did UC, she was scared shitless. That's when I knew she took this shit seriously. Up to and including my very last undercover deal, I was petrified each and every time. Over the years, I learned to overcome and manage that fear, but I used to laugh when Bambi would say, "I'm not like all you guys who seem to handle this stuff without ever being scared." It didn't help that during basic academy and any subsequent advanced training, we were constantly reminded of some of the tragic failures in our agency's history. Ariel Rios, Alex D'Atri, Eddie Benitez—among others, those names stayed with us. All three agents had been shot in the line of duty, and in the cases of Ariel and Eddie, killed, in Florida in the early 1980s during the drug wars.

One of Bambi's earliest solo buys could have gone south very quickly. She was purchasing heroin from a guy known as Crippled Joey. They called him that because he had one leg longer than the other and walked funny. He didn't like the name, but it stuck. The normal deal was, Bambi would roll up in her wired-up UC pickup truck, and Joey would jump in. They would chat for a couple minutes, exchange money for dope, and Bambi would leave. Complete with crystal-clear video and audio recordings. We call that a slam-dunk guilty plea.

On one of her buys, she arrived at the house Joey was dealing out of, but this time instead of Joey, the main bad guy that Joey sold for came out to the truck. It was hard for Bam to conceal her excitement. Going hand-to-hand with the big guy was a godsend. He walked up to the truck, and asked, "You Shelly?" She said, "Yeah. Where's Crippled Joey?" The dealer said something like, "He's out doing shit for me. He told me you were coming. Come on in."

As operators we have the leeway to go off script, but we try not to. Mostly because the cover team has a list of possible responses based on the op plan, and when you go off script, they have to adjust.* Bambi made a quick judgment call to go inside the house to do the deal. She could have refused and said she didn't have time, or any other number of excuses, but she saw the opportunity to get inside the house, wander around. She could identify all of the players in the house, get eyes on where the dealer kept his dope, and maybe see if the people inside were armed. All of this would lend itself to securing a search warrant after the buy.

Immediately upon entering the house, Mr. Big locked the front door behind them. Red flags went up; Bambi's mind was racing. In a nanosecond, she had to assess a potential escape avenue as well as the increased threat of personal harm. She quickly wondered how the cover team would get in if she gave the distress signal.

Operational planning often covers specific tactics to be used during an agent extraction and/or the execution of a buy bust. Everything a UC does when in proximity to a violator can have consequences. Something as simple as making sure the door is unlocked so that the team easily can make entry may factor in. The lighting in a room or background noise or music can be a factor. Each encounter holds its own specific challenges.

---

* Operation plans always have been a part of any field op. We used to just throw something together to keep the bosses off our asses. Dates, times, locations, manpower assignments, and bust/distress signals. After the Waco report came out and ATF was flogged for substandard ops planning, every operation was required to have a detailed op plan approved beforehand, including UC, search and arrest warrants, and sometimes surveillances. In practice, it's a pain in the ass and slows agents down considerably. That's why UCs sometimes draw outside the lines.

Things that most people don't normally think about or pay attention to can be critical to a UC.

(When Alex was shot and Ariel was killed in a Miami hotel room, one of the last things to happen was that the door was locked behind them.)

Bambi protested to the violator: "I ain't planning on being here that long."

He said: "I just didn't want anybody just walking in on us."

Bambi accepted his response and followed him down the hall. She stayed on alert because there were other people in the house. Lots of them. Babies, babies' mamas, stoned dudes, and chicks sprawled everywhere. Bambi kept her wits about her and was in and out in minutes.

Speaking from a personal perspective, I never liked going into the violator's house. It's his world, and I could have no idea what was going on inside, but I, too, have pushed the envelope. In this case, because Bambi kept her cool, did the deal and got out, ATF scored. Instead of just being able to arrest Crippled Joey, and maybe or maybe not getting enough probable cause (PC) to hit the house, we got it all. We secured a warrant for the house and arrest warrants for the main guy as well as Dipshit Joey or whatever they called him. There were multiple violators in the house, and thanks to Bambi, the search warrant team knew the exact layout of the house and where the dope was kept. Bam took some pretty evil players off the street.

. . . .

One of my most prideful and memorable experiences when I finally got cut loose happened close to home, in Marin County, California. During my first tour with the San Francisco division office, Joe Stafford asked me if I wanted to cut my teeth and get a little UC experience. Of course, I jumped at the chance. Joe was one of the most senior, respected, and experienced agents in my squad. Although he wasn't officially my training officer, he took me under his wing. He told me I'd be doing the UC for the

Marin County drug task force. The task force was made up of cops from all over the county, including from my hometown, Novato.

We met at the San Rafael Police Department for the briefing, and Joe introduced me around as people arrived. I was sitting with my cowboy boots propped on a desk when Novato Police Sgt. Mike Poole entered the room. He shook the hands of Joe and the other ATF agents, and started to walk by me. I could tell he recognized me, but he didn't know from where. He kicked my boots off the desk and asked the others, "Why is the snitch sitting in on our briefing?"

The entire place erupted into laughter, and Mike was confused.

I stood up and said, "Fuck you, Poole. You want me to do this deal or not?"

He spun around to find himself staring straight at my US Treasury badge and credentials. He was seriously slack-jawed and stuttering. When it hit him, he threw a huge bear hug on me and we caught up. See, Mike had been a patrolman when I was running around Novato being a juvenile dickhead. He not only had arrested me several times but also had one occasion to arrest my father for DUI, which included a pretty good beating. Rest assured, my father earned it, took it, and never held a grudge. In fact, Mike Poole, my dad, and I had cocktails on several occasions long after all of that.

But now I had joined the "A" team. My parents and friends were so proud of me. There was only one problem confronting me. Being assigned to the San Francisco field division put me back in my old stomping grounds. I'd been able to keep my childhood indiscretions secret because California law allowed me to. My mother had been smart enough at the time to have my records sealed, so legally I could deny any of it had ever happened. What I couldn't do was hide my past from people I'd known and the friends I'd run with back in those days.

There were some awkward moments that couldn't be anticipated but had to be dealt with. While in a bar meeting with a fairly violent violator in Santa Rosa, I had one such experience. I had gone to a Catholic high school. My former vice principal/priest walked into the bar with a couple other people. He was in civilian clothes, but I recognized him and turned away so hopefully he wouldn't recognize me.*

When the violator went to the bathroom, I decided to defuse the potential for compromise right then and there. I walked over to Father Finn. He looked up and immediately hugged me, which means he wrapped his arms around the 9 mm pistol in my shoulder holster, which caused him to lurch. While still in the hug, I whispered quietly but clearly, "I'm a police officer, and I'm undercover right now." He looked puzzled but nodded and turned back to his table.

After the violator left, I went back over to Father Finn and his group, showed him my big-time federal credentials and said, "Thanks, Padre. Yah done good." I said. "See, I'm not a bad guy anymore." He replied, "Good, because I'm not a priest anymore."

From the stories he told to his friends that evening as we visited, I could tell the ex-padre was proud of who I'd become. But seeing him again highlighted the issues that arise when any agent works in his or her hometown. What do you do when you run into old friends? Are they good guys, or are they bad guys? Do you tell them what you do for a living or give them the canned story? Do you pursue a case vigorously against a good friend and childhood buddy? Can he or she blow your cover? I knew a whole lot of people from my childhood, and most of them were fuck-heads. I never gave any of it much thought until shortly after I went into the field working and also started getting my name known among local

---

* Father Finn once suspended me for smoking weed in the parking lot at lunchtime. My punishment was detention on the weekend and to clean the school office. While cleaning his office, I found the pipe he had taken from me in his desk, still filled with weed. It wasn't the worst detention I ever did.

law enforcement. Actually, most of the old-timers in local law enforcement already knew me—just not as an ATF agent.

Having terrorized Marin and Sonoma counties as a kid, my name was quite well known by the local constabulary. As word got out and I reestablished my name as a cop, my ATF agent partners and I would find ourselves in a tavern now and again, where I would have to sit and listen to the local cops tell story after story to my fellow agents about what a total asshole I was as a kid. One such night, I was with Joe and Larry, and we were going to the Hilltop to meet some cop for drinks on the way home. I never thought to ask, and they never thought to tell me who we were meeting. We walked in, and sitting at the bar was Novato Police Officer Yugo Innocenti. The same Yugo Innocenti who had a dozen years earlier shoved a shotgun in my face and threatened to blow my head off. Joe and Larry walked up and shook his hand, and then stepped aside and said, "Here's our new agent." Yugo stared. I stared. After a pause, he threw a kind of bear hug on me. He said he couldn't believe this shit, and went on to tell me that he had always liked me and hoped I would grow out of my bullshit. He asked about my mom and dad, and then began the nonstop stories to Joe and Larry, all of which started with: "Let me tell you how fucked up this kid was."

I admit that I felt a sense of pride: number one, that I had, in fact, grown out of my bullshit, and number two, that these senior agents were seeing me as somewhat of a local celebrity. The four of us drank and laughed until another party known to me entered the bar.

There were only two open seats, both close to where we sat. The guy in a shirt and tie who sat down a few spots away from our group was none other than Joel Thomas. Back in the day, Thomas and his brother were a couple of the biggest dope dealers, burglars, and strong-armed robbers in town. What made it worse is that Thomas was one of my old running mates.

He didn't pay us much attention and ordered a drink. I thought: "What the fuck do I do?" I was sitting with a cop who had busted him and his brother at least half a dozen times. Joe and Larry, both senior agents having worked this area for a dozen years, also knew the brothers and had investigated them on federal firearms charges. I just sat there and tried to get small, but Thomas eventually looked up, noticed Joe and Larry, and muttered something like, "Lovely, of all the bars, I have to come to the one with not one but two ATF fucking assholes." I think it was Joe who shot back, "Go fuck yourself, Thomas, and where's your faggot brother? In prison?"

Now I really wanted to get small. As a side note, it always was suspected that Thomas and his brother had burglarized my parents' house and stolen my mom's antique jewelry. For many years, because I was running around with these types of people, my parents believed I had something to do with it. I did, but only by association. Needless to say, we hadn't remained friends after the burglary. I'd fantasized about this very moment, coming face-to-face with Thomas or his brother and either beating their asses or arresting them. Now here I was with a badge, and I didn't have a clue what to say or do, so I just sat there. It wasn't a minute or two longer before Thomas noticed Yugo and couldn't keep his mouth shut. He said something like, "I didn't know ATF guys hung out with punk-ass patrolman, because best I recall you can't catch shit."

Yugo stood up and in his thick-ass Italian accent, not using his indoor voice, said, "I knowa thisa, you and youa fuckin' brother are justa fuckin' burgalers."

Thomas stood up as if he was going to do something, which he wasn't, and looked over and finally saw me. I could tell his mind was reaching, and it finally clicked. He said, "What are you doing with these assholes, Cefalu? Snitching on your friends, I guess?"

I pulled my credentials out of my pocket, flipped the wallet open so my badge hung down, and said, "Well, kinda."

He looked at my badge and then back at me. "Bullshit."

"Nope, fact," I told him. "And I promise I'll be seeing your ass again."

He drank down his drink, threw a ten-dollar bill on the bar, and muttered, "Fuck all you motherfuckers," and walked out.

We laughed about the irony, and Joe and Larry proceeded to name all of my childhood friends as past targets of their investigations over the years. Thank you, Lord, and thank you, US Marines, for getting me the hell out of there, or my name would have been in that group.

. . . .

All the way across the country, other "out of the cage" scenarios were playing out with friends of mine. In Savannah, Georgia, on any given day you could find Dino, Bambi, and her partner Randy running the streets. Dino had lined up a guy in his sights for a pipe bomb purchase, so he asked Randy to come along. This particular violator also had a contact for a machine gun. As is often the case, they met the violator at a trailer. Not a mobile home trailer but a pull-behind-your-car trailer.

Upon entering the trailer, they saw materials for making bombs. They also observed black powder spilled all over the floor and the violator with a lit cigarette. This was all they needed to excuse themselves to avoid blowing up with the violator. They walked out and sat in the Ford Ranger pickup truck they had driven to the deal. After a few minutes had passed and no explosion, the violator walked out to the truck carrying a gym bag containing several pipe bombs.

There were only two seats in the truck, and Randy was driving. Therefore, he was wearing the wire. Dino jumped in the truck bed. The plan was to drive the violator to another guy's house to try to secure the machine gun. They were trying to make it a two-deal day. (I think the most deals I have ever done in one day was three.)

As they were driving down a rural road out in the country, the violator said, "Hey, watch how good this works." Before Randy could respond, the violator lit the fuse on a pipe bomb and attempted to throw it out the window—except the window glass was shut all the way, and the bomb bounced onto the floor of the truck. The violator quickly grabbed it, rolled down the widow, and chucked the bomb out. Meanwhile, Dino was sitting in the truck bed looking toward the tailgate, clueless to what was happening in the cab. He saw something shiny fly past his head, followed by a huge explosion. The fuse had burned down quickly. Another second or two, and that bomb could have exploded right next to Dino's melon.

The agents decided to be satisfied with the one deal on that day and to arrange for the machine gun deal at a later date. After they went back to the office and cleaned themselves.

. . . .

Some agents would be let out of the cage only to turn and run right back in. Mark was one such agent. After a couple of years in the field, he figured out he was not the best suited to prowl in the nasty underbelly of the criminal world. His plan became to do anything and everything to be the one handling the snakes rather than to be one of them. This probably was good for him and good for the field, and it was often said that if the boss stopped too quickly, Mark's head would go right up his ass.

In the 1980s, California's Campaign Against Marijuana Planting (CAMP) was in full swing. It was a multiagency effort to eradicate marijuana fields in Northern California, with most law enforcement divisions dedicating a few officers/agents to the effort for several months. It was hard, dirty, dangerous work. Marijuana fields were identified prior to the harvest season and then visited during CAMP raids, when we were dispatched in teams to the locations and either helicoptered in or dropped as close to the field as possible. We had to hike in, cut the plants, and drag them out. We were faced with terrain, snakes, and bugs. Occasionally, we sat on an active site to arrest the growers, who protected their crops with booby traps and, often, armed guards. Overnight teams had to hump their provisions in for an extended stay.

Mark was assigned to one such team. We were staying at one of the hotels rented out to just cops for weeks on end.* We would meet early in the morning, and get assigned to teams and briefed on our locations. Mark showed up to the morning briefing where we all were in camo and raid gear, bulletproof vests, and hiking boots. His attire: collared polo shirt, silk slacks, shiny dress shoes. He was assigned to a small team that couldn't spare even one man, so he had to hump it that day in all his finery. It was the damnedest thing I ever saw. Since he did have the boss's ear, he was replaced by a no-shit street agent within a day.

. . . .

During those early days, my mom and dad were beside themselves that I had risen to such a prominent position after the hell I put them through as a kid. They showed me off like an organ-grinder monkey, and I was good with that. They loved all the agents.

One night a bunch of us were out drinking, and I apparently had too much. The crew drove me to my mom's home, where I was staying until I closed on my first house. They came in to say hi to my mom, and she offered to make food for everybody. It was midnight and they respectfully declined, but she was having none of it. There was my mom, a tiny 105 pounds, "ordering" some serious old-school special agents to park their cars and not to leave her house until they put something in their stomachs. The agents complied.

---

* We weren't very well liked in the Emerald Triangle, as evidenced by all of our tires being slashed one night.

CHAPTER 7

....

FREEDOM

Most UCs work under minimal oversight. Usually, a daily check-in with your group supervisor is sufficient. Drop by the office once a week and do your reports of investigation (ROIs), make your court appearances,* fill out your time sheet on time, and you're golden. But as a result, UCs don't experience the grounding effect of cop morals and values that are reiterated by regularly comingling with fellow cops. More of the UC's time is spent living among the bad guys than the good guys, and it gets easier to be consumed by an investigation. Picture it this way: An undercover operator has a gun, a badge, a fake ID, a

---

* UCs often do not have to appear in court until the case is over, when it matters less who sees them. The case agent and others make the regular court appearances to secure warrants or tracking devices, et cetera. If a UC has to appear in court for an interim matter, they sometimes enter the building clandestinely or through secure access areas to avoid burning their cover.

non-government-looking car or bike, some sort of backstopping, and quite often a covert bank account or credit card. His boss only knows what the agent wants him to know, and likewise with a spouse or significant other.

Such freedom can be a blessing or the kiss of death.

I remember my dad sitting me down over cocktails one night. He told me he was so very proud of what I had become. Then he caught me off guard by saying, "If you're going to be a cop, be the best, most honest cop you can be." He followed that with, "If you're going to be a crook, be the best you can be, but please don't be both." I thought his comments were directed at me because of my youthful bullshit. Then I realized he wasn't necessarily talking about me but more likely referring to his days growing up, when police corruption was almost expected. It was easy to put my dad's concerns to rest. I had become the cop who picked up a dollar bill while on patrol and turned it in as found property. I didn't even feel comfortable accepting free coffee at Dunkin' Donuts, although I did. When we hit the Hells Angels in 1987, via a joint ATF and FBI investigation dubbed Operation CACUS, we seized three million dollars from a club member's residence. I was alone in a room with all of the cash before it had been documented. That kind of shit never crossed my mind. Breaking the law was no longer part of my behavior. For the first time in my life I didn't have to look over my shoulder, and I liked it.

Although, there always was a line for a UC to walk. Early on, while refining my UC skills and traveling within our small circle, I befriended several local police department special squads. They often called on me to provide UC services outside of ATF jurisdiction and with no ATF involvement. According to policy, UC operations could be conducted only within strict reporting parameters. Following this protocol would have required me to refuse the special squads or significantly delay their operations to get the necessary ATF approvals. Therefore, I did what we all did. I did the undercover work and prayed like hell nobody got shot and nothing bad happened. While working the Black Biscuit Hells Angels case (a high-stakes infiltration of the gang in Mesa, Arizona, in 2001 that resulted in numerous convictions), Bird crossed the US border into Mexico to make a meeting to advance his credibility with the club. Crossing an international border for a law enforcement action without approval is as big a policy violation as you can make. We were experts at hanging our asses out to get the job done.

When I came on with ATF, as mentioned, agents had a slew of collateral duties. Some were evidence custodians, some were interstate nexus experts, some were in charge of office-assigned equipment. Some had to do collateral investigations (the term used for a request from one field division to another to conduct a follow-up investigation) or relief from disability investigations. Luckily for me, I had pretty darn good bosses in the early days, and they made me do *all* of those duties at one time or another.

To begin with, my training officer, Joyce Seymour, gave me every shit deal on the planet, and I love her for that today. I learned the job from the bottom up. Joyce had more than fifteen years with the ATF and had been heavily involved in the 1977 Golden Dragon investigation in San Francisco's Chinatown after a bunch of local gangbangers shot up the restaurant, leaving five bystanders dead and eleven wounded. My next boss, Lou Bristol, immediately made me the evidence vault custodian. That one pissed me off. I'd moved over to the task force right after the takedown of the 1987 Hells Angels case. We had a huge vault at the drug task force, now filled top to bottom with evidentiary guns and ammo. Every time a gun had to come in or go out for the lab or court, I had to be there and document its movements.

Meanwhile, as the trials got underway, the hallways of the courthouses were filled with Hells Angels—for months. As various law enforcement personnel passed daily through those same hallways, the palpable animosity in the air was directed mainly toward ATF.

At the end of the Hells Angels trials, there was evidence that needed to be returned to its rightful owners. I was extremely uncomfortable with returning any gun to any Hells Angel for any reason. I bitched to Lou, but his answer was, "That's part of the job." The then vice president of the Hells Angels Oakland chapter was a guy known as Cisco Valderrama. He had a shitty reputation as a menacing individual, could afford a high-dollar attorney, and he had never been convicted of a felony and therefore was not prohibited from owning a firearm. So I had to make arrangements to return a trunkload of firearms to the VP of an organized crime group.

The morning I had arranged to transfer the firearms to Valderrama's attorney, Lou came over to my desk and handed me a stack of Mylar stickers used by ATF.

"I thought you might like some of these," he said, and then just walked away.

I met with the attorney in the sub-basement of the federal building to turn over the firearms—nice firearms, expensive firearms. After completing the mounds of paperwork to effect the change of custody, I rolled out a big cart with all of the guns on it.

"Are you kidding me?" was the attorney's response.

Each and every gun was adorned with a shiny ATF badge–shaped sticker that would take considerable time and effort to remove. Sometimes it was the small victories.

Needless to say, I never liked returning firearms to criminals. It went against every fiber of my cop being. And every time I had to meet a Hells Angel or any scumbag, they would see my face. The one that caused me damn near ulcer-level stomach cramps was returning a firearm to Chucky Diaz.*

---

* We didn't yet know that he was one of the Angels responsible for the Grondalski murders, but let's just say that Chucky and I had a history.

Chucky, being a no-shit degenerate criminal, was convinced I had a warrant for his arrest and was nowhere to be found. I finally called Valderrama and told him if that fucking asshole Diaz wanted his pistol back, he'd better call me. Valderrama offered to take receipt, but I declined just because I could. Finally, Chucky called. We made arrangements to meet on the side of the road in Richmond, California. I made him sign the paperwork and then handed him the gun. He said "Fuck you," and I returned the sentiment.

· ·

When you are finally cut loose from training and free to operate independently, the first thing you want to do is produce. You stop asking permission for everything you do, and just do it. It's a liberating feeling to no longer be the "rookie." The tendency is to run out, find a violator, and make your first UC buy on your own. Darren Gil and I were no different.

Before we taught the class from hell, Darren was one of my first partners and friends in ATF. While we both were still FNGs, Darren and I met a violator trying to sell a machine gun. This guy was a felon, just out of prison, and a huge narcotics user. We scrambled to get our story together, which seemed simple enough to concoct: we were security and hit men for major marijuana grows in Northern California. We would learn after this caper that maybe we should put more thought into our cover stories.

We met the guy at a local fleabag motel to talk prices and negotiate for a later meeting when he would bring the weapon and we would bring the money. He never showed up and wouldn't return our pages. It looked like our first UC together was a bust. No biggie, these things happen. However, when you open a formal investigation, you enter the subject's profile in the Treasury Enforcement Communications System (TECS) so law enforcement will be aware that the individual was a target at some point in his life. This protocol allows other law enforcement to call and get the background on the violator.

After the Loma Prieta earthquake in the San Francisco Bay Area in 1989, one of our ATF squads was kicked out of their office across town because the building was so badly damaged. For the short-term, the Metro squad was co-located in our office. No big deal, except for two things. First, we were two squads in an office barely big enough to house one. Number two, and probably the biggest rub, was that the SF Metro group supervisor did not like me or Darren. He actually directed his group not to discuss their ongoing investigations with us. To our surprise, the Metro group opened a case on the same guy Darren and I had met for the machine gun. The guy's profile was right there in TECS, but out of competitive bullshit, the Metro team refused to confer with us.

As we later found out, Metro's undercover agent was not aware of this guy's previous lack of credibility. ATF frowned on letting a violator take money on a promise to return later with the product. In this case, the violator had promised two silenced pistols. The Metro UC let the violator walk with the money and, of course, got ripped off. The ballbusting that followed courtesy of Darren and me was unrelenting.

Fast-forward a couple of weeks. The call came into our office that the Napa County narcotics team had found the guy and were set to do a dope deal with him (probably with our money). Darren and I decided to race up there and hook this asshole up. The problem was, Metro had the warrant, and their boss would be none too happy to know Darren and I were going to arrest him. We walked into our supervisor's office (he was aware of the rip-off and the nature of the infighting) and asked him if we could go get this guy. His response was, "What are you waiting for?" As we were hauling ass out the door, he added, "You may want to turn off your radios and pagers." After we left, the Metro supervisor stomped into our boss's office and demanded he order us back. Our supervisor made several attempts but could not reach us . . . bahahaha.

Darren and I met with the Napa narcs, who agreed that once they had the dope, they would signal us and we could apprehend the guy. The signal came, and we walked up the block and then up the walkway, staring straight at the violator, not expecting what happened next. He recognized us—as the two buyers/hit men he'd ditched in his machine gun scam. He jumped behind one of the narcs and started screaming, "Call the cops," "Help me," "They are gonna kill me!"

He fell down trying to get away, and when Darren and I laid hands on him, we intentionally waited a few seconds and then showed our badges and told him he was under arrest. He let out a loud moan and said, "Thank God."

. . . .

Still pretty early in my RatSnake career, the San Francisco Police Department (SFPD) intelligence unit was on the trail of a convicted bank robber who later would elevate his status to cop killer. Long story short: ATF initially was called in because the suspect had acquired many of his firearms under a fake ID. Although I was new to the agency, the boss figured it would be a good way for me to learn our firearms tracing system and do a little legwork. Nothing too fancy for the new kid. It just goes to show—you never know what lies out there when you open a case.

Ted Jeffery Otsuki, a.k.a. Mark Taira, was a very, very bad man. In fact, he was the most dangerous violator I ever dealt with. After determining his true identity, the case approach changed drastically. Otsuki/Taira was a former federal convict whose specialty was takeover bank robberies. Shortly after being released from Leavenworth, he was identified as the subject who had been casing the Brownsville, Texas, DEA office. His plan was to rob the office of all its stored drugs. After being confronted by law enforcement regarding malicious intent toward the DEA office, Otsuki fled to San Francisco, where he joined up with a former inmate from Leavenworth. Our investigation ultimately revealed that he planned to take a bank executive hostage, strap a bomb to his body, and demand ransom. We knew this because his roommate told us of his plans, and we recovered the bombs from a rented storage locker. Locating that evidence shed light on his intentions and prompted Otsuki to flee again, this time to Boston, where a bizarre set of events led to him murdering one Boston police officer and wounding another.

While Otsuki was still in San Francisco, I got a 3 AM phone call asking if I could meet the SFPD gang unit in the Mission District. This is where I first met Lt. Dan Foley, commander of SFPD's intelligence and gang unit, and otherwise known as "the Toad." Dan had risen through the ranks as a detective after helping to solve the Golden Dragon restaurant murders. While working that case, he had gained respect for ATF.

Dan's team needed a UC guy to hang out in an X-rated peep show theater and follow a designated subject to his apartment. I had no time to call my bosses, so I just did as the SFPD asked. The subject was the room-mate of Otsuki. Tailing the roommate led to his arrest, and he sang his heart out. He was visibly shaken and clearly terrified of Otsuki. The items seized from the apartment included bulletproof vests, pipe bombs, and machine guns—evidence that ultimately led to the arrest and conviction of an FBI Top Ten Most Wanted cop killer. Because Massachusetts didn't have the death penalty at the time, and because everybody agreed that this son of a bitch should never see daylight, ATF prosecuted him as well under the Armed Career Criminal Act. This is rarely done, but in Otsuki's case, after he serves his life sentence in Massachusetts, he owes another life sentence to the feds.

My bosses were very happy with my work on the case, and I never had to testify, so they also were none the wiser about my off-the-books

UC that night. I did get a letter of commendation from the Boston police commissioner. And whenever I needed something from the SFPD guys, they were Johnny-on-the-spot.

. . . .

My nighttime UC for the SFPD was something of an exception in that prepping for an undercover assignment most often is a highly methodical process. Deciding how you will dress. What you will drive. What you will say. You need to have abort, distress, and bust plans all in place. The smallest detail can tank an operation and sometimes has. Imagine meeting a guy you've previously done some business with and have established some sort of relationship with. Maybe on previous meets you introduced a female agent as your girlfriend or fiancée, but you show up on this particular occasion sporting a wedding band. This after you spent the first few deals telling him how you never would get married again or how your ex-wife was such a bitch. These types of self-inflicted operational security (OPSEC) issues can make the job a lot harder.

That's why agents always have a partner or a case agent double-check their physical persons before they go out the door. When I graduated from college, one of the first in my family to do so, I ran out and bought the nicest class ring I could buy. It was gold with a diamond and the scales of justice on it. It sat in my jewelry box for the remainder of my career.

Undercover agents come in all sizes and shapes. There are no set-in-stone traits, skills, or characteristics that guarantee you will be a good or a great undercover operator. Probably one of the most glaring and best-known comparisons would be the differences between Bird and me. Bird is a big man, extremely calm, soft-spoken, and affable. I am of average build, loud, brash, and high-strung. Not because we planned or practiced it, but our natural good cop/bad cop looks and demeanors may very well explain our relative success on joint operations.

Compare the Ragin' Cajun Milton and/or Bambi to me, and most would agree we are contenders for the "aggravating son of a bitch hall of fame." As RatSnakes, we all adopted personas that made us feel safer when moving within a criminal environment. For Jay, it was an over-the-top appearance, with tattoos, braided goatee, and a shitload of rings and bracelets. For me, it was long hair, earrings, tattoos, and occasionally a black eye patch. I found that when I wore the eye patch, violators were more distracted wondering whether or not I had an empty socket under there than worrying about me being a cop. For Milton, well, it was just being a scraggly bastard. Gundo vacillated between '60s hippie and rode-hard biker. Some of the black agents went with street bling, sports jerseys, and earrings. Our Hispanic brothers and sisters sometimes favored buttoned-to-the-collar (Soreno gang-style) flannel shirts and dungarees. We all wanted to blend in, but we also knew it had less to do with appearance and much more to do with attitude and game, in other words, our ability to sound and act like criminals without actually being criminals.

The exact street lingo you employ is critical. It's the little things that can get you, like talking to a violator and answering his question with "10-4." Or instead of referring to a pistol or rifle as a gat, or some steel, you instead accidentally say sidearm or Roscoe. That's cop talk, not bad-guy talk. When I was in Atlanta, I spent a lot of time working in the inner city, mostly in the projects, buying dope and guns. I happen to be Caucasian, but the common greeting of "What's up, my nigga?" was accepted street slang and didn't raise any eyebrows. In that context, the phrase wasn't viewed as a racial remark and was used interchangeably between blacks and whites. Then I walked into a first meet with an Aryan Brotherhood member who recently had been paroled, and the familiar phrase slipped out. Time seemed to stop as this white supremacist motherfucker stood up, took a step toward me, and said, "What the fuck did you just call me?" On that occasion, pretending humility was the best option. I said, "My bad, brother. I was just fuckin' around." He said, "Don't ever call me a nigger again, or we are going to have problems."

My fake humility paid off, and he ultimately spent ten years in a federal penitentiary being called way worse, I'm sure.

It is situations like this that make UC such a stressful endeavor. You can never stop thinking and yet have to appear as if you don't have a care in the world. Again, it's all about having game. Case in point, in the mid-1980s I had not yet been to the ATF Academy and as such my undercover contact with violators was prohibited, or at least extremely limited. I was working to build a case against an armed methamphetamine "cooker" in Sonoma County. My informant advised that he could make a direct introduction for a purchase of some meth and a couple stolen guns. I hadn't been in San Francisco long and did not know the other agents very well or who to approach. Back in those days, new agents were to be seen and not heard. I was treated a bit differently because I had a fair amount of prior experience. My training agent, Joyce Seymour, guided me through the process and paperwork of setting up a UC meet. She said that since Joe Stafford and another agent, Jim Smith (Smitty), worked up north a lot, she would ask them to help out.

I wrote up the plan and met with Joe and Smitty and the narcs from Sonoma who would be covering the deal. We were good to go, and I was looking forward to getting my first UC case under my belt. We showed up at the briefing, and my undercover, Agent Smitty, walked in and I almost seized up right there. He was wearing a button-down oxford shirt, polyester-blend slacks, and hard-soled polished dress shoes. It was a rainy night, so he also was wearing a two-hundred-dollar London Fog raincoat, with an umbrella tucked under his arm. He was tall, a bit overweight, and had short salt-and-pepper-colored hair and a beard. I was speechless. He was going to roll on down into the white ghetto part of town, waltz into a meth cook's house looking like Lord Fauntleroy, and buy guns and dope?

We finished the briefing, and Smitty threw a wire (transmitter) into one pocket and a Nagra recorder in the other and set my plan in motion. I was still in shock. This wasn't what I thought undercover work looked like.

Smitty was very close to retirement, which put him around fifty years old. Well, I watched a badass do badass stuff that night. Hell, I'm not even sure if he brought his firearm. He walked in, made small talk, told the guy he didn't have all night to fuck around, and walked out fifteen minutes later with an ounce of meth and two stolen pistols.

Later during that same period of time, Smitty's partner, Joe Stafford, was tagged for another UC deal. It wasn't mine, but I got to help with the surveillance. There had been a significant hijacking of brand-new in-the-box Beretta pistols, and one of Joe's snitches had a line on maybe purchasing them. Based on our intel, these violator(s) were probably mobbed up, meaning they were likely Mafia-connected guys. I'd hardly gotten my mind around the Smitty deal, half deciding it was a fluke, so imagine my surprise when Joe showed up to the briefing wearing a polo shirt, corduroy sport coat, faded jeans, and penny loafers—no socks. He might have been the most handsome man any of us had ever seen and was a damn scratch golfer. I remember thinking that with my bell-bottom jeans and long hair, maybe I wasn't cut out for this UC stuff after all.

Equally bizarre to me was that the plan called for Joe simply to meet the violators for drinks and go from there. Joe was driving an undercover Cadillac borrowed from the local narcs, and he proceeded to a high-end bar on Fisherman's Wharf where we easily could surveil him and monitor the wire. After shooting the breeze for a bit, the two violators and Joe strolled out and went across the street to A. Sabella's, one of the finest seafood houses in San Francisco at the time. They commenced to have dinner for so long that Joe had to excuse himself and go to the restroom to change the battery in the wire. To top this all off, he paid for dinner with ATF funds. I was immediately back on the undercover train. I could do *this*.

Joe met the violators again the next day to purchase the pistols. We executed a buy bust and recovered all but two of the stolen guns. To say I was in awe of Joe's skills would not be nearly strong enough.

. . . .

Of course, undercover operations didn't always go so smoothly, even for greats like Smitty and Stafford, but sometimes it was good enough that they went at all. I'm reminded of a friend and former cop who came to ATF. She was smart and aggressive. Her very first undercover buy went anything but well. Kelly was supposed to meet the violator to pick up a pistol for her "boyfriend." The deal had been set up by said boyfriend, who actually was an informant.

The details are sketchy to this day, but there was a breakdown in relaying GPS directions to the violator's location. The cover team ended up surveilling an address on South Main Street while Kelly was headed to the same house number on North Main Street. By the time Kelly realized that she was at a different location than the cover team, the violator already was approaching her vehicle to invite her inside. She didn't know if the cover team could hear the wire, and she couldn't call them to say where she was. So, she did what any good UC would do. She walked in, made the deal, recorded it, and walked the hell out, knowing she was in for some shit talking when she finally got back with the team. By any standard, it was a bush league operation and really bad things could have happened, but they didn't and that is how we learn. For her troubles, Kelly earned the nickname Special Agent Magellan.

As Kelly did in setting up her buy, a UC invariably will rely on the use of informants. Working with CIs does not create the best-case scenario, but these individuals oftentimes are vital to an investigation. They can give introductions or vouch for an agent's criminal credibility. Working informants and working the street gives UCs a definitive edge over most traditional investigators. You pick up street talk and intel that you file away for later use. The pitfalls of using an informant are obvious. You now have a criminal who knows who you are. The best UCs in the business are pretty much experts in informant control. They know exactly the right blend of the stick and the carrot. Those who don't understand how to work an informant are placing lives at even greater risk.

The Outlaws Motorcycle Club had its roots in McCook, Illinois, and by the 1990s the gang had chapters nationwide, including in Atlanta, Georgia. At the time, I was assigned to the Atlanta gang group, and during the Outlaws takedown by ATF, DEA, and Atlanta PD, street intel proved helpful. You won't find this kind of intel in any ATF or police manual.

While a search of the Outlaws' clubhouse and compound in Atlanta was being conducted, one of the Outlaws who was handcuffed behind his back, consistent with policy, was in obvious agony. He wasn't complaining, but I knew from street intel that he had suffered a severe injury from a gunshot in the past. He was being guarded by DEA agents. As the case agent and senior agent on the scene, I walked over and told him to stand up.

"If you fuck with me, I will shoot you where you stand. Now turn around," I told him.

He did as told, and I moved the cuffs to the front.

This pissed off the DEA agents, and they raised hell and called their boss over, but I told them, "This is my prisoner, so fuck off."

At that time, we were temporarily housing federal prisoners at Douglas County Jail, a nonsmoking facility. When the Outlaw asked where he and his buddies were going to be processed and I told him Douglas County, he sighed.

"I guess you wouldn't let me have a smoke, right?" he asked me.

Over the further objections of my DEA counterparts, I gave him a cigarette and lit it.

There was a method to my madness in showing the biker some street respect. The cops had won. The bikers all were going to prison. I didn't need to show this Outlaw how tough I was.

I had to get to court to get ready to process the prisoner. I called my partner Steve Kosch over and told him to stay with this prisoner and that if he acted a fool, to shoot him. Kosch nodded. I had a pack of smokes with three or four in it; I tossed them to the prisoner, he nodded at me, and I left.

The reason I haven't named this particular biker is because I was called to the US Attorney's office early the next morning under a shroud of secrecy. When I got there, my DEA counterparts were already there, and so was the same biker, in handcuffs, sitting next to his attorney.

The US attorney said to me, "He wants to cooperate, and he wants to work with you."

The biker looked over at the DEA guys and said, "I ain't working with those fucking assholes."

. . . .

It may sound great, but let me say that some of the hardest and most challenging ops to be involved in are those that are coed. Aside from being tactical, cover identities add another layer of security to keep agents' families away from the ugly world UCs travel in. But to work closely in a UC role with a member of the opposite sex inherently creates issues at home. Nobody wants to think about their spouse working in a highly charged environment, oftentimes acting in their undercover roles as boyfriend or girlfriend. Then you have to explain that you're taking off your wedding ring because "it doesn't fit my role." This is not to say that UCs couldn't and shouldn't be trusted as faithful spouses. However, perception gets pretty close to reality when the spouses are at home bathing children while the agents are at a bar schmoozing violators.

Just as those before me had done, I took it upon myself to help up-and-coming UCs through support and encouragement. Lori was one such agent and a competent one, although she didn't have much UC exposure when we worked together the first time. We had been invited to a biker party in Macon, Georgia. It was supposed to be an in-and-out, get our faces known, and just talk some shit for future contacts.

The weather got shitty, and we had been drinking. Neither of us wanted to ride two hours back to Atlanta in the rain on a motorcycle. The president of the club had taken a liking to us and offered to let us stay in his motor home. Our other choice was to run around in the middle of the night, in the rain, to find a hotel. We took his offer, and he didn't mention that there would be another biker couple sharing the motor home. There we were in the roles of boyfriend and girlfriend with no real option but to suck it up and sleep (yes, *sleep*) in the same bed. We preserved our cover and agreed never to speak of it again.

Maybe there should be a rule that only single guys and gals can do UC work. It's really not fair to the families. The vast majority of my UC meets were at night, when other moms and dads were going home to their families. I really don't know why so much nefarious shit happens at night. Maybe it's written somewhere in the gangster handbook.

"Dad, are you gonna be at my football game tonight?" my sons would ask me. My answer was the same every time: "I am planning on it." They soon learned what that meant. Even though she knew the answer, and knew how much it aggravated the shit out of me, my wife would always ask, "What time are you going to be home tonight, honey?"

Across the state, a similar scenario would be playing out with Bambi and her boyfriend. "Ya wanna go out tonight, baby?" the boyfriend might say. "Sounds good. I'll call you later," Bambi would reply, knowing a machine guns deal she'd been working for months might go down tonight, but it's easier not to get into details with the boyfriend. Hell, the deal might not happen anyway. At the same time, Bird's cell phone would be blowing up. It was a violator he'd been trying to meet with for days. But he couldn't answer the phone at the moment because he had two crying babies in the background, and such an error would surely compromise his cover.

It was the same drill every day: Make sure the pistol was loaded, gather badge and credentials, kiss the wife, kiss the kids, and roll toward the office to tackle the mound of paperwork from last night's deal. Cops whined about paperwork, but all that paperwork meant we did good. It meant the deal went. It meant somebody was going to jail.

I'd walk in the office late because we'd been out late the night before.

"Hey, Boss, morning."

The boss would say, "Don't sit down. The SAC wants to see you."

The SAC would be pissed because we'd spent so much cash buying guns last night and he wanted to know why we didn't buy bust the guy.

"Tell him he would know if he'd read my fucking reports," would be my answer.

After repeating all the details to the SAC, ASAC, and operations officer, I'd be allowed to go back to work—now that a particular boss had shown me how much he knew about undercover, even though I was certain he never did a UC case worth mentioning in his whole career.

The other UCs would start rolling in. High fives would go around over coffee and a debriefing.

I always looked at debriefing as a constructive way of identifying how everybody on the deal fucked up. We could all too easily say, "Hey, the deal went down, and we all went home. Damn, we are good." The problem was that we might not be so lucky next time. So we aired out every aspect of the operation: planning, execution, the undercover, the cover team, the equipment. Then it was on to somebody else's deal, and so it went.

Invariably, some agent would set a deal for Friday afternoon, during rush hour. You haven't had your patience fully tested until you've had to do a rolling surveillance during rush hour in a metropolitan area.

Some operations never got the go-ahead. There were many reasons for this, with safety usually at the forefront. Unfortunately, sometimes it was just inexperience and fear on the part of management. My supervisor shut down one operation because the sun was setting and he didn't want me to be doing undercover after dark. I was so pissed. The only response I could come up with was, "Are you shitting me? That's your fucking reason?" He didn't appreciate my response, and certainly it was disrespectful and I apologized. But these kinds of decisions can have broader impact. In this case, I had another agency's Special Weapons and Tactics (SWAT) team acting as my UC cover team. I'd called on agents to come in from out of town. I used up a lot of resources and lost credibility based on my representations.

The supervisor's decision to pull out also created an exit dilemma for me. It's always a gut call about how long to wait for the bad guy. Don't wait long enough, and said bad guy won't agree to meet you next time. Wait around all day without a good reason from the bad guy, and you brand yourself as either a punk or a cop. Bad guys don't keep schedules. They slither in the dark and in the shadows. They are always late and always undependable. Picture yourself being a bad guy, running around doing bad-guy stuff. You've agreed to meet me to sell me a fully automatic machine gun. You call and say you got shit goin' on and will meet me two hours later, which I resist, but playing the role of another bad guy, I ultimately agree. You are going to expect a good reason if I call you back and try to reset the deal for tomorrow at daylight.

After a long day such as this, it was back home to the family, by now having missed the kids' birthday parties/football games/bedtime. The wife/husband/boyfriend/girlfriend would be understandably tired and pissed off at having to deal with things on their own—again. Of course, I realize that many people in various professions work long hours and juggle work and home life. There are, however, only a select few professions that include the pressure of morphing into a different identity and entering/ exiting a dangerous, criminal world each day before heading back home to the spouse and kids.

. . . .

One common character flaw of UCs who lived this lifestyle was their inability to say no. There were many reasons for this tendency; the most pressing was that we lived for the rush. It's what kept us going and, to a certain degree, defined us. When you had established a name for yourself as a good operator, more and more people requested you to do their UCs. If you said no too many times or in a critical situation, it might be the last time they asked. Finally, it had to do with ego. The more successes you had working undercover, the more you started to believe you could do it better than anybody else.

Whatever the reason, saying no can save your life. I don't know that for sure because I don't ever remember saying no. When all of us were early in our careers, we took every gig that came down the pike. It wasn't a competition, but it sure looked like one. I was calling Gundo; he was calling Bambi; and Dino was being called by everybody. The outcome we risked was a destructive type of burnout.

Undercover agents act out their lives in little bit parts. RatSnakes describe the corollary effect as "personality fragmentation." Although it has not been specifically identified in the *Diagnostic and Statistical Manual of Mental Disorders*, fifth edition (the recognized bible of mood disorders published by the American Psychiatric Association), personality fragmentation is a real thing. Not to be confused with a diagnosed multiple personality disorder, personality fragmentation can be a net result of too much UC exposure, swiftly moving in and out of acted roles without sufficient recovery time. Who am I today? What am I buying from this guy? Where did I tell that guy I am from? When those lines begin to blur, bad things can happen.

The mental and emotional agility required to do UC work also means the agents experience prolonged and heightened stress. One might say that the type of freedom intrinsic to doing UC work comes with a cost. The law enforcement community has worked to develop supportive programs, sometimes even leading to interventions. ATF provided an Employee Assistance Program (EAP) and peer-support resources. In my time, most of us leaned on our families, friends, and other RatSnakes. Drinking was one coping method. Mostly, though, we just ignored it. See, everybody around us may have perceived the impacts of long-term exposure, but often we agents were the last to recognize it in ourselves.

Chapter 8

....

"OH, SHIT" MOMENTS

'm sure that every UC who ever lived can rattle off their top ten "oh, shit" moments. Here's mine, including some from personal experience and some courtesy of my fellow RatSnakes around the country.

#10. MARIN COUNTY, CALIFORNIA

You will not be well served as an ATF undercover agent if you panic at the sight of a firearm. You probably won't survive your twenty years if having a gun pointed at your face freaks you out too much to function, because in the life of a RatSnake, that can be a frequent occurrence. I broke my gun-in-the-face cherry before I ever came to law enforcement. I was thirteen years old and helping an older friend, Bruce, clean up and bag a couple pounds of marijuana in exchange for some cash. I asked to use the bathroom, and Bruce pointed down the hallway. On my way to the bathroom, I passed through a living room where several older people were hanging out. One greasy-looking, long-haired dude had his foot up on a chair. Without a word or warning, he pulled a pistol from his boot, pointed it at my face, and asked, "What the fuck are you doing here?"

"I'm with Bruce," I squeaked.

They all laughed, and he put the pistol back in his boot and pointed to the bathroom. I didn't need to pee anymore.*

#9. OUTSKIRTS OF KANSAS CITY, MISSOURI

Shortly before ATF became a bureau in 1972 (when it was still the ATF division of the IRS), Pat Kelly took his young trainee, Bob Harper, on a classic UC operation. They wanted to get close to a well-known firearms trafficker. The problem was, he was serving a short stint in the county jail. Pat said, "No problem. We are going to jail." Bob wasn't all that keen on the plan, but what the hell, he was ATF. With the help of a local detective, they were placed in the same pod as the violator and passed themselves off as car thieves. They were only supposed to be there for a few hours before someone posted their bail, but something got screwed up and they ended up spending the whole night in jail. It paid off though. The violator gave them his telephone number, told them he would be out in a couple of weeks, and that they should call him.

When it came time to get in touch with the violator, Pat was tied up

---

* The greasy guy with the long hair was none other than Hells Angel member Charles "Chucky" Diaz. Now you know why I had stomach cramps when, years later, I had to give him back his firearm. Diaz is now is serving a life sentence, having narrowly avoided the death penalty for the Grondalski quadruple homicides in Fort Bragg, California.

on another case. Bob was still new, so Pat reached out to Virgil Walker, another experienced agent and ATF legend, to help make arrangements to meet the violator. They hit the jackpot. The violator told them that he had a fully automatic Thompson submachine gun to sell.

Known by many other nicknames, the deadly "Tommy gun" was invented by US Army officer John T. Thompson in 1918 and became an infamous weapon of choice by the military, law enforcement, and criminals during Prohibition years. Fully automatic guns—meaning the weapon will continue to fire as long as the trigger is depressed and there is ammunition in the chamber or magazine—are one of the most strictly regulated classes of firearms today. So much so that they cannot even be manufactured anymore. The fully automatic firearms that are legally possessed in the United States are the last we will ever see. They must be registered through the Treasury Department, special transfer taxes paid, and a thorough background completed. However, there is no shortage of bootlegged or black-market converted machine guns on the streets. Most semiautomatic firearms easily can be converted to fire fully automatic, which is a serious felony. Machine guns and submachine guns still are widely used by special military and police SWAT teams for close-quarters operations.

Virgil and Bob met the violator out at a small secluded farm, where the deal was done under a porch light, because the guy didn't want his neighbors to see what was going on. The agents examined his firearms and conducted a field test (a technique used to determine whether a firearm will fire fully automatic without actually firing the weapon). It usually is a good technique to ensure you're not duped into buying a semiautomatic, but it's not foolproof. A semiautomatic gun is self-loading but requires a single trigger pull for each shot, creating a much slower rate of fire. Because of this fact, semiautomatic guns carry less street value than fully automatic guns, and in the United States can be legally owned and sold by private parties.

Virgil and Bob bought the gun and headed off down the road.

When they were almost to the office, Virgil, who was napping in the back seat, suddenly bolted upright and yelled, "Let me see that fucking gun." Bob almost drove off the road. Virgil turned on the dome light and said, "Son of a bitch." He had remembered seeing a memo come through the office warning agents about replica Thompsons. The knockoffs field-tested properly but weren't machine guns. Virgil and Bob had just handed over $250 of ATF's funds—about $1,600 in today's money—for a legal gun.

The next day, they reported to the boss what happened and his response was simple: "You better go get my fucking two hundred and fifty dollars back or write me a fucking check."

Of course, it wasn't the boss's money, but shit would roll downhill if agency funds were lost to a blown deal.

Bob was in shock and turned to Virgil and asked, "What are we going to do? I don't have two hundred and fifty dollars."

That amount was about half a month's pay at the time.

Virgil told Bob to go eat lunch and then meet him out in the parking lot. When Bob got back from lunch, Virgil was sitting in his government car and told him to jump in. A sawed-off shotgun lay on the front seat. Bob didn't ask, and Virgil didn't volunteer. He just said they were going to get the boss's money.

The violator worked at a service station in the next town over. When they arrived at the spot, Virgil waved the violator over to the car. When the guy bent down, Virgil grabbed him by the collar and pulled him halfway in through the open car window and stuck the sawed-off shotgun in his face.

"That piece of shit you sold us was fake, but this one is real. We want our money back," Virgil said.

The violator started emptying dollar bills out of his pocket onto the front seat. Hell, he even gave them his change counter, but he was about fifty dollars short. Virgil and Bob made him get into the back seat, and they drove to his mother's house where the violator got the rest of the money. They dropped him off back at the service station and returned to the office.

The boss was a little shocked when Virgil and Bob handed him the buy money, but he didn't ask any questions. Virgil returned the shotgun to the evidence vault and it was never spoken of again.*

#8. MARIN COUNTY, CALIFORNIA

I've already explained that undercover agents often wear concealed transmitters, both for agent safety and to record conversations for use in court. Working with a transmitter requires a certain level of focus. If you turn it on too soon, the battery may die before the violator shows up. If you turn it on too late or forget to turn it on, you miss the conversations altogether.

A good undercover constantly is aware of the status of the transmitter. He does a sound check before going to meet the target. A transmitter has a fairly short range but gives the cover team real-time audio so they can hear a distress or bust signal. As I've said, violators often are undependable and don't show up when they are supposed to. Or they show up and then need to leave to get the guns or dope after they see the money. The UC always needs to know the time available on the batteries and must be able to turn the transmitter on and off to save battery time.

On one occasion, I was working with a bunch of local cops in Marin County. My supervisor at that time was not very aggressive or very skilled at undercover work. In fact, he hated it. Suffice to say, not many of the guys liked him.

---

* Needless to say, they never brought charges against the violator for the fake Tommy gun they bought.

This particular deal was on-again, off-again. During one of the down periods while waiting for the violator to call back, we all were in a concealed parking lot drinking coffee and talking shit. My supervisor was sitting in his car by himself. One of the officers asked, "What's wrong with your boss?" I blurted out, "He's just a big pussy and only out here because he's required to be."

I heard the squelch break on the PA system in my boss's car, and then: "Cefalu, your wire is still on. Come over here and see me."

Oh, shit.

#7. SAN FRANCISCO BAY AREA

Everybody loved Spike Gleba. By the time I came on, he had started to glide toward retirement. He wasn't burning up the world by then, but word was he used to. Spike would help any agent, any time. I had secured a search warrant on some gangster's house and we were spread thin, so I asked Spike if he could help me. He said he would if he could find his gun. That was a running joke, since if he wasn't helping on somebody's case, he'd rather be clipping recipes out of the *San Francisco Chronicle*.

Well, he found his gun, but I later wished he hadn't. In those days, we would fill up a bunch of government unmarked cop cars and race up to the front door and all pile out and kick in the door. It was fun but not very efficient, depending on the size of the street, available space, and traffic. This day, we raced in and whoever was driving the car Spike was in slammed on the brakes. Spike was holding his .38-caliber revolver with his finger on the trigger (a no-no), and accidentally squeezed off a round inside the car. Aside from the other agents' eardrums, the only thing that died that day was the police radio in the car.

#6. ATHENS, GEORGIA

One time, we were searching a building where a burglar alarm had gone off. After scouring the entire one-story structure, there was only one place left to look: the attic. I slowly ascended the ladder, using my flashlight to see ahead. Another Athens officer, Ray Chinn, was right behind me. I peeked up and shined my flashlight around and couldn't see anybody. However, there was a big industrial heating unit blocking about half of the attic. I had to climb up and straddle the rafters, inching across until I could see behind the heater. Ray shined his light for me so I could focus on the potential threat. After I cleared the area behind the heating unit, I turned around to slowly make my way back to the ladder.

I hollered at Ray, "Clear!"

When Ray heard the word "clear," he shut off his flashlight, and I couldn't see where to put my foot. The next thing I remember was lying flat on my back, on the main floor, having crashed through the Sheetrock ceiling.

Ray hollered out, "Hey, Vince, are you okay? Where are you at?"

He had gone back up the ladder to see what happened.

I said, "I'm down here, you stupid motherfucker."

"How'd you get down there?"

"Not funny, dude."

#5. ATLANTA, GEORGIA

Considered ballsy and innovative, UC operators often were the proving ground for new techniques, tactics, and equipment. One such tactic that was being tried around the country in the 1990s was the use of remotely detonated flash bangs—grenade-like devices that create a brief, bright flash and a loud explosion—as a distraction during takedowns. Hey, I'm the first one to try new and crazy shit, but this one had several of us raising an eyebrow. ATF's Special Response Teams are the equivalent to police SWAT teams. The flash bangs were being used in conjunction with our SRT deployments, and the idea was as follows: We buried or otherwise concealed flash bangs immediately adjacent to where the undercover deal was going to happen. Our Explosive Technology Branch (ETB) guy would be present and have the ability to remotely detonate the stun grenades. As the UC exited the area, but before the violators could leave, we'd set off three bangs simultaneously to completely disorient the bad guys and then rush in to arrest them.

On this day, we isolated the deal to the very back of a mall parking lot, as far away from the public as possible. We had surveillance everywhere. The UC was supposed to buy the guns and dope, walk back toward his vehicle, and then give the bust signal. At which point, *kaboom*. The violators would be temporarily incapacitated, and the SRT would swoop on them. That was the theory.

What actually occurred was the UC gave the signal, the bangs were initiated, and all hell broke loose. The bad guys thought they were being shot at. They jumped in their car and hauled ass, driving over curbs to avoid our surveillance vehicles that were attempting to block their escape. The violators headed straight to the main entrance of the mall, bailed out of their vehicle, and disappeared.

In all fairness, we actually had used that technique several times successfully. But we decided after that caper that our tactic needed more work.

#4. SOME COUNTY, GEORGIA

Before encrypted and scrambled signals were in use, it was a very real possibility that wearing a wire could be detected by a cheap RadioShack radio frequency (RF) detector. There are many other pitfalls to wearing too much or the wrong electronics. There are some accounts of the wire creating static in a nearby television or radio. Some transmissions actually have been captured over a police scanner. Imagine hearing your conversation blasted live over a scanner in the violator's living room. That's one more reason why placement of the wire was important. You needed to be able to shut it off instantly.

In the late 1990s, I was working a case against a dirty deputy sheriff, clearly not my fave thing to do. However, the informant was another deputy, so the boss assigned the investigation to me. One day while communicating with the CI on my cell phone, while the CI was on a cordless house phone, we got severely compromised. Apparently, our call was broadcast over a baby monitor frequency and right into the violator's scanner. The only other possibility our tech guys could come up with was that the violator, being a friend of the informant, may have secured the phone frequency at some point when he was at the CI's house.

The violator immediately called the CI and recounted our entire conversation. That created a shit storm. We believed the violator was capable of violence, so security had to be put in place for the informant. Then we had to locate the violator and lock him down until we could get a search warrant. We did both of those things and ultimately recommended federal prosecution for possession of an unregistered Title II firearm. Such highly lethal weapons—machine guns, short-barreled shotguns and rifles, explosives and other incendiary devices—are federally regulated by the National Firearms Act (NFA). Because the sheriff at the time was fond of the deputy/violator, ATF was asked to defer prosecution/discipline to the sheriff's office. We did so, but our team never felt good about it.

#3. CASTRO DISTRICT, SAN FRANCISCO

When I was just getting my investigative legs under me during my first years in San Francisco, I was pumped when the then head of the San Francisco Gang Intelligence squad called to make me an offer. I'd provided UC support on many of their cases, and now they were offering me an introduction to a highly placed informant.

The CI lived in the heart of the Castro District. The Castro had become a mecca for gay rights in the 1960s and '70s, so I was not surprised to find out that this informant was a flamboyant gay man. He was referred to me because the gang guys knew I was actively working the Northern California white supremacist movement as it was linked to allegations of firearms trafficking.

The CI was cordial, well educated, and provided information for money. It took months to establish trust, and although he never said it specifically, I deduced that he had a background in government intelligence. As I developed the case against various extremist groups in Northern California, including the Aryan Brotherhood, the White Aryan Resistance, and the Ku Klux Klan (KKK), this informant wanted me to meet with two guys who, he said, had intimate knowledge and contact with members of these organizations and others. I by now trusted him and told him to set it up.

When the CI got back to me, he was very specific about how and when the meet was to go down. It involved a late-night rendezvous and code words and shit like that. It stunk of setup. To make it worse, I was told to go alone. Like that shit was ever going to happen. I reached out to one of the gang investigators I knew, and he said he was familiar with these guys, and this was legit. He said that safety wasn't an issue. Just the same, I had my partner Darren Gil staged up before the meet as a backup.

Initially, I only met one of the guys referred by the CI. We chatted and felt each other out, and he gave me his address and we agreed to meet the next day with the second individual. I still didn't know their names, but since the meet was going to be at a residence I was fine with it. Suffice to say I wasn't the only ATF agent listening to the next day's conversation. Yes, I was wearing a wire, and I had another agent close by. This meeting was creepy and for good cause. The two men had great intelligence on the people I was investigating but refused to go on record or testify. Not even for money. They merely were doing their part to help law enforcement. I told them I was concerned about all the secrecy, and they looked at each other, and the one guy put his finger up, signaling to wait just a minute.

He left the room and came back with a box of heavily redacted government documents from the US State Department, the Department of Defense, and the Central Intelligence Agency (CIA). Looking over the documents, it became immediately apparent that they referred to a well-known and subsequently exposed government covert operation in the 1970s, and these two men were the principals in that operation. Due to the nature of the documents and the prior actions of these guys, I was resistant to report or use any of the information they provided, and I told them so. Their information, identities, and background were more than likely highly classified. This meant it would be damn near impossible to use them or their information in a criminal trial. One of them handed me a business card from a lieutenant colonel at the National Security Agency (NSA). He said, "Call him. He will vouch for us."

When I got back to the office, I researched the NSA to see if this was a good phone number for their public exchange. Anybody could print up a fake business card. RatSnakes did it all the time. I'll be damned, the number was good. I called the colonel and explained what I wanted to know. He in turn asked for my call-back number, no doubt to verify who I was. He called back shortly and said, "Whatever they told you, you can take to the bank. I guarantee it." Then he hung up.

I remember sighing and thinking that I had come to ATF as a normal and reasonably well-adjusted guy who just wanted to catch bad guys. FMTT,* I really didn't need all this cloak-and-dagger shit. It was just too damn scary. In the end, I pursued the investigation without further utilizing the informants.

#2. SOUTH ATLANTA, GEORGIA

Whenever round tabling an upcoming deal, we always would anticipate the worst-case scenario so we had a contingency for every conceivable situation. There were, however, those cases where you walked away scratching your head and asking, "What the fuck just happened?" One case I'm still scratching my head about to this day happened in South Atlanta in the mid-1990s.

A licensed firearms dealer had cooperated with ATF for years, reporting suspicious firearms purchasers. Depending on the violator and their background, we would either let the sale go through, surveil them away from the store, and effect the arrest, or actually put an agent behind the counter to try and elicit where and to whom the guns might be going. Sometimes we would surveil the violators and their cargo to the guns' final destination.

In this case, a violator was flagged by the federal insta-check background check. At the time, this was a fairly new process and we (the government) were still working out the kinks. After identifying the violator, I went back to the office and ran his criminal history. The report showed

---

* Fuck me to tears.

LEGENDS

Les Robinson, front and center. One legendary agent. (Photo courtesy of Les Robinson.)

Seen here holding a photo in which he also appears (*far left*), Robinson worked one of the early Hells Angels infiltration cases in the 1970s. An ATF Hall of Famer, *fo sho*. (Photo courtesy of Les Robinson.)

Old-school revenuers. Special Agent John Rice (*left*) ran the ATF Academy class where I trained. (Photo courtesy of Dawn Maestas, John's daughter, and Neta Rice, his wife, who was like a mother to many ATF undercover agents. "Momma Neta" saved our asses more than once.)

John Rice (*center*) and fellow agents shutting down an old-time bootlegger's still. (Photo courtesy of Dawn Maestas and Neta Rice.)

Being a special agent is cool, but being the first-ever female SA in ATF is the coolest. This is Jo Ann Kocher being sworn in by Eugene Rossides, Assistant Secretary of the US Treasury, in 1972. Rex D. Davis, then Director of ATF, is at left. (Photo courtesy of Jo Ann Kocher.)

Breaking new ground: SA Jo Ann Kocher at target practice in the early 1970s. (Photo courtesy of Jo Ann Kocher.)

VINNY

Semper Fi.

Bein' the *real* police in Athens,
Georgia, in 1984.

Receiving the Ariel Rios Award. It also was my first time at public speaking. Yep, I choked.

Shooting

From page one

gan gave officers a simple lesson on facing a man armed with a knife — don't try to disarm the man in hand to hand combat, he advised.

Farnam watched and noted. "We teach knives in hands of even amateurs are so deadly that if a person intends to use it, you are justified in using deadly force."

Both men are with Executive Security International in Aspen, Colo., a private institution for the training of bodyguards and other professionals in the business of protection. A native of Los Angeles, Calif., Duggan is president and owner of the business. During the 1960s and early 1970s, he was a guerrilla in Latin America and became familiar with Marxist methods.

At the County Police Department tonight he is expected to offer a program on terrorism, something he said officers in Athens could encounter because of the foreign dignitaries who visit the University of Georgia.

Both Duggan and Farnam were complimentary of persons responsible for providing this additional training to local police.

"Everett (Chief E. Price) has professionalized his department and he made a committment in training," Farnam said.

In the county, Farnam complimented County Commissioner Walter Padgett. "If it wasn't for Walt Padgett this wouldn't have happened," he said.

Price said he has received good feeback from officers on the training. "Our people have been giving it good reports," he said, adding that this is the only place in the state to offer such a training program.

Photo by ELLEN FITZGERALD
ATHENS PD OFFICER VINCENT CEFALU FIRES SHOT
Officers' Shooting Assessed As 'Outstanding'

Some things I did really, really well.
(Photo by Ellen Fitzgerald and courtesy of OnlineAthens/*Athens Banner-Herald*.)

PAGE 12

Photo by WINGATE DOWNS
APD OFFICER VINCE CEFALU ESCORTS ESCAPEE ANTHONY POPE
The Suspect Led Officers On Two Foot Chases Before Being Taken To Jail

Damn, I had to chase this thug down twice in one day.
(Photo by Wingate Downs and courtesy of OnlineAthens/*Athens Banner-Herald*.)

Runnin' with the big boys: Early in my undercover career, I was an instructor for ATF Special Response Team (SRT) training.

Some of my first training officers, who taught me the craft of UC work. *From left*: Bill Eastman, Ted Baltas, and (RIP to them both) Larry Williams and Ed "Spike" Gleba.

I got my crazy honest. Luv you, Mom! (Photo courtesy of NorCal Skydiving.)

RATSNAKES ON THE LOOSE

Jay Dobyns, Chris Bayless (*center*), and me back when we were UC toddlers.

SA Jimm Langley: The 1980s weren't kind to any of us.

Here's a rare moment: a RatSnake in uniform. Yep, that's Box.

Me and Bird dirtied up: Never very pretty but always COOL.

The KKK in the 1980s: I never expected this shit when I signed on with ATF.

Infiltrating the KKK: The *not* cool part of my job.

All in a day's work when you're a UC: Here's Gundo (*right*) rockin' the Godiva look to prove his stones to an outlaw motorcycle gang.

Okay, it wasn't *always* all work. Sometimes you lose a bet and end up painting your partner's toes. Here I am pampering Bambi.

With ATF Group Supervisor "Uncle" Ron Mitchell: The greatest boss I ever had.

DEPARTMENT OF THE TREASURY
BUREAU OF
ALCOHOL TOBACCO & FIREARMS

EDWARD J. VERKIN
RESIDENT AGENT IN CHARGE

600 LAS VEGAS BLVD. S.
SUITE 650
LAS VEGAS, NEVADA, 89101

TELEPHONE: (702) 388-6584
FACSIMILE NO: (702) 388-6460

To: Vinnie – UC
Extraordinaire
Champion of the People

RAC Verkin was the best, and a smart boss.

I was that whistle-blower. I took an oath, and I meant it. (Image courtesy of *Townhall* magazine.)

TOGETHER AGAIN

Decades of ATF undercover history: (*from left*) agent-turned-author William "Billy" Queen; Box and Carmen, two greats who were in it with me from the beginning; and Charlie Fuller, who had worked during the Miami drug wars and was my partner in Atlanta.

Clearly denying whatever I'm being accused of.

From left: Jay Dobyns, Alex D'Atri, me, and Gundo. Three knuckleheads and a legend.

Hanging at a Willie Nelson concert with Congressman Jim Lightfoot and Nancy Lightfoot.

With SA Butch Brewer, an ex-cop and agent, and one of
the hardest-working partners I ever had.

Time off with my buds, Bird and Box.

Carmen (*right*) and Robyn: The far better halves of Box and me.

SA Dobyns and myself: Okay, we *may* have had an adult beverage or two.

Bambi: "I have not yet begun to drink."

With SA Pat Kelly, a.k.a. the Godfather, at Pam's #1 cop bar. Loved me some Patty.

No Angel either: Channeling my inner Bird. Who wore it best?

To RatSnakes past and present: It's been a wild ride. Catch you on the other side.

an arrest in the early 1970s for first-degree murder, somewhat surprising, but there was no disposition listed, which was puzzling. Any time a person was convicted of a crime, the originating agency was supposed to follow up with the outcome. If the person was found guilty, there was supposed to be another set of fingerprints on file and a description of the sentence. At face value, we did not have proof that this individual was even a felon or prohibited from possessing a firearm.

The jaw-dropping aspect of this case came several hours later, when I queried the National Crime Information Center (the centralized crime-tracking database maintained by the FBI) regarding further identification and disposition of this individual. Communication with NCIC almost always was done via fax or a telecommunications messages. Only rarely were such interactions done in person or via personal contact between NCIC, the FBI, and the investigating agent. So when our secretary said, "Vince, line one—it's NCIC," I gave my office partner a quizzical look.

The person on the phone from NCIC said: "You don't have the guy you think you have. The guy you think you have is sitting on death row awaiting execution."

Say whaaat?

We told the gun store owner to put the guy off for a little while and just to tell him his background check hadn't come back yet. Then a flurry of fingerprints and photos began flying back and forth over the teletypes.

My boss, and his boss, and his boss's boss's heads were spinning. It took hours to figure out just what was going on. The records in the system for this guy were in shambles. As it turned out, he in fact had been convicted of a double homicide in the 1970s. He was sentenced to death and sat on death row. However, in the mid-1970s, the death penalty was ruled unconstitutional for a brief period, and everybody who was on death row at the time had their sentences commuted to life, including the members of the murderous Charles Manson family. Since this particular violator's sentence had been commuted, he became eligible for parole and had, in fact, been released from prison. We had a convicted murderer on the loose whose crimes were so heinous that they warranted execution, and now he was about to buy some firearms.

Once we pieced it together, it was all hands on deck. We weren't going to take any chances with this guy. It was decided I would conduct the transaction with him, and we would immediately arrest him inside the store.

The arrest went without incident, and I'm reasonably certain I will go down in history as the only ATF agent to arrest a condemned prisoner. Whether I am or not, the situation was so high profile that then President Bill Clinton mentioned it in a speech, affirming the new background checks system worked—although in this case, the system almost didn't work. Because of Georgia state law at the time, if they merely had revoked this violator's parole, he would have been sent back to prison for only one year. ATF and the US Attorney's Office decided to prosecute him as an armed career criminal, exposing him to fifteen years to life of federal prison time. He was convicted and received fifteen years.

#1. NEW ORLEANS, LOUISIANA

Charlie Smith and I went to the ATF Academy together, and we worked The Teams (SRTs) together. Charlie had been a standout college football player with a heart and demeanor as big as his biceps. I never heard Charlie speak ill of anyone. I remember thinking early on that he was going to be a great ATF undercover, but I also remember wondering, "Is he too nice for this job?"

Over the years, Charlie participated in several lethal encounters. The most well known of these was as a member of the New Orleans SRT on February 28, 1993, when he found himself in the fight of his life during the raid at the Mount Carmel compound of David Koresh and his Branch Davidian followers outside Waco, Texas.

I sat helplessly watching the shoot-out unfold on national television while on standby with the Atlanta SRT. We knew something huge was going to happen, but for operational security reasons, we had few details. When my pager went off to call me in from standby, I immediately knew something had gone horribly wrong. My team hit the ground and remained there until the tragic fire that engulfed the compound. My most pressing personal concern was for my fellow agents and friends, Charlie being one. When my team arrived in Waco, I finally saw him upright with no bullet holes in him, and I smiled in relief. By all eyewitness accounts, Charlie took the fight to the armed and violent criminals that fateful day.

Charlie's lethal encounters didn't end at Waco. Later, he was confronted once again with one of the most terrifying aspects of being a RatSnake: having a gun pointed at your face at point-blank range without knowing if the violator on the other end has the stones to pull the trigger. As said, many of us endured these occasions, and for me, as I narrowly avoided shitting my pants in each case, I conditioned myself to believe that if the perp was going to pull the trigger, they would have, and so I merely went on to work the problem. On this occasion, however, Charlie saw it differently.

It was late at night, and I was at home when I got the phone call from another agent: "Charlie Smith was just in a shooting. He killed the guy. He's fine."

As a trained peer-support member and a friend, I was intimately aware of the turmoil that would follow for Charlie, both personally and professionally. At the moment, I also knew the most important thing: Charlie was okay.

As I got a few more details, I wanted to call Charlie right up and say, "What the *fuck* were you thinking?"

Instead, the next morning I said, "How you doing, brother? You okay?"

"Yeah, man," he said. "I'm good."

"Dude, what the fuck happened?"

"I'd met these guys a couple times. We had a couple deals under our belt."

That was a red flag. Having done multiple deals with a specific violator without incident could lull an undercover operator into a false sense of security.

"Dude," Charlie went on, "I thought we were cool. We were in a public place. Cover team was super close. It was a buy walk, so it should have been a cakewalk."

A buy walk is a technique where the agent and the violator exchange money for the product, and the violator is allowed to leave with the money to be arrested another day.

"Brother, if it was such a damn cakewalk, how come you had to kill the guy? What the fuck?"

We both laughed, but nothing about this was funny.

"I walked up to the car parked right there on the street in public view. I shook hands with both guys. It was just like the last couple times, but then the driver got kinda weird. He started asking me over and over, 'You got the money?' I told him, 'Yeah, you got the guns?' But we'd never had this weirdness before."

"Okay, and?"

"We did the back-and-forth a couple times, and the driver pulled a pistol so fucking fast I didn't have time to blink. He reached across the front of the passenger seat, pointed it straight at my face and said, 'Give me the fucking money now.'"

"What happened after you gave him the money?"

Charlie paused for a very long time.

"I didn't give him the money," he said.

"What the fuck, Charlie?" I screamed into the phone. "What the motherfuck?"

It is a hard-and-fast rule in undercover work that you do *whatever* you have to do to get home safely at night. Money can be replaced. Dope can be recovered. Guns can be seized down the road. I was damn near speechless, because Charlie knew this. He had done this type of operation a hundred times.

Charlie was very quiet, and then he said, "Vince, I knew he was going to kill me. I could see it in his eyes. I knew the cover team would never get there in time. So, I ripped my pistol from my belt and got off the first shot and hit him right in the head. He got a round off before he died, and it went through the windshield inches from his partner's and my faces. I backed away, thinking that the partner may try to shoot me. Instead, he took off on foot, and the cover team caught him moments later."

"I love you, Charlie," I said, realizing he'd done the only thing he could and still make it home that night. "I'm sorry it shook out that way, but he made the decision. You did your job."

Never again did I think Charlie was too nice for the job. He was found to be justified in his use of deadly force and went on to rise through the ranks of ATF.

BONUS ROUND: MACON, GEORGIA

In 1995, Jay Dobyns and I had, in record time, gained direct undercover access to the Iron Cross Motorcycle Club, more accurately described as a gang. Not only had we gained access, but we were invited to their clubhouse—a big deal as it was normally reserved for friends and close associates.

Our early and rapid success may have gone to our heads.

UC agents often carry wallets containing "wallet clutter." If a violator ever had occasion to look inside the wallet, at a quick glance it would appear to contain the things a normal bad guy might have: driver's license, pictures, traffic citations, and other misleading clutter.

I'm laying most of this on Bird, because I recall it being his idea. But I also remember thinking, "This plan is brilliant."

Well, it wasn't.

The plan was to hang out and drink with the gang president, "Lil Rat," and other gang members at the clubhouse. Whenever we decided to leave, Bird would "accidentally" drop his wallet on the floor for them to find. They would rifle through the wallet, and the contents would support our story and give us immediate credibility with the club.

The next day, Jay and I got called to Lil Rat's tattoo parlor. Bingo. We were high-fiving and pretty smug when we got the call, because we knew exactly why we were summoned to the shop, or so we thought. We arrived to find the shop closed midday, and that was not a good sign. Someone unlocked the door to let us in, and the entire club chapter was there, numbering about ten gang members. The mood was serious, and I immediately assessed exits and went over target selection in my mind, just in case this went to shit.

The Rat, as we referred to him, said, "Vinny, sit right there. I'll get to you in a minute. Bird, come with me."

Bird briefly glanced at me as if to say, "Be ready," and disappeared into Rat's office with Lil Rat and the club's vice president. I sat out in the lobby, smoking cigarettes with the other eight club members, and endured what only could be described as a not-so-subtle interrogation. Approximately fifteen minutes later, Bird exited the Rat's office, and Lil Rat motioned me in.

What happened to me is exactly what had just happened to Bird. I sat down, facing Lil Rat, with the club vice president standing behind me. The Rat had Bird's wallet on the desk with all its contents spread out. As

I sat down, he reached in his drawer and placed a loaded .357 Magnum revolver on the desk.

"Do we have a problem?" I asked.

"That's what we're here to find out," said Lil Rat.

I mimicked his action and placed my .45-caliber semiautomatic pistol on the desk. It's generally not good when the guns come out, but it's not always guaranteed to be bad.

Lil Rat slid a picture from Bird's wallet across the desk to me. "Who's this?"

The picture was one Bird had acquired over the course of his career, depicting two Outlaws Motorcycle Club members out of Chicago holding a naked woman in the air as she spread her legs for the camera.

"Who are these guys?" the Rat asked again, referring to the bikers in the picture.

"How the fuck should I know, and where did you get Bird's wallet?"

"He left it at the clubhouse the other day. I know those two Outlaws, and one of them is dead. I need to know where Bird got this picture."

"Well, ask fucking Bird then."

"I did, and Bird said from the chick in the picture."

Wanting not to show weakness and trying to reestablish some high ground in this scenario, I said, "Well, good, you figured it out. I got shit to do. I'm gonna bounce."

"I ain't done yet," he said.

In my sometimes overly aggressive way, I said, "Can we just hit the high points, please?"

He didn't particularly like that response. He slid a business card from Bird's wallet over to me.

"What's this about?"

The card was that of a neo-Nazi KKK group known for its violence.

135

These are often used as calling cards by violators, so the possessor can show an affiliation to the organization.

"This card has a tack hole in it," said Lil Rat.

My attitude was getting worse by the second, and I think I responded, "What the fuck?"

"It looks like a card a cop would pin to his trophy board."

Damn, this guy was a smart motherfucker. But I guess my indignant look worked, and he said, "Meet us at Whiskey River (a regular watering hole for bikers and rednecks) for drinks tonight, and I'll bring Bird's wallet back."

We walked out of his office, shook hands, and Jay and I left.

Outside, Jay whispered to me as we mounted our bikes, "Don't say nothin'. We'll talk back at the crib."

When we were alone, Jay explained he was pressed by Lil Rat to identify the woman in the picture and produce a phone number. Jay spat out the number of an ATF female UC based in Chicago. Now all we had to do was advise her of the scam before Lil Rat got to her.

Jay called her right away, and it turned out Lil Rat also was ringing her.

She merely said to Jay, "I got this, guys," and hung up.

Well, she did good, and all was well when we met the club members at Whiskey River. Jay got his wallet back, and the gang paid for all our drinks all night long.

Just, damn.

CHAPTER 9

....

MORE WITH LESS

I once showed up for a briefing wearing a T-shirt that read "Drink Smoke Shoot," fully planning to change shirts before I went to make the buy. That was right up until one of the other agents said, "You don't have the balls to wear that shirt on the deal."

As any bad guy would know:

DRINK SMOKE SHOOT = ALCOHOL TOBACCO FIREARMS = ATF

Yep, I wore the shirt. The violator thought it was hilarious. After we arrested him, I said, "Dude, I gave you every chance I could."

He didn't see the humor.

Then there was the time Bird was at a public restaurant, negotiating a murder for hire with a bad guy. The violator was describing how and where he wanted a bomb placed on a vehicle to kill his ex-wife. Right in the middle of this guy literally drawing on a napkin, Bird pulled out his Spider-Man PEZ dispenser and asked the guy, "Hey, you want a PEZ?"

The guy stopped talking, stared at Bird for a minute, declined the candy, and continued detailing his vile plot. This violator was arrested soon after this meeting, once he had committed to the plot.

Sometimes we tossed in those little one-liners or did things to get a laugh from the cover team or just to fuck with the violator. We'd mention one of the cover team member's names so they would hear it over the wire. The guys literally would place bets before a deal as to whether or not I could get the violator to say "Joey Buttafuoco," which was my bust/ distress signal of choice in the 1990s.*

Cops always will harmlessly prank each other, but it goes without saying that today's cops, and ATF agents specifically, would not be able to function in the way they have come to know if the clock were somehow turned back. In the twenty-first century, we can talk to each other anywhere on the planet. We have digital and encrypted electronics, and we can see each other while talking on a cell phone or other device. In the 1980s, our budget was shit. We barely could keep gas in our vehicles and afford ammo to train with. Managing to record every UC deal would have been the perfect scenario. I've mentioned the challenges of using the boxlike Nagra recorder with its reel-to-reel tapes. "Kel kit" transmitters were our alternative to the Nagra and equally flawed. Kel kits were about the size of a pack of cigarettes, so a bit more concealable. We often would deploy both, meaning you had to hide the two devices on your body. The higher up on the body you wore the transmitter, the farther its range.

---

* Joey Buttafuoco became infamous in the early 1990s after his underage girlfriend confronted and nonfatally shot his wife with a .25 semiauto pistol. Buttafuoco subsequently pleaded guilty to statutory rape and was charged with various other crimes over the years.

A Kel kit had one wire coming out of it that was a microphone and one that was an antenna. It could transmit several blocks in a city and a little farther in open spaces. It had a short life but could be recorded remotely by cover agents. Kel kits came with a big suitcase-like carrier that housed the receiver, an external speaker, and a standard-size cassette recorder. When using either type of transmitter, you never expected to get a good recording and did not depend on it solely for safety. They failed more often than not. The reception was generally scratchy and cut in and out. We had special devices to boost the transmissions, but those rarely worked either.

We didn't have cell phones until the 1990s. We used pagers and pay phones to communicate. At one point, we did have one cell phone for our entire group of twenty agents. It was heavy, worked intermittently, and was about as big as an airline carry-on bag.

Our surveillance cameras were standard 35 mm manual operation, with a variety of magnified lenses. Ideally, we would set up in a UC van or vehicle and take long-range photographs. If we were really lucky, we might get some video. Over time, the violators became acquainted with our vehicles and tactics, so it was rarely as simple as parking a van down the block and pulling back the curtain to take some pictures.

Our tech guys got creative in advancing our electronics and how to conceal them. The good techs all had a RadioShack charge account and tried every possible way they could think of to make life easier and safer for UCs. When the Sony Walkman became popular in the 1980s, we used them to conceal recording devices. Some of the ideas were right out of *Star Trek* and didn't always work at the time. But remember, we all laughed the first time Orbit City denizen George Jetson talked to his wife over a TV screen. The point is that the tech guys tried hard and kept trying. With the advent of encryption, microchips, and microwaves, our resources improved. I will not go into those advances here because some of that technology still is in use in the field. But don't be surprised down the road if you hear about a chip implanted in an agent's body to act as a recorder or transmitting device. I say that partly tongue-in-cheek and partly to freak out any bad guys reading this book.

My favorite story of innovation came from my favorite boss of all time, "Uncle" Ron Mitchell. Ron was a decorated Army Ranger from the Vietnam War. His father was a retired FBI agent and probably would have rather Ron joined his team, but it was good for us that Ron chose ATF. When Ron was a young agent in Macon, Georgia, he managed to make several hand-to-hand buys from a prolific and notorious bootlegger. ATF didn't just want to arrest this violator for selling moonshine, they wanted him for manufacturing too. They had been trying to find the location of his still or warehouse for years, but this bootlegger was cunning and impossible to follow. Ron's team scheduled another large buy from him, and he wanted to meet and see the money first. The violator scheduled the meet at night, so the surveillance team couldn't follow him without headlights giving away the tail.

Somebody, I'm sure it wasn't Ron, because he wasn't that smart, came up with a plan. One of the agents hooked a coffee can filled with phosphorous under the violator's vehicle. They had poked pin-sized holes in the can so the phosphorous would slowly drip out like a trail of glowing bread crumbs. Then, Ron sat on the hood of the G-ride* holding a black light, guiding the driver as to which way to turn. Eventually, they came upon the violator's hidden location and his storage shed full of illegal liquor, and they also found his still.

---

*   G-ride = a "G"overnment car usually only used for UC or a UC's assigned vehicle during an operation.

Les Robinson and his partners set the standard for shoestring investigations. By the time I met Les, he had been a boss for years. When I reported to the San Francisco drug task force, Les was the OCDETF coordinator. He was a short, barrel-chested guy who came to ATF via the US Marine Corps and Salinas, California, PD. He had a gravelly voice and a hard exterior appearance but actually was a mild-mannered, soft-spoken guy.

In the 1970s, as a young ATF agent in San Francisco, Les brought one of the first, if not *the* first, RICO Act cases against the Hells Angels. His case would qualify as the initial attempt at infiltration investigations. This was at the height of the Hells Angels' presence and criminal activity in Northern California. They were attracting significant attention throughout the state related to arrests, drugs, prostitution, and violence, and the motorcycle club had been designated an organized crime organization by the State of California. No one agency at the time had the ability, manpower, or resources to attack the problem.

In coordination with state authorities, the ATF San Francisco field division set up a Hells Angels task force with the sole purpose of investigating each and every violation committed by these guys, even misdemeanors. The Hells Angels never had received that sort of scrutiny, and they didn't like it. There were Angels getting arrested every week for one thing or another. It was draining their defense funds and disrupting their businesses. So the Angels approached the leaders of the task force with a proposal. This was one for the books (no pun intended). The Angels' leadership proposed that if an Angel was in jail for a nonviolent misdemeanor, the club would relinquish a firearm in exchange for getting the charges dropped. A deal of sorts was struck and there were a little fewer illegal guns in Hells Angels hands.

Even as a young boy, I'd seen the Hells Angels show up at town events, scaring the shit out of the citizens, including me. They rolled into town on their loud bikes, walked down the streets shoulder to shoulder, and expected people to get out of their way—and people did. In my hometown of Novato, the annual Western Weekend came complete with a carnival and parades. One year there were stabbings, shootings, and bar brawls that shook our little bedroom community to the core. Much of the violence and disruption to the festivities was attributed to the presence of the Hells Angels, and the event was cancelled for the next year.

Working in San Francisco and Oakland, Les, Doug Gray, Jess Guy, and some other agents hatched an aggressive plan. Les had made some inroads into the Hells Angels in Oakland, but in order to get in close with the bikers, the agents needed bikes. ATF had none at the time. Les lobbied for funds to purchase motorcycles and was met with a brick wall. ATF already was pinching pennies because rumors were swirling that the fledgling agency might be disbanded. Finally, the regional director (the predecessor to the special-agent-in-charge designation) gave Les and his crew three hundred dollars to kick off the case.

Les and his team started spending more time around the bikers, furthering their seedy connections. Next thing they knew, they were being sold cheap motorcycle frames and stolen motorcycle parts. The Angels liked to show off their motorcycle mechanic expertise and would work with the agents to build their bikes. All the agents needed to do was buy the beer. That came out of their own pockets because they had to drag out that three hundred dollars. As the case progressed, the regional director lamented that he couldn't figure out how they were making advances so quickly with such a tiny budget. Les's team was producing evidentiary guns and dope and bombs and never-before-gained intelligence on the bikers. The director had no choice but to throw a little more money their way. He began to support the operation that would embed ATF in the biker's intelligence community, forming a hate/hate relationship for decades to come.*

The ATF undercovers got so close to the bikers that Les was invited to Sonny Barger's wedding party. By then Barger was president of the Oakland Hells Angels. Manpower and funding still being an issue, the agents were told to start winding down the investigation and move on to other priorities. Nonetheless, working with the US Attorney's Office, ATF's investigation led to members of the Hells Angels being indicted and charged with the new, but as yet to be widely used, RICO statute. The simple description of the RICO Act is that the organization is criminally liable for the sum of the crimes committed by its members. It wasn't quite that simple. In the end, that early RICO case failed, and individuals were prosecuted for far lesser violations. But ATF had dipped into the club's legal funds and put the Hells Angels on notice: the Hells Angels weren't the bogeymen, ATF was.

. . . .

ATF was unique in that it truly relied on its boots-on-the-ground agents. From what I saw, other agencies were more structured and oversaw investigations by committee, whereas until ATF moved from Treasury to the main Justice Department, agents remained very independent and agile. Maybe too agile at times.

In the early 1970s, an ATF agent I will call Gene—since neither one of us knows if the statute of limitations has run out yet—was involved in a joint operation between ATF and DEA. Gene/ATF had been approached by DEA to make a sizable marijuana purchase. ATF kicked in some funds, but DEA put up most of the buy money. The informant took Gene to

---

* At the risk of sounding arrogant, ATF became *the* clearinghouse for outlaw motorcycle organization intelligence to this day.

meet the seller, who had five pounds of just-harvested, uncured or "wet" marijuana. Gene bought the marijuana and turned it over to DEA. At that point, DEA and Gene were thrilled. The next morning DEA called, not so fucking thrilled, and wanted their money back. The substance wasn't marijuana. This was a huge problem for Gene because the bosses already were pissed at him for getting duped into a bogus moonshine buy.

Determined to get the money back, Gene stuck the informant in the car along with the bad grass and went to see the seller. After a brief confrontation, and a gun possibly being jammed in the seller's face, the seller turned over all the money he had, but it wasn't the full amount. So at gunpoint, Agent Gene put the CI and the seller into his car and headed for the supplier's house. At this point, an argument could be made that one armed robbery and one kidnapping had occurred—all in the name of justice. Okay, that's the best justification I could come up with.

Upon arriving at the supplier's house, the seller knocked on the door, while Gene stood on one side of the seller and the informant on the other. When the supplier answered the door, with a chain latch on, and the seller told him what had happened, his response was, "Tough shit." Gene reached through the door and grabbed the supplier by the hair, which came off in Gene's hand. It was a wig. Next, the door was kicked in and the return of the money was requested. The supplier gave up what he had, but it still wasn't enough. Gene then escorted the informant, the seller, and the supplier to his G-ride at gunpoint.

What are we up to now? Two "possible" armed robberies, two kidnappings, and a breaking and entering?

The supplier said he would take Gene to the source's house. The knock on the door was repeated, this time with the supplier knocking while flanked by Gene, the CI, and the seller. An elderly man answered the door and said he was the source's father. He went on to explain that his son had died overnight and that the police had just left. Gene walked through the house and observed that the police had recently been there. At this point, he decided that DEA would have to accept partial repayment, and he ended his alleged crime spree.

. . . .

Around the time Agent Gene was making criminals question their career choices, the Symbionese Liberation Army, known for kidnapping heiress Patty Hearst, was on ATF's radar. The FBI already was working the kidnapping by the time ATF opened a separate case on the SLA, which had racked up a slew of federal firearms and explosives violations. In those days, the competition between ATF and FBI agents often was adversarial. FBI agents had money and politics behind them, but we had the results behind us. They also had a reputation for not sharing intelligence, which caused unnecessary overlap on investigations.

The bizarre twist of events that followed Hearst's abduction, in which the nineteen-year-old, reputedly brainwashed, cooperated with her captors and committed armed robbery, had the nation riveted. Meanwhile, ATF agents throughout the state were scouring streets and alleys, looking for any clues to the whereabouts of the SLA and Patty Hearst.

A story was circulating around ATF San Francisco that I believe implicitly, because it was told to me by ATF legend Larry Williams, and went like this: ATF had targeted several members of the SLA in Berkeley and the East Bay prior to the Hearst kidnapping. They had generated enough probable cause to execute several search warrants for high-powered weapons and explosives. However, the FBI had approached ATF and asked that they not advance the search warrants because the FBI also had a case on the SLA, and ATF's actions could screw up their case. ATF leadership acquiesced. Months later, the Hearst kidnapping occurred.

As one of the ATF agents chasing the SLA around, a seasoned investigator named TK had developed an informant. TK had major cases under

his belt and also was a reserve officer in the US Air Force. When his informant convinced TK that the terrorist group was holed up in the thick
forests of Northern California, TK, known for thinking outside the box,
saw fame on the horizon. Leveraging his contacts at the Air Force and his
official position as an ATF special agent, he was able to mobilize a U-2 spy
plane to take aerial photographs of the hidden location. If Hearst's kidnap-
pers were there, TK would be the guy to solve the biggest case since the
1932 Lindbergh kidnapping, not to mention one-upping the FBI guys.

Unfortunately for TK, the information didn't pan out. Oh, well, that
was the cost of doing business, he thought. The price turned out to be a
little more than TK had factored in. A two-hour flight of a U-2 spy plane
cost approximately thirty thousand dollars, or at least that was the bill that
ATF was handed. TK stayed in the weeds for a while after that one.

. . . .

Since ATF wasn't funded well enough in the narcotics arena, no matter
how we did it, we usually had to solicit funding for dope cases from other
agencies. We often partnered up with local narcs, the DEA, or, as a last
resort, the FBI. Part of the reason we shied away from partnering up with
DEA and definitely the FBI is because we were Treasury and they were
Justice. Their policies often contradicted ours when it came to firearms.*
Most of us preferred to work with local narcs. But either way, we often
found ourselves soliciting (begging) participation from an outside agency.

I'll put this out here right now. When I originally started pursuing
a federal law enforcement career, DEA was my first choice. I just wasn't

---

* FBI's operational policies are far more restrictive when it comes to day-to-day cases
involving guns. They don't like guns and try to avoid introducing guns into any
transaction or undercover deal. Under Treasury, we were far more aggressive. Simply
put, we wanted armed bad guys at the meet. The FBI would shut down meets if they
knew a bad guy was coming armed. Pussies.

theirs. However, as the years passed, I realized that was a blessing in disguise. In the 1980s and '90s, DEA went through a transformation. Their bosses married up with FBI leadership. Their core focus shifted from street-level narcotics to major cartels and targeting money laundering. It became harder and harder to find agents in their ranks with any significant UC experience, and even harder to find a DEA boss who would help fund an ATF undercover operation. They were super good at historical cases and wiretaps but weren't very interested in street crime.

Unfortunately (for me), I had targeted one of the big four biker clubs, and there was surely going to be a lot of narcotics purchases before it was over. I needed an extended commitment for drug purchases. The local departments weren't really set up for long-term cases, so I bit the bullet and hooked up with two DEA agents; one was an acting supervisor and one was a task force cop detailed to DEA. When these types of cases start up, there is a bunch of jockeying for power over the day-to-day decisions and the direction of the case as well as the control of informants. It can be extremely challenging when there is a wealth of seniority and experience in the room, but there has to be a shot caller. These things move too fast to run by committee. As the ATF case agent and the one who initiated the case and developed the informant, I was in position to be the lead. DEA thought that since they were throwing money and a little bit of manpower at it, they should call the shots or at least have equal say-so. The task force guy was an Atlanta police officer, but he didn't have a long history of working informants, and he never was going to side with me (even if I was right), because he was trying to get a job with DEA. And the DEA case agent was just a prick who didn't like me or ATF. He thought I was a cowboy, and I thought he was a ladder-climbing pussy, but we were stuck with each other.

From the start, the informant despised the DEA team because they treated him like a snitch and never let him forget it. No matter how much this guy did for us and tried to color inside the lines, they felt that reminding him constantly that he was a scumbag was somehow helpful. That actually was good for me, because our rapport was good and he listened to me. One night, we had a deal scheduled at the gang's clubhouse. That was the Holy Grail, because if we could prove they were using the property as a place to sell drugs, we (the US government) could seize and forfeit the house. This was key because all the members of this club going north or south on runs used Atlanta as a waypoint.

As was the norm, we equipped the CI with a recording device but not a transmitter. In the biker environment, club members were paranoid and suspicious. As mentioned, we didn't have good enough technology to conceal transmitters, and our transmitters all looked like fucking transmitters. Hell, even our recording devices in those days weren't all that covert.

To give some context, when utilizing a CI, garden-variety dope deals go like this: Meet the informant, search him/her to make sure they aren't taking drugs into the deal. The only money they are allowed to take into a deal is government money so they won't be tempted to buy some personal-use dope. Brief the CI on how you would like them to steer conversation for the best evidence in court later: elicit a confession, even if it's in street lingo. Give them a recorder (and/or a transmitter) and send them in. We normally set a time limit so the cover team outside doesn't stay there all night while the CI parties with the violator. In and out is the perfect scenario.

This particular night was different from the beginning. It was a Halloween party, and a shitload of bikers would be roaming the clubhouse and surrounding area, making it very hard for us to surveil the area. Once inside the clubhouse, the club VP started ordering the CI to do things to set up for the party. The target violator called the CI at the clubhouse and said he would be a couple hours late. That started the drama between DEA and the CI, and ultimately me that night. The only way we could communicate with the CI was through pager codes or if he called us from the pay phone inside the clubhouse. The DEA guys insisted on an update call, even though it was reasonable to think that the bikers may have bugged their own phones.

The CI got the page to call, and he did so, surrounded by bikers. He spoke in code, letting us know that it would be a couple hours until the target would get there to complete the purchase. The DEA guys wanted to be home with their kids trick-or-treating. So did my guys, but too fuckin' bad. It was dark out, and the deal was now pushed to around 10 PM. At about 10:01, DEA wanted me to page the CI to call again. I told them to chill the fuck out. This informant already had done a bunch of these deals and did well. By 11 PM, the DEA guys were losing their fucking minds. The bad guy hadn't gotten there yet, and they were ready to shut the deal down. The problem was, they had some sort of hard-and-fast rule (actually, I don't believe it was a written policy, just the DEA guys being fucking dickheads) that they couldn't/wouldn't leave the recorder or the money.

They wanted to call off the deal, and I wasn't going to have that. So there we were out behind a shopping center, out of public view, but literally screaming and yelling at each other. The CI had used the pay phone to call out to us twice. At some point, I had to think that someone inside the clubhouse was noticing this. The DEA guys continued to insist they get their equipment and money back. It's not optimal, but in some cases I have left the equipment and money overnight with a CI if he or she couldn't break away from the bad guys.

When the CI called again, the DEA case agent took the call. The shit he said nearly spun my head off. He wanted the CI to walk to the back fence of the compound and throw the money and equipment over the fence. This plan presented a host of problems, safety-wise and every other fucking-wise. One of us would have to approach the fence undetected in the dark, with dozens of partying bikers just feet away inside the fence. Then the CI would have to casually meander back to the corner of the compound without attracting any attention. Then, when the violator showed up, the CI would have to explain why he didn't have the money for the dope he'd ordered.

With great resistance and anger, my partner, Steve Kosch, agreed to low-crawl up to the fence and retrieve the money and equipment. The CI wandered to the back corner and chucked the recorder over. Kosch heard some of the bikers call out, "What the fuck you doin' over there?" The CI replied that he was taking a piss. Kosch got the recorder and then crawled around in the dark looking for the money, still only feet away from the bikers on the other side. When he returned without the money, the DEA guys blew a gasket. It almost came to blows, and then the CI called again from the pay phone. He spoke in code and said something like, "Thanks for letting me borrow your lawn mower. Hope you got it back. I'll give you that money I owe you tomorrow."

We later learned that he hung on to the money because the guy with the dope was on his way, and the CI didn't want to deal with a public confrontation among his biker buddies and possibly incur an ass whipping. In the end, we got the dope and ultimately made the case in spite of the DEA guys' foolishness. The only thing we didn't have was a recording of the deal. Turns out, we didn't need it. Imagine my relief that DEA got their piece of shit recorder back while almost fucking up the entire case and maybe getting my partner killed.

. . . .

This next tale gives new meaning to the concept of "more with less." In the 1980s, the San Francisco Metro group was one of the most active teams in the San Francisco field division. It seemed like we were doing deals and serving search warrants seven days a week. We worked closely with state and local law enforcement, and in this case SFPD had identified a major narcotics suspect. Shelly was our UC on the case; she made contact and the violator agreed to deliver a kilo of cocaine. Not surprising since Shelly was a seasoned UC, but she also happened to be a gorgeous woman. I mention this only because I can't help but believe the violator was after more than money. He got that, but not in the way he may have expected.

One key to a successful undercover is controlling the location to your benefit. You try to choose a public place but not so exposed that it puts the community in harm's way. But public enough that surveillance teams can cover any escape routes, have good visuals at all times, and, in a perfect world, be close enough to video the transaction. We picked a large grocery store parking lot after hours. There were still plenty of cars around for the cover teams to blend in, but low citizen traffic. Many skilled narcotics traffickers use countersurveillance, so the cover teams have to meld with the setting. For this deal, we placed cover teams all over the area. As our teams got set up and made sure radio communications were working, Shelly made the call to the violator and relayed over the wire that the bad guy was en route. Shortly after the call, one of the surveillance units identified the suspect entering the parking lot in a black Grand Prix. *Go time.* The bad guy parked several spaces away from where Shelly was parked. She acknowledged him as he exited his vehicle, but he ignored her as he began crisscrossing the lot, walking in between cars, checking for cops. He was not going to get busted if he could avoid it.

He was headed straight for one of our cover team's vehicles. This was a problem. In the front seat of that vehicle was the cop's bulletproof vest with POLICE markings all over it. He had a loaded shotgun across his lap. This deal was going bad fast—or maybe not. What occurred next was nothing short of brilliant if not a bit crazy. As the violator got within eyeshot of the vehicle, the SFPD narcotics officer unzipped his pants, bared his penis, and rose up high enough for the violator to see him as he pretended to masturbate. We all watched, not knowing exactly what was occurring but prepared to pounce if the violator appeared to identify the officer as a cop. Instead, the violator stopped dead in his tracks, turned, and briskly walked back to Shelly's car to seal the deal.

When the violator related the story to her, Shelly laughed, and so did the other ten cops in vehicles stationed around the parking lot, listening to this over the wire. Shelly made the buy, and the violator was immediately arrested. He pleaded guilty and was off to prison. The narcotics officer's on-the-fly technique never made it into the official police report. Nor did I ever emulate the strategy.

Hilarity aside, the parking lot scenario demonstrated the continual need for UC agents to improvise, adapt, and overcome in order to see an operation through. It almost was guaranteed that no matter how many contingencies we planned for, we would forget the one that invariably popped up. Such was the case when I was called upon by some agents from the Birmingham, Alabama, field division to assist in a UC operation that dropped us right in the middle of the largest KKK rally in the country.

At the time, Bart, Turbo, who had worked the Warlocks infiltration, and Futvoye, a.k.a. Foot, were working some hardcore white supremacists out of Alabama and Florida. They were invited to attend the rally but felt some local ATF contacts would be helpful if the case eventually spilled into Georgia. With the necessary approvals in place, we found ourselves at the foot of Stone Mountain surrounded by thousands of Klan members and associates. The KKK and supporters stood inside the fence. Outside the fence were hundreds of cops. Both sides were armed to the teeth. It didn't get real scary until right at dusk. That's when the hoods came out, armed patrols around the fence started, and sixty-foot-tall wooden crosses were hoisted. The scene was right out of a movie.

It was a successful mission. We gathered great intel and solidified our position with the violators, and then we got the hell out of there. The boys were scheduled to leave the next day, and I put on a barbeque at my house.

As I recall, copious amounts of JD were consumed that night. Foot had flown in and spent the night at my house. In the morning, both of us a little "tired," I drove him to the airport.

When we arrived at the airport, Foot realized that he and Turbo had the exact same carry-on bag and they somehow got switched the night before. They each had the other's credentials, which were the only thing that allowed an agent to carry their firearm onboard an aircraft. Foot's luggage already had been checked, and he had a deal planned back home the next day and needed his gun.

I'm embarrassed to say that this was the best we could come up with. I went through security carrying both our guns, and once we'd cleared security, we went to the bathroom, where I passed his pistol to him under the stall. I cringe even today when I think of the bad things that could have happened pulling that bonehead move. Luckily, we didn't have to find out, and nobody else ever found out. Until now.

. . . .

Let me tell you about Joe Plummer. He was everybody's favorite prosecutor—humble, smart as shit, aggressive as hell, and he was never condescending to the agents. Early in my career, I was involved in a very strange case, actually two separate cases, involving the CIA. In Atlanta, my then partner Bill King and I happened upon this weird case, and to this day I am thankful Joe Plummer was the assigned assistant US attorney. We needed all of our combined skills to navigate this one.

We had received information from multiple firearms dealers that a man and woman were purchasing huge caches of firearms, ammunition, and virtually every firearm-related accessory known to man. Preliminary investigation revealed that the male was a prior convicted felon. He would therefore accompany the female to the purchase site, decide what would be purchased, and then step aside while the female completed the transaction. A "straw-man purchase" is illegal, but that violation in and of itself wasn't a top priority for ATF unless the purchase amounts were in the tens of thousands of dollars. In this case, the couple bought hundreds of thousands of dollars in firearms. That got our attention.

As we started to investigate, we first wanted to know where a seemingly average couple got so much money. Secondly, what did they possibly want with so much armament? A run-of-the-mill gun collector wouldn't be purchasing dozens of reloading presses, cleaning kits, holsters, and such. They also wouldn't be buying dozens of guns in a single transaction. Investments? Maybe, but again, where was all the money coming from? We started around-the-clock surveillance on this pair. They lived in a middle-income neighborhood north of Atlanta, on a cul-de-sac with few to no good vantage points for surveillance, so we reached out to our tech guys in DC and asked for some type of concealable camera to place in the woods across the street from the couple's house. When we received the package and opened it, we busted out laughing. The techs had sent us what was supposed to look like a squirrel's nest: a camera attached to a football with leaves glued all over it.

It looked like a football with leaves glued all over it. Time for plan B.

Our next best idea was to use a drop car, an innocuous vehicle outfitted with a camera trained on their house. We dropped the vehicle up the street from their home and got eyes on them. The very first morning that the vehicle was parked there, the two violators walked straight up to the car, located the camera, and then notified the local television news station. We turned on the morning news and there was a reporter with the violators, filming our camera filming them. That was when we knew we were dealing with something pretty nefarious.

We were going to have to up our game, and how the hell were we going to get our vehicle out of there without being on the evening news? Needless to say, we had to get creative—at four o'clock in the fucking morning—to retrieve our vehicle undetected. Simultaneously, we had identified multiple storage units rented by the couple. Financial records showed that the two had a long history of back-and-forth financial transactions with parties in South Africa. This thing was getting bigger and weirder by the day. Joe, Bill, and I wondered the same thing: Could this be a covert government operation? Before continuing our investigation and dedicating even more expensive assets to this case, we needed to know whether or not we would be shut down or have the case halted because our two suspects were acting in concert with the government and/or on behalf of the South African government.

You don't just stroll into the local CIA office—if there even is a local CIA office—and ask what they're up to. ATF and the US Attorney's Office had liaisons to the CIA, and any and all inquiries or interactions went through very formal channels. Eventually, we massaged the necessary people with the necessary requests and arranged to meet with a representative from the CIA.

This shit was getting spooky. We were told to meet an unnamed person at a nondescript civilian office space. None of us ever had done this formally and had no idea what to expect. When we arrived at the sparsely furnished office (it appeared to have been thrown together and was probably vacated after our meeting), a man awaited us. We explained everything that we knew. When we asked questions, he redirected with his own questions. I don't think the guy answered one of our questions. We walked out, scratching our heads, not knowing any more than we did when we went in.

Several days later, Joe called us into his office and advised that we had received formal word that we "could proceed with a criminal investigation." That was it. No other information, and there would be no further communication with the CIA on this matter. I guess that was all we really needed to know, but it would have been nice to receive a little information from them. It was unlikely they weren't at least aware of and/or tracking the international money transfers. In the end, we arrested the man and woman and charged them with a slew of violations. They pleaded guilty, and we seized all of the guns and ammo. Normally, that would be a victory. But we never found out what they were up to, and it was on to the next case. Since we arrested them before they could attempt to transfer the guns internationally, if, in fact that's what they were going to do, we will never know. In this case, we agreed with the bosses. If we had drawn the case out to track them to a port facility or a transportation hub and lost the guns, we would have been putting the public at great risk. My educated guess? There always has been a buttload of money to be made in international gunrunning.

. . . .

For a good twenty years, between the 1970s and 1990s, times were lean for ATF. Despite its numerous successes, the agency didn't grow much and resources remained slim. We didn't have fancy SWAT trucks like are used today. Our mobile command centers were small RV-type motor homes, and we didn't have huge vans to load up with agents to go on a large raid. It wasn't really practical to come screaming into a neighborhood in ten or twelve police-type unmarked cars. But we had to be able to flood an area quickly with enough agents to safely conduct a raid, so sometimes the conga line of police cars was the only way we could get enough manpower on the scene. It was really hard to sneak up on a search warrant location with a dozen Crown Vics, the standard unmarked police vehicle of many PDs. So we often used a rented panel moving van. As alluded to above, that worked well for a lot of years, until the ghetto dwellers started to figure it out. We used to laugh that there was no way of knowing how much dope got flushed down the toilets in the projects just because somebody was legitimately moving out using a U-Haul truck.

During the late 1990s, I was assigned back to where my law enforcement career started, in Athens, Georgia. There had been an increase in narcotics trafficking and firearms-related violence in the Classic City, and ATF offered to help. I was the logical choice for this assignment. It was old-home week, except that all my former patrol partners were now big-shot bosses, but that was a good thing because I had instant credibility. We put together yet another ad hoc task force and married up with the Athens-Clarke County PD narcs. This marriage turned out to be extremely successful. After a year or so of taking down some of the worst gangsters in Athens, we started hearing chatter on the streets that ATF had sent about twenty agents to Athens and the dealers should not carry guns because fed time was no joke. Truth be known, I was the only ATF agent there with any regularity, and I was partnered up with about ten highly skilled and motivated local cops. But all the street thugs knew was that their buddies were not going to local lockup and instead were taken to Macon and charged by ATF. We had to take them to Macon simply because that was the federal judicial district governing Athens.

I had befriended some of the newer narcs—one in particular, a hard-charging former Marine named Billy Stotts. He was fairly new to the business but would work night and day, and he loved working dope cases. There was a particularly elusive horrible bad guy in Athens we wanted. This man, Boris, had evaded charges and arrest for years. Mostly because everyone was afraid to testify against him but also because of where he lived. Boris's house sat up on a hill, where he could see cops coming from every direction. Amazingly, I was able to twist a dealer's arm and get an introduction to Boris. That was the easy part. At that time and place, a drug dealer would have been suspicious of a healthy-looking white boy wanting to buy crack cocaine. To start with, I put the word out through our snitch that I wanted powder coke.* Just meeting Boris at his house was huge. I could take pictures, secretly, of course. I could identify lookouts and violators. I could document vehicle information, and, if I was convincing enough, I could buy dope.

Boris was known to be armed, and he had armed lookouts, which made my bosses nervous because of the logistical challenge. We couldn't get surveillance units close enough to hear or see what was going on. The powers that be agreed to let me make one meet without backup. Amazingly, Boris immediately latched on to me—and my money—and agreed to sell me an ounce of powder. We bullshitted for a few minutes, and I asked if I could come back but without the snitch. I told Boris that I didn't like people knowing my business. He said sure, just to call before I came. Due to the success of the first transaction, my bosses relaxed. Although I noted it in my report later, I hadn't made a big deal to my bosses about the .45-caliber pistol Boris had stuck in his belt.

Powder coke didn't hold the same penalties as crack, so I wanted to segue into crack buys. At the next meet, I told Boris that my buyers were just taking the powder and making rock anyway, so if he had any rock, I could make more money. He was a well-known crack dealer and enforcer, so when I went down that road, he made some comment that basically said: Stupid ass white boy, the only reason I even sold you powder was because you asked.

I was equipped with a hidden camera and a recorder, and we were able to identify everybody in the house and capture pictures of those who were armed. The goal was to make a couple buys, and then up the quantity—and then tear their shit down. But we still would need to get a team close

* Powder coke was seen as the expensive drug of choice for elite whites. Cocaine in crack form was far cheaper and also far more addictive—and easier to sell to inner-city types. Requesting powder coke was the only way for me to approach Boris because he wasn't going to believe I was smoking crack.

enough to the house to prevent the dope from getting destroyed and all the players disappearing into the wind before we could make arrests. Or worse, give them enough time to set up and shoot it out with us.

I recalled my days of pulling into the Atlanta projects in a U-Haul or Ryder van. At first everyone thought I was insane when I suggested using a van, which by this time was synonymous with the po-po. But I explained: We would set up one more buy, do the buy in a rental truck, and desensitize the bad guys. Let them see me in the van and remove their fears. Then, use it for the raid.

We discussed and agreed: No guts, no glory. Or as Jay Bird always would say: Jesus hates a pussy.

I called Boris, told him I needed another half ounce of crack. I said that I was helping my sister move shit, and I'd cut away in a little bit to pick it up. I went on and on about how I was tired of moving this bitch in and out of houses every time she dumped a boyfriend. He laughed and said he could relate.

We secured the necessary search and arrest warrants, wanting to be ready to serve them the next day. We could drag the moving story out for only so long. Then I rolled up in front of the house in a U-Haul van with my window down, so Boris's lookouts could see that it was me. I signaled one of the lookouts that I needed to see Boris. He walked his fat ass down the steep driveway and came over to the truck. He was laughing. He reached in through the window and handed me my dope, and I handed him the buy money. I asked when I could get a couple more ounces. He said, "Shit, my nigga', I got it right now." I said I'd be back the same time tomorrow, and he said okay.

The next day, we loaded up a bunch of cops and battering rams and all of our toys in the back of the truck. I called Boris and said I was headed his way. This time I would drop the truck into low and drive it all the way up to the front door of the house like a modern-day Trojan horse. Things went perfectly until I got to the top of the driveway. It was raining hard, and as I put the brakes on, the truck slid a little just as Boris and his crew were walking out to meet me. Inside the back of the truck there wasn't much to hold on to, and a couple of the guys bounced against the wall of the truck as I came to a stop. That was it. Bad guys scattered in every direction. My guys unassed the back of the truck and started grabbing bad guys and made entry into the house. Boris was the number-one target, so I started out after him as he tore ass down the steep, muddy hill at the side of the house, hit the street, and kept going.

The time it took me to turn off the truck, set the parking brake, and make the decision to give chase allowed Boris a fifty-yard head start on me. I wasn't fast, but the day I couldn't catch his fat ass was the day I'd quit my job.

Well, that *was* the day. I hit that muddy hill at a dead run, tripped, and didn't stop tumbling and sliding until I had rolled about twenty feet into the street. Now I was about a hundred and fifty yards behind him. Luckily, my boy Stotts also wanted to lay hands on Boris and was right on his heels. I gathered myself, muddy and bleeding, and chased after Stotts and Boris, who had turned down an alley. When I caught up to them, Stotts was sitting on Boris, who was handcuffed, both of them panting like they'd run a marathon.

When Stotts looked up and saw me covered in mud, he busted out laughing. He tapped Boris on the shoulder and said, "Look at that shit." And then to me, "Where you been, boy?"

"Fuck you, Stotts."

Boris got ten years. Meanwhile, I had transferred back to the San Francisco field division. One night I got a call from a close friend of mine in Atlanta. Gooch started off by saying, "It looks like I'm going to make a career out of cleaning up your messes."

He always busted my balls, and I just laughed.

Gooch told me he was meeting Boris—who was now out of prison—to purchase a stolen pistol the next day. I couldn't believe it. What a small world, and Boris hadn't been out of prison that damn long. Gooch went on to make the buy and the arrest, and Boris was headed back to prison. Barely a month goes by now that Gooch doesn't call me to remind me how to do the job right. Fuck you, too, Gooch.

CHAPTER 10

. . . .

EXECUTIVE DOUCHEBAGS

fter the disaster of Waco, Congress wanted heads on a platter. Hell, even President Bill Clinton made wisecracks that basically equated to calling us the Bureau of Alcohol, Tobacco and Bubbas.* ATF was still a Treasury Department agency in the early 1990s, and its director was appointed by the Secretary of the Treasury. In fact, all four Treasury law enforcement agencies—ATF, IRS, USSS, and Customs—were budgeted

---

* At the 1995 Radio and Television Correspondents' Association Dinner, President Bill Clinton riffed on meeting with Vice President Al Gore and other White House staff to reinvent and consolidate the government. Clinton quipped: "We decided to do something for that group of constituents that's supposed to be so alienated from the Democratic Party. We want to combine the Bureau of Alcohol, Tobacco and Firearms with both the Bureau of Fisheries and the Interstate Trucking Commission." Fist pump. "We're gonna call it the Department of Guys." "1995 Radio and Television Correspondents Dinner." C-SPAN video (Program ID: 63940-1), 46:02. Aired March 15, 1995.
https://www.c-span.org/video/?63940-1/1995-radio-television-correspondents -dinner

by the Treasury/Postal Committee chaired at the time by Congressman James Lightfoot of Iowa, who did me the great honor of writing the foreword for this book. The congressman knew what ATF was capable of, and he was our strongest cheerleader when calls to abolish ATF got loud.

It didn't hurt ATF's cause that the Republican congressman was an ex-cop who'd worked in Tulsa, Oklahoma. But he alone couldn't save ATF, and he enlisted Dennis DeConcini, then Democratic senator from Arizona, to help keep ATF alive and undertake a massive restructuring. It was clear that the top ATF guys were gonna get axed after Waco. Lightfoot and DeConcini backed John Magaw for the role of ATF's new director.* Magaw was a hard-nosed Secret Service deputy director and, in his last couple of years with USSS, its director, with close ties to the administration; he was highly respected. ATF's top leadership was purged, and Magaw immediately began centralizing power and accountability. There would no longer be twenty-six SACs running their field divisions twenty-six different ways. Magaw wasn't perfect, but everybody knew who the boss was and what the rules were. With his credibility came administrative support, which brought funding. Our equipment was updated; we got newer and more suitable vehicles. Hell, we even got brand-new office furniture. Those were some good times. However, they wouldn't last long.

Magaw had no choice but to move up existing bosses. After the restructuring, there wasn't a deep bench when it came to experienced leadership. We now had SACs with maybe fifteen years on the job, translating to relatively light experience in this highly specialized, tactical field. In the old days, you had a hard time getting a first-line supervisor job with only fifteen years on. Director Magaw had started out as a state trooper for the Ohio State Highway Patrol before joining the Secret Service in 1967. He

* John William Magaw served as the fourth director of ATF from 1993–1999. Since becoming a bureau in July 1972, ATF has had twelve directors or acting directors, including Edgar A. Domenech, who twice served as acting director.

was seasoned but nonetheless new to ATF, and he had to listen to people inside ATF on how to implement his restructuring. Since there already was a contingency of former Miami bosses at the DC headquarters, this led to the "Miami mafia," as we referred to it. One after another after another, the Miami bosses moved higher up the food chain.

The way I saw it, the executive staff created a circle of loyalty that extended to each other more so than to the bureau and its mission. I was particularly not fond of the tactics of Edgar Domenech, who had positioned himself as assistant director of ATF, shooting for the big prize. Edgar was a good field agent, but as an executive, he created an us/them mentality between the field and HQ. Instead of HQ being there to support the agents who were risking their lives in the field, it felt like the other way around.

Admittedly, Director Magaw sort of set that tone early in his tenure with his response to the highly publicized "Good Ol' Boys" roundup. The annual gathering was started in southern Tennessee in 1980 by a small group of ATF and other Treasury agents. The week-long campout and barbeque originally was intended just as an informal RatSnakes reunion, but this thing grew to over three hundred attendees, including state and local cops and other federal agents. In 1995, the roundup was castigated in the media after at least one non–law enforcement person attended. The get-together was described as a highly drunken stripper fest, and there were allegations of racism characterizing the event. After an investigation, the Inspector General's report found the opposite. There were one or two racially motivated signs and/or a short comedic skit. No ATF agents were directly involved in those incidents, which were conducted in privately rented campsites. When the ATF organizers had found out about this fuckery, they'd immediately shut it down. The troublemakers had been confronted and told to knock that shit off.

However, the microscopes were on ATF after Waco and Ruby Ridge and would be for a while. Magaw, still relatively new as director, brought down the hammer and vowed to fire every agent in attendance at the roundup. No one from ATF was fired for participating in the gathering that year, but by pandering to the media rather than showing trust in and publicly supporting his agents, Magaw drove a wedge between HQ and the field.

Aside from issues created by restructuring that haunted ATF for a good decade going forward, if likewise looking backward, it's also true that many at the SAC level and above had come over from the fairly quiet corridors of the Treasury Department's Alcohol Tobacco Tax Unit. If they hadn't come directly from the old ATTU, they were trained by those who did. Most of that set were just as happy when they were wearing the old green uniform, and they didn't like ATF's dope or gun jurisdictions. Their history and training often colored their vision of what ATF should be. It was typical to blame the bosses and the senior executive leadership at HQ for all that was wrong in the field during those years. That sentiment was misplaced in some cases. But there is no disputing that ATF leadership made it easy to blame them. They hadn't grown at the same pace as the agency. Frankly, the horror stories of decisions made by some in senior leadership would fill another book. My intent is simply to illuminate some of the avoidable obstacles that field agents, specifically UCs, were confronted with over the years while merely trying to do their jobs.

I was involved in one tragic example of my bosses' unwillingness to enter the drug world as it related to our investigations in the twentieth damn century. ATF's narcotic-purchase budget back in the 1980s was laughable, and DEA normally wouldn't come out to play for small-level deals. My bosses had a mind-set that had been ingrained in them for a decade or more. The HQ point of view was very clear: "You wanna buy dope, go work for DEA."

I am going to be intentionally vague when describing what occurred. I was asked to meet an inner-city gangster who had a sawed-off shotgun for sale. Sawed-off shotguns are covered under the National Firearms Act and carry stiff penalties for possessing an unregistered one. The altered weapon is particularly deadly because it has a much wider shot pattern and the ammunition is launched faster than it would be if the barrel were full length. The informant said I needed to buy some crack cocaine to establish my credibility with the violator. He felt it would be too suspicious if I showed up to buy the sawed-off first time out.

My SAC at the time was a rigid old-school revenuer who wished we were still working moonshine. I asked for three hundred dollars to make a crack purchase and additional funds to secure the shotgun. The informant was not reliable enough to trust with that kind of money, so my SAC insisted I do the deal. Then he authorized me to buy only ten dollars worth of crack. I was going to meet a no-shit gangster and ask to buy a single hit of crack, but then I had five hundred to eight hundred dollars to buy the shotgun. Can you say COP?!!! The long and short of it was that there was no immediate way to bridge the huge gap the boss's directive would drop me into. So, I walked away from the deal for the time being. For various reasons, walking away was a fairly common occurrence, and in this case I was fine with it. I was busy with other shit.

I wish I had fought harder for the money. Two weeks later, the same violator committed a murder for hire of a woman in front of her children on Thanksgiving Day—*with a sawed-off shotgun*. I was crushed. Had I gone through with the purchase, the violator would have faced ten or more years in a federal penitentiary. From what I knew, that violator would have sold out his mother and might have given up the murder-for-hire scheme for a deal on his charges. I/we will never know.

It wasn't just my bad damn luck at getting ignorant SACs and ASACs, because it was happening all over the country. ATF was promoting so fast that they couldn't groom new bosses quickly enough. Definitely not all but many of those who rose through the ranks in those days didn't like working as street agents, and they weren't good at it. I had one ASAC in Atlanta who tried to micromanage even the most basic of agents' investigative activities. One time he called me while I was standing outside a grand jury room and told me not to testify. He didn't think I had satisfied the elements of the crime, meaning I hadn't proven all of the facts needed for a conviction. Yet he'd already signed off on the case as ready for prosecution. While I was arguing with him on the phone, I got called into the grand jury room. I hung up and went in and testified. The defendant pleaded guilty and went to prison for ten years. I got your elements hangin', Mark.

. . . .

Magaw left ATF in 1999, and a disturbing and ultimately destructive trend started. The next appointed director was an ATF attorney, Bradley Buckles.* I'm sure he is a smart guy, but he knew dick about fieldwork. It came down that supervisors now would be required to attend a two-week, first-time supervisors' school. That was fine, but the school included almost no mission-related training. Nearly the entire two weeks was devoted to procedures for disciplinary actions against agents and how to handle discrimination and retaliation complaints. Again, this set a tone and the priorities.

I've talked a lot about leadership needing to understand what it's like to work in the field in order to effectively manage active agents. Let me

---

* Bradley A. Buckles joined ATF's Office of Chief Counsel in 1974 and became chief counsel for the agency in 1995. He was deputy director under Magaw from 1996–1999 and director of ATF from 1999–2004.

reiterate that police work and certainly UC work requires those in the field to navigate a gray area laced with danger. The type of individual who can survive and operate in such an environment does not respond well to nor does he or she respect a too-rigid management style. A UC has zero respect for a boss tucked away in an office somewhere who puts both an investigation and lives at risk by making ill-advised calls during an operation.

One of the better acts of douchebaggery happened while I was riding with my group supervisor in his car during an operation in Atlanta. The ASAC had insisted that the supervisor call him and place the cell phone on the car seat so the ASAC could monitor activities in real time. Of course the ASAC had every right to come out and monitor or even oversee any operation he wanted to. What he didn't have a right to do was expect the supervisor to effectively oversee the operation while talking back and forth to him. Instead of being laser focused on the UC operation and directing the agents' actions on the ground, the supervisor was busy giving the play-by-play over an open mic. I don't know who was the biggest douchebag boss that day, the ASAC or the supervisor for giving in to such a shit order.

Police officers throughout time have been given discretion in the field so that good judgment can prevail when a gray-area decision has to be made, often on the spot. In other words, an officer needs to wisely balance the letter of the law with the intended spirit of the law. For example, one of the greatest challenges for an undercover agent is to know when to walk away. That choice might be made because the violator is full of shit or for the simple fact that the crime does not rise to a level that will merit federal prosecution. It also could be just a gut instinct that something is wrong.

As a young undercover, I was asked to infiltrate a particular violator's circle. The information was that he had a fully automatic machine gun for sale.

Should have been a no-brainer, right?

Wrong.

Further investigation revealed that the violator was a twenty-year-old returning veteran from the first Iraq war. The soldier had an honorable military record, including being a Bronze Star Medal recipient. The gun was a war trophy he'd taken and brought home. Against the law? Yes, of course. (It was previously overlooked when returning World War II heroes brought war trophies home.)

It became obvious to me and others that the military is very good at dealing with and disciplining their own. The US attorney agreed. But my ATF bosses at the time saw the case as a slam-dunk prosecution. So, without advising the bosses, those of us working the case quietly teamed up with the Army Criminal Investigation Division (CID) and confronted the soldier. The machine gun was taken into custody without incident, and the case was closed. My bosses blew a gasket, but justice prevailed.

On another occasion, I was tasked with helping to execute a search warrant on a former Vietnam veteran and Green Beret. His wife had gotten pissed at him and turned him in for having—you guessed it—a war trophy hanging over his mantle. Rather than kicking his door in, we introduced ourselves and explained the gravity of the situation. The ex-soldier readily abandoned the machine gun. Case closed, and we were able to preserve the dignity of another war hero.

We got our asses reamed for that one too.

Whereas my first boss, Bill McNulty, was one of the best. Mac, as we all called him, had come to the San Francisco office right after the MOVE bombing in West Philadelphia in 1985. Rumors abounded that Mac had a hand in the police raid on MOVE's compound, which resulted in the deaths of eleven people, including children. He never said, and I didn't ask.

Mac loved the job. He would go on every operation with us. He wasn't there to watch us but to participate. I was still on newbie probation, and there was one senior agent who was fucking with me unmercifully. He had a chip on his shoulder, and everybody knew it. One day I'd had enough, and I told the other agent if he fucked with me one more time, he and I were going to the parking garage to work it out.

Mac came over to us in the middle of the office. I figured I was in deep shit. The senior agent immediately said, "Did you hear him threaten me, boss?" Mac said, "Yes, I did, and I heard how you were talking to him as well." The agent asked, "Well, what are you going to do about it?" Mac said, "I guess I'll take both of your phone messages since you two are heading for the parking garage, right?"

Needless to say, I would have followed Mac to hell and back.

. . . .

Bradley Buckles's directorship lasted far longer than I had expected. Then Edgar Domenech was named acting director for a brief time in 2004, and his boys ran wild under his leadership or lack of. From my vantage point, all of our growth and progress under Magaw had stalled. Fallout from the 9/11 attacks had also highlighted US interagency disputes and lack of cooperation. Additionally, several high-profile domestic bombings had produced OIG reports that ATF and the FBI weren't playing well together. The following year, in fall of 2002, President George W. Bush created the Department of Homeland Security and moved ATF out of Treasury and under main Justice. Our director would now be appointed by the Attorney General. We were done for at that point, in my opinion.

In 2004, John Ashcroft appointed Carl Truscott, another trusted Secret Service executive, to head ATF. Hey, at least Truscott wasn't a lawyer. Edgar was pissed. With his Miami mafia entrenched in all the top positions, Edgar had assumed he would be appointed director.

Truscott started spending on a new headquarters building at such a rate that it took the project way over budget. He had stereos and TVs put in the executive washroom. He ordered a custom-made conference table at the price of tens of thousands of dollars. The spending abuse went on and on, and Edgar, once again in the role of deputy director, saw the opportunity to seize control. He started documenting the abuse of power and resources and then anonymously leaked information to the media that led to an OIG investigation. Everybody in the field knew that Edgar ratted out his boss. My issues with Edgar are many, but, as he was quick to say, if ATF doesn't retaliate, then why did he need to hide behind anonymity?*

Truscott resigned in 2006, and Edgar was made acting director for the second time. He again didn't get the full promotion. Instead, in that same year, US Attorney Michael Sullivan was appointed as the next ATF director and served in the role until 2009. This was the first time we had a director who would fill dual roles. Mr. Sullivan remained the US attorney in Massachusetts and served as our director, commuting between the two jobs. It was insane. Edgar was removed from his deputy director role and alleged that Sullivan had retaliated against him. Some call it karma. I just say: you reap what you sow. The director has every right to pick his second in command; in Sullivan's case it was Ronnie Carter. ATF paid Edgar off and he went away, so some good came out of it.

---

* As alluded to earlier, in 2005, I spoke out publicly against corruption and illegal wiretapping sanctioned by senior personnel within ATF. Sadly, blowing the whistle resulted in a lengthy dispute with the agency for which I'd worked for twenty-seven years. Edgar Domenech and HQ vigorously fought my contention that retaliation against me had occurred when I exposed corrupt practices by some individuals.

Those familiar with an ATF operation dubbed "Fast and Furious" know that the gunwalking scandal ran deeper than a few individuals and was linked to the fatal shooting of US Border Patrol agent Brian Terry in December 2010. I don't intend this book as a tell-all, nor do I wish to dwell on my argument with ATF, but I will say more about the failed operation and my legal case in chapter 17, "The Cost of Doing America's Business."

Steve M. of the agent foursome who had infiltrated the Warlocks biker gang—rode the Edgar Domenech gravy train while it lasted, and ATF just kept promoting him. For a time, Steve was my boss, and he tried to have me fired. I ultimately prevailed, while he eventually retired in obscurity. I have no problem pointing out that his ego got in the way of his tactical judgment. One of the worst decisions by Steve that I personally watched unfold was the 2007 Laotian undercover case known as Operation Tarnished Eagle. Steve was the San Francisco field division SAC at that point, and he sanctioned and took personal interest in the case.

The case being developed involved Harrison Jack, a retired Army Ranger and lieutenant colonel who had served in the Vietnam War, and former Royal Lao Army Major General Vang Pao, who were believed to be conspiring to overthrow the communist government in Laos. Vang Pao had emigrated from Laos to the United States in 1975, after communists seized power of his homeland and vowed to annihilate indigenous Hmongs who sided with US forces during the Vietnam conflict. Many Hmongs had fled to the Laos jungles for decades after the war. An ATF undercover posed as an arms dealer, claiming he could deliver millions of dollars' worth of weapons—including automatic rifles, antitank missiles, rockets, and explosives—to a US-based Hmong group led by Vang Pao and Jack. The group allegedly then planned to smuggle the arms to Laos, where the Lao government had increased its campaign against the Hmong.

The host of charges that would be brought included weapons violations, conspiracy to kill and kidnap foreign nationals, and violation of the US Neutrality Acts. The Neutrality Acts make it illegal for an American to wage war or attempt to overthrow a country at peace with the United States. To my knowledge, Operation Tarnished Eagle was the first and only Neutrality Acts case involving ATF.

The problem with the case from the get-go, and I told Steve so over the course of several weeks, was that it stunk of entrapment. The main defendant was a Laotian war hero in his seventies. We had a completely inexperienced UC agent and a cadre of new hires, also inexperienced, pursuing the case that ran on for months. The only guns involved in the investigation were the props provided by ATF, and, in fact, when search warrants were executed against members of the Hmong group in California's Central Valley, there were no firearms seized. Just one black rhino horn.*

Arrests had been made, and Steve did what Steve always did. He called the media and invited Director Sullivan out for the press conference. In the end, the case was dismissed with extreme prejudice, and the judge was none too happy with us. Public sentiment lay with the Lao Hmongs, whose plight was highlighted after the case went public.

. . . .

Here's a flashback. I've told about the night years ago at Pam's #1, when I was first welcomed into the snake pit and there was an agent who spent the evening talking about how great he was at UC work. Fathom a guess who that was. Years later, when ATF created an undercover pool, who of all people was sitting on my interview panel? Right again. This was in the 1990s, and I was working in Atlanta at the time. Factor in that I had openly called this particular agent out for his self-serving, back-stabbing, self-promoting ways, and you know how my interview went. Of course, all three bosses on that panel had significant UC exposure—ten or more fucking years ago.

----

* The Convention on International Trade in Endangered Species of Wild Fauna and Flora (CITES) entered into force in 1975 and became the only treaty to ensure that international trade in plants and animals does not threaten their survival in the wild. Of course, ATF had no way to prove the rhino horn was taken after 1975. The whole thing was embarrassing.

I was not accepted into the program, needless to say. Far less experienced junior agents were selected. The irony was that being snubbed by the pool panel didn't impact my life or case work even a little. I continued to work more UC around the country than anybody else in my field division. I made the same money as those who made the cut. All in all, I had bought more guns, more explosives, more dope, and (off the job) likely gotten way more pussy than all three of the bosses on my panel put together. That made me smile, but I laughed my ass off when they denied Bird's assignment as well. Who were they shitting? Bird didn't make the A team? He laughed, too, because we were both up to our asses in UC work.

Around that time, there was an FBI task force supervisor who had asked for my UC participation. That in and of itself was a miracle because the FBI bosses tended to hate my ass. But then this knucklehead shut down an operation because—wait for it—the violator was known to be armed and was bringing a gun to sell to me. That may have been one of the dumbest things I ever heard come out of a cop's mouth. I truly thought I had fallen down the rabbit hole.

. . . .

Part of my frustration with some bosses stemmed from the simple fact that taking on the UC persona and accompanying duties was hard, especially for young agents. While UCs were respected—but not always loved and admired—by the hard-charging, ass-kicking field agents, the same couldn't always be said when it came to the bosses. The RACs could view UCs as a liability and even a stumbling block in their climb up the management ladder. For too long, an outdated mind-set prevailed: big cases, big problems; little cases, little problems; no cases, no problems. This was never clearer to me than when I first reported to Atlanta in 1991. I was a fast-tracker in the agency. I attributed that mostly to a good work ethic and the influence of the senior agents and my San Francisco boss, Lou

Bristol, who had demanded that I learn how to do the job right—the first time. At any rate, in record time, I was promoted to the highest level a street agent could achieve. I literally was promoted thirty days before I was even eligible, which caused some ruckus at HQ because they had never encountered that.

To make matters more complicated, I was simultaneously promoted in two cities, twenty-five hundred miles apart. I was promoted to GS-13 in Oakland and Atlanta with the exact same report date. I opted for Atlanta, and the agency honored my decision. I was a new agent with a new wife and two new babies. California was getting too damn expensive, and my wife was bitching about being too far from her home in Georgia. After the folks at HQ figured out how to delay my Atlanta promotion for thirty days, and meanwhile un-promote me in Oakland, I said goodbye to my folks in the San Francisco Bay Area and headed east.

The Atlanta SAC had a reputation for being a micromanaging, old-timer moonshine cop from the early days. Oh, boy, I thought, but I'd survived Ron Wolters, my micromanaging ASAC in San Francisco, so I could survive this guy. As was customary when traveling to your new office during your government-sponsored house-hunting trip, I went in to introduce myself (to kiss the ring) to my new SAC, a guy named Tommy Stokes.

I put on my best suit, the only one I had, and walked into the division headquarters office, where I was greeted by several of the administrative staff ladies. Their response was all I needed to know: This wasn't Kansas, Dorothy. One of the ladies said "He's in the last office on the left. Good luck!"

Stokes was on the phone with his back to me, and when I reached his door, he swiveled around in his chair, drawing on a cigarette while talking on the phone. He flashed me a look of disdain and then left me standing there for ten minutes while he clearly was just shootin' the shit with somebody. Finally, he hung up and loudly said, "Come in." I walked in, hand outstretched. He briefly stood to shake my hand. As he sat back down, he said, "Get a haircut and lose the fucking earring. This ain't California."

I would go on to be the bane of his existence and he mine for the next four or five years that he remained my SAC.

At the time, I thought to myself, well, at least my group supervisor probably will be better. Nope. My new supervisor was dead in the middle of a class-action discrimination lawsuit against the ATF. The lawsuit, brought on behalf of two hundred and forty black ATF agents, was finally settled in 1996, with a large award, payment of the class's attorneys' fees, and a promise that the ATF would overhaul its procedures for hiring, training, discipline, and performance reviews. Ironically, he seemed to favor the black agents in his group over the white ones by his words and deeds. I knew something was different when I showed up to the office before we were open for business one morning and found my supervisor and every black agent in our group behind closed doors in the conference room. Later that day, he mentioned to me in passing that they were conducting a Bible study. I didn't believe that, but I told him I didn't care.

This same supervisor later complained to the ASAC that I had Klan literature on my desk, and he was offended. Coming from San Francisco and having worked alongside black agents that I considered brothers in arms, I was offended. What I actually had on my desk was a *Time* magazine with an article highlighted about the KKK. The article mentioned the case I'd worked on and applauded ATF's enforcement efforts against the Klan. The ASAC agreed the supervisor's claim was crybaby bullshit, but ATF was under the gun and acted scared of anything to do with black agents. The ASAC asked me to put the magazine in a drawer, and I did. I was frustrated at the lack of possibility for the two-way trust that is so critical in UC work, let alone my supervisor actually having my back.

. . . .

In contrast, here's how it's supposed to be done.

Bird and I had gone to Las Vegas to start a long-term undercover operation. We were both in the doghouse for various and sundry minor violations
back at our home offices. This Vegas case might just get us back in the bureau's
good graces. We got our feet on the ground and began making UC contacts.
One night, Bird didn't feel like going out, so I went to a casino to play poker.
Back then, many of us carried our firearms and credentials in those hideous
fanny packs. Bird called them "hey, shoot me first, I'm a cop" bags. It was
kind of true. It seemed like every cop on the planet was using them.

Knowing I'd be at the poker table for hours and this big ol' fanny
pack wasn't comfortable, I took it off and strapped it to my chair. I won't
belabor the stupidity of that. Yep, got up, went back to the UC apartment
several hours later without my gun and badge. By the time I realized what
I had done, I blew every red light to get back to my seat at the poker table.
My fanny pack was gone. I had fucked up huge. A cop losing his gun is
bad; an ATF agent losing his gun is horrific. By policy, you must report
this to IA within two hours.

This is exactly when you need a skilled and level-headed boss. In this
case, it was the Las Vegas supervisor, Ed Verkin. I called him about 1 AM
and woke him up. When I told him what had happened, his response was
to say calmly: "Let's sleep on it, see what happens."

Sleep? Was he fucking kidding me? He said he'd call me in the morning and we'd figure it out, and meanwhile "don't do anything stupid like
calling IA until you talk to me in the AM."

Ed called me in the morning to see if I'd heard anything. Nope. He
was heading into the office in about an hour and said for me to meet him
there to start getting our story together. I was done. I saw my career going
out the window.

In reality, it was probably just going to be days off, but I didn't need any more screwups right then. We have always said among ourselves, "God loves ATF agents and drunks." Well, that day it was true. No sooner had I hung up the phone at the undercover apartment when the phone rang. To this day, I do not know how the local police got our UC number, and I don't care. The caller said, "This is Carol from Las Vegas Metro, and we have an Agent Cefalu's badge and gun down here. May I speak to him, please?"

My mind was racing, but out of instinct I didn't confirm or deny and merely asked if I could have a callback number to confirm this was Metro PD. After all, the apartment was *supposed* to be a UC location. She gave me her extension, and sure enough it was Metro. I only confirmed who and where she was, and the next thing you heard was me and Bird burning rubber out of the parking lot.

Bird said, "You better call Verkin." As it turns out, Ed was about ten minutes away from notifying IA. Many bosses would have been speed dialing IA to cover their own ass the minute I told them what had happened. Ed called me in after I had retrieved my property and simply said, "I don't want to ever hear this discussed. Do you understand me?" I said, "Yes, sir," and it was forgotten, until now. Sorry, Ed.

. . . .

You probably can imagine that the bosses in my day rarely asked RatSnakes to fill in for supervisors. When they did, it usually was short-lived. In my case, it only took the bosses a few tries before they realized they should never make me the boss for more than a day or two. Not because I was bad at it, but because I was really good at it. It's hard to explain the general mentality back in those days, but I would describe it as often a very draconian environment—and I wasn't known for being a yes man.

When I was in Atlanta, I worked under a particularly self-consumed ASAC. It was said he'd made his management bones by driving the director around. Anyway, my supervisor was going out of town for a month, and this ASAC made me the acting supervisor. I think he thought he could keep closer tabs on me and maybe slow me down a bit. Wrong, Two Dogs.

My second day in the seat, the ASAC called me, agitated, and asked, "Who approved that operation last night?" I said that I had. He went on to scold me, saying I didn't have the authority, blah blah blah. While he was rambling on, I pulled out the ATF directive that said I *did* have the authority. He stammered something about the Atlanta field division having additional internal policies. I told him I had a binder with the Atlanta field division policies in it, and asked if could he direct me to the policy. He said it was verbal and common knowledge to the regular supervisors. I replied that I wasn't aware of that policy, and we hung up.

Day three in the boss seat. I hadn't had my first cup of coffee, and the ASAC had called and was yelling on the other end of the line. Who had authorized this gun buy expenditure? Agents couldn't be allowed to just spend funds as they saw fit, he said. I told him I had authorized the buy, and might I pass along his "job well done" to the field agents? He got louder and said: "Don't get smart with me, Cefalu." I asked if he needed anything else. He commenced to chew my ass and advise me of yet another verbal policy I was not aware of.

Day four. Yep, the ASAC called again, this time to say he was assigning a junior agent to serve as acting boss for the remaining twenty-six days. He thanked me for doing a good job. Everybody thought that was funny as shit and believed it was a new Atlanta record. I was off the hook, but what always had me shaking my head when shit like that happened was that I'd been replaced for *doing my job*.

. . . .

JT was another one of those overly interfering boss types. Back when he'd been an agent in Las Vegas, he'd regularly jumped other agents' cases, and that trend continued after he was promoted. As the SAC, he was and always would be within his right to review and sign off on any undercover operation. What he clearly should not have done was try to direct and make discretionary judgments from a thousand miles away while the operation was live, which is exactly what he did.

I had just been transferred back to the San Francisco field division after thirteen years. As one of the senior agents in the division and the most experienced UC, I immediately was sent to Reno to work with and oversee a gun show undercover operation that had commenced months earlier. The case was being worked by a couple of brand-new agents. They seemed to be making some good contacts, even if they were slightly over-aggressive and lacked focus. Their networking concept was sort of the shotgun approach, which doesn't generally work all that well. But, hey, not my circus, not my clowns. I just tried to support them as best I could.

At any rate, they had made contact with a gun dealer at the show who had agreed to sell them a converted machine gun. Upon my arrival on the case, the meeting and purchase price had already been set. All that needed to be done was for the two young case agents to brief the cover teams regarding the buy and takedown.

Just prior to the briefing, the supervisor called me and the two UCs aside and said, "The SAC says Cefalu goes in with you guys, or you don't go." My head damn near spun off. Before the new guys could say anything, I screamed at the supervisor, "Did the SAC hit his fucking head?" We all lodged our complaint with the supervisor, who wasn't known for standing up for his guys. Just as those before me had done, I felt it was my job to take the heat for the new guys. I told the supervisor: "I ain't doin' shit until I talk to the SAC," and he said, "Go ahead."

The reason this was such a shocking development is that No. 1: I had never heard of such a thing. No. 2: It presented so many possible bad outcomes it bordered on moronic. No. 3: JT already had signed off on the previous plan. I had never met the violator, we had no rapport, and introducing a new face into a deal that's already been set up runs everybody's anxiety level way up. Especially the bad guy's.

When I got JT on the phone, it was a short call. I screamed, he screamed, and it ended with him saying: "This is nonnegotiable. You go in or call off the deal. You guys choose." I took our SAC's position back to the two young UCs and told them my opinion was to call off the deal. But being a couple hours away from what I think was going to be their first-ever UC machine gun buy, they were willing to take the chance. So, we modified the plan, briefed, and went for it. You can only die once, right?

As we all fully expected, not knowing who the fuck I was, the violator was none too happy to see me, and he said so. I made a couple attempts to smooth things over, and he wasn't having any of it. The two undercovers were staring at me as if to say, "What the fuck do we do now?" I made the command decision to extract myself from the deal and told the UCs I'd meet them at the bar later. I exited, and upon clearing the immediate area, got on the radio and updated the supervisor and cover teams. I remained out of sight but very close in case a distress signal was given. A few minutes later, the two UCs exited the building with the machine gun, the violator following behind them. One of the UCs gave the bust signal, and a clean arrest was made without incident.

I knew what was forthcoming was not going to be a "good job" or an "attaboy." It was going to be a major ass chewing from JT for deviating from his plan. Ah, the joys of being a UC. Sure enough, JT told me to get my ass back to San Francisco and be in his office the next morning. I was so pissed and was getting no backing from the supervisor, and I told JT, "I'm two hours away. I can be in your office tonight, motherfucker," and hung up. After the debriefing, the supervisor called me aside and said, "You really shouldn't have called the SAC a motherfucker." I told him I didn't give a fuck. He said, "Now we both have to be in his office in the morning."

I know the title and much of what I've said in this chapter will piss off some of my bosses who read it. But hey, fellas, if the shoe fits.

On the other hand, I've mentioned Lou Bristol. He was one of the old guard and a peacemaker who treated all his people well. I worked under Lou in the 1980s when I was with the OCDETF group in San Francisco. He always asked a little more of me, but in exchange I was treated more like a veteran than an FNG. He also took the time to teach me the job of being an investigator and not just a cop. He taught me the most valuable lesson of all: Learn the policies and learn the paperwork. Those two things repeatedly saved me for the rest of my career.

Because Lou knew the job of being an ATF agent better than anyone, he would sometimes piss his bosses off. I heard him tell an ASAC and a SAC more than once, "You can't do that. It's against policy," and he always was right. Shortly after I left San Francisco, Lou was transferred to the field division headquarters in a bullshit admin position. Apparently, some bosses didn't want people in the field who knew more than they did. That transfer would ultimately prompt Lou to retire. I was angry at the bureau for letting that happen to him. Little did I know that sixteen years later I would meet with a similar demise.

CHAPTER 11

. . . .

HAVE GUN, WILL TRAVEL

The old undercover pool and its successor were created to help rapidly identify an agent with a specific skill set to fit a particular UC role or plan. For example, if a case required transport of a load of stolen guns across state lines for a violator, you might want a UC who could drive an eighteen-wheeler or an agent who had a pilot's license. Maybe you needed a Spanish-speaking black guy or a woman who could ride a motorcycle. We relied heavily on networking within our little RatSnakes world.

There was no regulation or policy mandating use of the UC pool. In fact, most UC requests were made agent to agent. So it really didn't matter if you were in the pool or not. The pool was just another resource in case a particular agent didn't know somebody to reach out to. A typical request for a UC went like this: Somebody would call one of us and ask about availability and willingness to take on a particular role. Then the requesting agents, SAC, or ASAC would call the UC agent's SAC or ASAC and formally request their assistance. Normally, it would be approved without issue. Once in a great while, an SAC might resist letting one of his superstars go work for another field division.

Being the UC for outside agencies always presented a give-and-take scenario. Some of our federal policies were too strict for the locals, and some of theirs too loose for our liking. We usually met in the middle. I have to admit, it was pretty empowering to be the "hired gun."*

During the 1980s, the US Marshals had an annual fugitive roundup code named Operation Falcon. It was an all-hands-on-deck affair, and all federal and local agencies contributed manpower for this operation. I was always assigned to the Marshals' covert ops team. They would use me to get close to suspected fugitive houses. I might knock on a door, pretending to look for somebody who didn't live there. Or I'd curl up in the street wrapped around a whiskey bottle. The Marshals used and abused me in those days, and I loved it. It got me on two episodes of the TV show *Cops*. I'd tell my mom to watch when I was going to be on. She'd say, "Let me guess, you're the one all blurred out." True. But hey, the hired guns got the good gigs.

Very unexpectedly, I was asked by the Atlanta FBI office to be the UC on a fairly high-profile coke and gun deal. The FBI supervisor hated me, and I hated him right back for the empty suit he was. But he had no choice: He didn't have anybody skilled enough, and I was the only show in town. I suspect that I also was expendable if it went bad.

I was getting ready to meet three Colombians in a hotel room for a kilo of coke and a machine gun deal. FBI SWAT would be covering me from the next room. As a rule, I wasn't thrilled when it wasn't ATF covering me. But it was the FBI's case and their money, so their rules.

I always attempted to lower my anxiety before a meeting by using

---

* My business cards had "Have Gun, Will Travel" printed on the back.

controlled breathing and mental preparation. If you could stay calm, it was easier to work the problem. This would be a meeting in a hotel room with known violent gangsters, and this exact scenario had met with some disastrous results over the years.* I was particularly anxious. Luckily for me, the ATF group supervisor, Louis Quinonez, was an old friend of mine with an ample background in undercover work. It was not uncommon for me and others to say a prayer before going on an operation. In this case, Louis did the honor. After some prayerful words, he ended it with, "If this goes bad for you, Vince, please say hello to Jesus for me." The FBI guys gasped. I looked at Louis to see his sly grin, and my anxiety went away.

The Colombians called and said they were running late. I had about an hour to wait, which could ratchet my nerves back up. Louis didn't want me to just pace back and forth in the hotel room, so he opened the door between my room and the cover team's room so we could chat and share a cup of coffee. The cover team could warn of anyone approaching the room well in advance.

After standing around shooting the bull for a couple minutes, the FBI SWAT team leader called Louis and me over for a sidebar. Apparently, when communicating with the cover team, I'd dropped the "F" bomb a couple times. The team leader said he was a Christian man and didn't appreciate my language. Louis immediately put his hand on my shoulder and squeezed tightly, as if to say, "Don't throat punch him, Vince."

"Several of my team were offended as well," said the FBI team leader.

---

* The tragic shootings of ATF agents Ariel Rios and Alex D'Atri have been mentioned earlier in this book. In 1982, five drug and gun dealers met with the undercover agents at the Hurricane Motel in Miami to sell large amounts of cocaine and machine guns. The violators grew suspicious and opened fire in the hotel room. Special Agent Alex D'Atri was wounded five times and survived. Special Agent Ariel Rios died as a result of his wounds. The two violators were convicted of first-degree murder, assault, and firearm charges. Ten other defendants also were convicted on related charges.

Louis squeezed my shoulder harder.

I wanted to say, "Fuck you, I am a Christian as well," but I didn't. Nor did I say, "Why don't you or one of your pussy team members come on in here and do this UC?"

I made the buy without incident. The FBI cover team performed like pros. Bad guys in custody and dope seized from the vehicle they arrived in. FBI buy money secured, which probably was the only thing the FBI boss cared about. This case illustrated some of the shit that non-operators didn't always understand. See, the one absolutely unique aspect of being an undercover operator is that you were alone. There always were people close by to help, but no human is faster than a bullet. UCs don't get to go into our world with guns drawn. We don't get to wear heavy ballistic vests. We don't bring specialized protective equipment, flash bangs, or body bunkers.* So, when the tactical boys tried to weigh in too heavily on how to run a UC, our normal response was thank you, but how about just shutting the fuck up.

This also is why I always felt more comfortable doing UC work for other ATF offices and state and local police. They understood and appreciated our contributions and the inherent risks. There were requests from certain departments and/or individuals to which my reply was an instantaneous yes. One of those individuals was Bambi's partner, Randy Beach, based out of the Savannah, Georgia, field office. If Randy was asking, it was an important case, and he took the job seriously. One time Randy called; I said yes, figuring I'd go to Augusta, where he needed me, make a buy, afterward party with Randy, probably Bambi and Dino, and go home.

I got to Augusta, and Randy brought me up to speed. A multiagency

---

* Also called ballistic shields or ballistic blankets, body bunkers are the handheld bullet-resistant shields used by law enforcement.

task force had been in place for a couple years, working up and down the Eastern Seaboard on a large arms trafficking case. Randy's team all had been burned, i.e., their cover was blown, while working the case for so long. He wanted me to meet one of their targets, even though he thought it was unlikely the violator would agree to meet or deal with me. Randy introduced me to his CI, and we put a plan together.

I not only met the trafficker, but he agreed to sell me a fully auto MAC-10. We set a next-phase plan in motion, which would be a buy walk. In the hierarchy of my most intriguing buys, I thought this one was way down the list. I went in and bought the gun and agreed to meet the violator later. This is where it got weird.

A day or so afterward, I was back at my home office, when Randy paged me "911." He wouldn't talk over the phone and just said he needed me back in Augusta ASAP. I cleared it with my boss, jumped in my G-ride, and hauled ass. When I got to Augusta and met with Randy, there were several bosses at the office.

This was real bad, Randy said, and then he dropped the bomb.

"Vince, wanna know where the last place that MAC-10 was documented to be?"

I said, "This is what you had me drive four hours for? To reveal the trace results on one gun?"

He calmly said, "We had already recovered that particular gun."

My mind was swirling, trying to figure out where he was going with this. Then he said, "The last place that gun was documented as being was in the FBI's possession."

WTF? WTF? WTF?!

I gestured for him to keep going. I hadn't noticed at first but now understood why IA was in the room. After hearing all the theories, I asked, "What now, and what does this have to do with me?"

They wanted me to reinitiate contact with the violator and try to arrange another buy, and then attempt to garner information about the last gun. This would have been a buy bust, but ultimately, I could not reach the violator. I later learned he probably had left the country. I never heard and never asked what they ever found out about that MAC-10. Simple buy walk, my ass. I should have just assumed if Randy was involved, "weird" was involved.

. . . .

TV shows can have the cops meeting the bad guy, gaining his confidence, and making the buy and arrest in a forty-minute time frame. In reality, every undercover operation requires planning, paperwork, more planning, and more paperwork. When embarking on an undercover operation outside of our area of operation, we had to do a lot of advance legwork and address a number of questions. For instance, how long did we expect the operation to actively continue? This led to concerns about funding. Which field division would pay the related expenses? Would it be funded out of headquarters? Who were the violators? Did the UC have any prior exposure to this violator(s), location, or organization? What special equipment, electronics, or vehicles might we need? What backstopping or identification would the UC need? It could take days, weeks, or sometimes months to attempt to answer in advance every question that might arise.

In discussions of undercover work, you will hear much about round tabling. To keep everybody on the same playbook, this often was done formally with all participants present, including the bosses. Most of the real planning went on unofficially between the affected agents as well as those who possessed special knowledge of similar cases. We would want to know what had previously worked and what had not. Some of the planning sessions could get quite heated. There were large egos and widely diverse personalities in the room. There was vast experience in the room.

We didn't hold back our opinions, and we didn't always agree. I sometimes had in the back of my mind: "Hey, you guys learned about criminal shit in cop school. I *was* a criminal and know this shit firsthand."

I was never a huge proponent of long term UC operations for a number of reasons. Although we had many successful long-term UC cases, they brought more peril than working narrowly targeted violators. The longer an agent is undercover, the greater the chance of compromise. The longer that agent is away from fellow cops and family, the more the lines can blur. Many long-term cases just don't pan out for one reason or another, and many precious resources can be squandered on those cases. To be clear, this was my personal position and not always shared by my peers or the bureau. The good thing about so many agents having input was the diversity of ideas. Sometimes that led to a case being called off by agreement of all the factions.

I also was not a true believer in OMO long-term cases. Again, this was my personal opinion. It can be argued that all 1-percent club members are guilty by association.* I wouldn't disagree that they are of questionable character, and they choose to associate with criminals, but that doesn't make them all criminals. In contrast, *all* Mafia members are criminals. All narcotics-dealing street gang members are criminals. Bird and I often lamented that ATF was too consumed by all things biker related. Over the years, neither of us thought the big biker infiltration cases were a good use of resources. Yet, Bird worked one of the longest, most notorious biker cases in the bureau's history.† Even I relented at the request of others and did my own long-term biker ops.

---

* Outlaw Motorcycle Organizations such as the Hells Angels or Outlaws Motorcycle Club often are termed "1 percent clubs," since the other 99 percent of motorcycle riders generally are law-abiding citizens.

† Jay Dobyns tells about this case in his book *No Angel: My Harrowing Undercover*

Once I was working a long-term UC in Gainesville, Georgia, when the Mexican informant we were using had to step away for a while. He could, however, make an introduction to the violator, who was holding a bunch of stolen guns and a kilo of coke. Our only problem was that the violator didn't speak English. So, drawing from the Core, we enlisted Dino. He was only a couple hours away and didn't have anything pressing back at his office.

Within a few hours, Dino came down from Savannah to help us out. We knew Chewy, the violator, wasn't going to sit on those guns and the dope for long. We got Dino briefed up and set up an introduction by the informant. The next day we hit the ground running. The violator agreed to meet Dino but would only bring one of the stolen pistols to the first date. We accepted, and the meet was set. My partner on this caper was Butch, an ex-cop and a very good investigator and experienced UC. We were supported by the guys at the Hall County narcotics unit, who were some of the best I've ever worked with.

We briefed, Dino got wired up, and off he went. The violator was on time, which almost never happens with drug dealers. He was introduced to Dino, and they immediately started speaking Spanish. Luckily, a couple of the task force guys were bilingual and were monitoring the wire and keeping us posted. Plus, Dino knew that not everybody on the wire spoke Spanish, especially the shot callers—me and Butch. Being an experienced UC, Dino mixed the conversation back and forth from English to Spanish to relay key info to us: the make of the vehicle the violator was driving, license number, make and model of the pistol, and things like that. It was pretty clear that Dino was buying a Bryco .25 semi-auto pistol—basically,

Journey to the Inner Circle of the Hells Angels (Crown Publishers/Random House, 2009).

in my opinion, one of the biggest pieces of shit handguns ever sold. They were heavy and not engineered for extreme accuracy.

Imagine our shock when the violator said he wanted $800 for this pistol, which could be bought brand-new for $175. Just like any deal in the real world, price and terms always are negotiable. In the underworld, it's expected that you argue about the money. If you don't, you're usually considered a punk or a cop. Butch and I laughed right up to the point when Dino said okay to the price without putting up a fight. Butch speed-dialed Dino—slightly unusual in the middle of a deal—and said, "You better not give that fucker eight hundred dollars, you fuckin' Puerto Rican." Dino just hung up and gave the violator the money.

In this situation, both Dino and Butch were right. A UC always must be mindful of the entrapment defense, which, in this particular case, would have gone something like this: "Ladies and gentlemen of the jury, which one of you in that jury box wouldn't jump at selling something for five times its value?"

What Butch and I didn't know was that Dino had protested the price, in Spanish, and the violator said he needed the cash right that minute but would cut $1,000 off the price of the kilo of coke when they met next.

What we also didn't know was that when the violator showed up, he hadn't come alone. He arrived with two other Mexican males. When they entered the ten-by-ten-foot studio, they locked the door behind them. To this day, Dino admits he didn't hear or see shit after that door lock clicked. The only thing Dino was thinking about was whether or not he could shoot all three dopers before they could get him. We never knew any of this until our debriefing because Dino's voice never changed inflection. UCs have to be able to multitask, and Dino was one of the best.

For years, we busted Dino's balls over that particular buy. His comeback was always: "Twenty years in prison, two guns, and a kilo of coke off the street. Not bad for a Puerto Rican, huh?"

Working as hired guns or otherwise, RatSnakes aren't always easily recognizable as the superstars we think we are. UCs have to realize that their appearance might be unnerving to others. We often were the only ones who knew we were the good guys. To everybody else we encountered, we were scary-looking street guys.

Box was transferring out of the academy and back to the field, and Jay and I were heading home after Box's going-away party. In other words, after a weekend of consuming lethal amounts of JD, Bird and I were hauling ass to Atlanta so he could catch a flight back to Arizona. We'd gotten up, said goodbye to everybody, and hit the road. No shower, no change of clothes, and hung-the-fuck-over. I was wearing cutoff jeans, no shirt, flip-flops, and hair down to my ass. Bird, well, Bird always looked like he just stepped out of the Special Housing Unit, a.k.a. SHU, for the worst of the worst at Pelican Bay State Prison.

Turns out, Georgia state troopers frowned on driving eighty-five miles per hour. We saw the trooper turn on his lights and do a U-turn in the median. It was clear that we were his target. When he pulled up behind us, our actions were slow and specific. We had multiple firearms in the car. Because of this and our appearance, our hands were on the dash, palms up. That apparently caught the trooper's attention, and he exited the vehicle with his Remington 870 shotgun, which, of course, elevated our anxiety. As the trooper got within earshot, Bird blurted out loudly, "We're cops."

It wasn't out of the ordinary for a trooper on this stretch of road to come across FLETC students coming or going. The trooper stopped short of my driver's-side window, leveled the shotgun in our direction, and commanded us to exit the vehicle out the driver's door. He said in his very deep, Southern voice, "I better see some goddamned badges pretty quick."

It worked out fine. No ticket was issued, and the trooper was last seen walking away shaking his head.

. . . .

As I've said, most ATF agents have multiple collateral responsibilities. Some include SRT work, hostage negotiator duties, or certified explosive specialist duties. This made it common on big roundups to keep running into the same folks. Unlike the FBI, we didn't have thousands of agents located in two or three states to call upon. If we needed a hundred agents for an operation, they would come from across the country. The reason for generally trying to hit all of the targets at once was to reduce the number of fugitives in the wind once word got out. We'd hit them first thing in the morning to catch them off guard and to reduce the possibility of a confrontation. Let's face it, who wants to fight first thing in the morning after drinking all night?

One raid I worked on was a roundup of the Sons of Silence motorcycle gang based in Colorado. Daryl and Blake, two of our best, had spent two years infiltrating the gang and perfecting dozens of criminal cases ranging from narcotics to firearms and explosive violations.* I was paired up with Milton the Ragin' Cajun for the duration of this operation, which lasted for days.

We had hundreds of agents and cops on this roundup. The night before, Milton and I were drinking in our hotel room. Milton was extremely distracted, and it only took me a few minutes to figure out why. This would be the first big roundup he would participate in since the Waco shoot-out. Milton had lost friends/brothers during the Waco raid, and those events affected him for the rest of his career. There were some

---

* A case is "perfected" when it is collectively agreed that the necessary elements of the crime have been satisfied and that the evidence is strong enough to convict.

basic similarities with the Sons of Silence raid that had him anxious. It was another huge operation, with hundreds of ATF agents staged at a local airport. We were going to execute on a rainy morning. One ultimately had nothing to do with the other, but for Milton, like many of those present during the Waco shoot-out, it brought back horrible memories. We talked about it briefly and then went to bed. In the morning, it would be business as usual.

Our SRT hit the Sons of Silence clubhouse at 0600, and that was everybody else's cue to execute their warrants. This gang had terrorized portions of Colorado Springs and also put our boys through two years of hell. We were on a mission to get as many in custody as fast as we could. Call it payback time.

Milton and I were assigned to the clubhouse with the SRT. The gang president was extremely hostile and noncompliant, so the SRT did what SRTs do: They lit him up with a beanbag. Direct hit to the chest. He folded like a cheap card table. Guess who had to stop the fun and escort him first to the hospital and then to lockup? Yep, that duty fell to Milton and me.

The guy spent the whole trip to the hospital explaining to us what motherfuckers we were and how we wouldn't be so tough without our badges. Milton was not known for his compassion for criminals, so I merely warned the biker he might not want to poke that particular tiger. When the violator was in the treatment room, the doctor came in. The violator was handcuffed and now proceeded to run his mouth at the doctor. The doctor opened the guy's shirt, exposing one of the nastiest pink, purple, and blue bruises I had ever seen. I kind of chuckled, which further set him off, and he tried to sit up. Only he was restrained by the handcuffs. So, instead he screamed: "That shit don't hurt, motherfuckers!" The doctor jammed a finger dead in the center of the bruise and said, "Really?" At which point, that biker shut his pie hole and went to jail like a good boy.

Once the overt phase of the operation (search and arrest warrants executed in uniform) was completed, Milton and I were called upon to go covert, a.k.a. UC. After the first two days of the roundup, we still had fugitives in the wind. Blake and Daryl provided a list of known hangouts for the Sons of Silence members, and one by one, Milton and I visited the bars and motorcycle shops undercover. We were able to track down a couple of the outstanding fugitives and get them arrested. The last place we visited was a bar under the control of the Sons, and we choreographed how to approach this location. Milton and I would insert ourselves prior to uniformed agents showing up. We could then document the patrons' actions and determine who might or might not be confederates of the club.

We entered the bar, immediately noticing support paraphernalia on the walls. The ATF raids were the talk of the bar. It was on everybody's minds.

After the bar filled up, the uniformed ATF teams showed up, locked down the parking lot, and assigned agents to the exits. Our guys immediately began identifying patrons and started basic interviews. Many of the patrons told our guys to fuck off. Others were more cooperative. Milton and I were in position to finger any patrons who stashed dope or chucked their weapons under a table. As a result, we made additional arrests, but we weren't done yet.

Next came the unofficial part of the plan. After our uniformed agents left, they went back to their rooms, changed into their civvies, and then came back and joined me and Milton in the bar. Free country, right? We could enjoy an adult beverage off duty just like anybody else. We all would be leaving over the next few days, and this was the last chance to have a little wheels-up party. The only thing unique about this one was that we held it at our enemy's tavern. We did so with great arrogance.

Bird, Gundo, Daryl, Blake, and others started coming into the bar. It didn't take the patrons or management long to figure out who we all were.

There were a couple low-key confrontations with a few patrons until they realized how many of us there were. Our message was clear: The Sons of Silence and their associates were out of business in Colorado Springs.

We were drinking and really feeling good about what we had accomplished. Then one of the band members made some sort of reference of support for the Sons, or an anti-ATF reference, I don't remember which. But that was it. Bird tapped me on the arm and said, "Come on." I didn't know what he had planned, but he was my twenty-plus-years partner, so without hesitation I followed him to the stage.

Bird took the microphone from the band member, who clearly wasn't going to say shit to him. Bird then announced that the reign of terror by the Sons in Colorado Springs was over. This was met with an equal amount of cheers and jeers. Some greasy biker type at a table close to the stage thought he was going to get involved. As quickly as he stood up to show his ass, Milton put a hand on his shoulder and told him to "sit the fuck down before I knock you the fuck out." The biker sat down.

I then took the microphone and simply thanked everybody for their support. I added, "The Sons of Silence's Colorado Springs privileges are hereby revoked."

. . . .

Was it fun being the central figure in a case? Of course it was. Despite the UC's pivotal role, most times the case agent was really the driving force. Case agents were responsible for everything from manpower to budgeting a case to scheduling surveillance and cover teams. There would be no opportunity to do undercover work if it wasn't for devoted case agents. The case agent had to be good at investigating and gathering the necessary intelligence and evidence to justify using undercover as a tactic.

Being the hired gun also came with a downside. Mr. or Ms. Cool Hired Gun UC was expected to follow through until the end. No backing out because you were scared. No changing your mind because you had a gut feeling. One such occasion presented itself to me in the 1990s. I'd come to ATF as a school-trained bomb tech and had a healthy respect for explosives, especially street or improvised explosives in the hands of untrained criminals.* In this case, I was asked to meet a John Doe who allegedly had a buttload of high explosives for sale.† Pete Beck was the case agent and admittedly didn't have much intel to go on, but there was an informant who would introduce me to the guy. Pete was a highly skilled investigator but, as was often the case, he didn't want to do the UC while also being the case agent. Because of the urgent threat to public safety, I agreed to meet a violator we knew almost nothing about. I wired up and met him in a public parking lot with a huge cover team. We arranged the meet after business hours to avoid possible civilian casualties if something went wrong.

I always hated doing explosive undercovers. Many times, the deals involved improvised explosive devices (IEDs), poorly made and very unstable. In this case, we were meeting an unknown person who was supposed to be bringing a sample of high explosives, without having a clue about what kind of explosives he was bringing or how much he knew about handling them.

Immediately upon meeting the violator, I got a really bad feeling. First, he was as big as a house. More disconcerting was his agitated state. He was sweating profusely and appeared to possibly be on meth. He stared me up and down, and then, without warning, he reached over and pulled my shirt up to see if I was wearing a wire. I tried to calm him down, thankful

---

* Athens PD had sent me to hazardous device school at the Redstone Arsenal at Athens State University.

† "High" explosives refers to compounds with a lower flashpoint but a much faster burn rate, hence the explosion instead of just hot fire.

that I'd taken the time to conceal the body wire well. He nervously shook my hand and said, "Sorry, man, I just got out of prison."

To maintain my bad-guy persona, I said, "What the fuck, mother-fucker?" and insisted on checking him for a wire. He agreed, and then tossed me a small brick of military-grade C-4.* The scenario went from possibly serious to no-shit serious. To this day, ATF has a hard-and-fast rule: We don't let guns or bombs "walk." I asked him how much more he had. The answer was: a trunk full. It would be disaster if that amount of explosives remained in criminal hands. We had to get all the explosives this guy had. I immediately made the decision to give him five hundred dollars for the brick of C-4. That far exceeded the street value, but I needed to get him to leave the explosives he was carting with me, and then entice him to bring me the rest. If I couldn't do so, we would have to arrest him on the spot, and we might never find the rest of the explosives.

We arranged for me to meet him later that same day. In the meantime, we identified him and his brother as violent bank robbers. While they were in prison, their mother had married a bomb technician from a local police department. Apparently, this officer had, over time, stolen explosives from police evidence and had the devices stored in his basement. That's how the bank robber got access to the explosives. This was all determined through the excellent efforts of Beck and the cover team, who followed the violator away from the first meeting.

The SAC was about to have a heart attack. He couldn't argue our tactics but knew if something blew up, it would be his ass. The second meeting with this violator was the most heavily covered in my career. We had bomb squads, life flights, SWAT teams, and an army of surveillance agents on

---

* Military grade C-4 is a demolition-grade, chemical-based explosive often used for razing buildings and other manmade structures. It has a higher shock point, so it won't explode if hit by a bullet in combat. One 11 × 2 × 1.5-inch (M112) block of C-4 can destroy a vehicle or significantly damage a light-framed building.

hand. The location for the deal became critical. Any explosives are potentially dangerous, but with improper handling by the bad guy, the cover team could be scooping me up with a shovel. We picked an old, deserted school parking lot as the location. This definitely was going to be a buy bust regardless of whether or not the bad guy brought all of his stash. The plan was to execute a search warrant at the mom's house right after the arrest.

The violator was on time. Again, he acted as if he was geeked up and paranoid, looking all around. I prayed my cover team would wait for my bust signal. I wanted to get the violator away from the explosives in case he had fight in him. When I walked to the back of his car, I remember thinking: "I'm going to shit myself." There were Claymore mines,* fuses, detonators, and enough high explosives to blow up a city block. Now, we both were sweating.

I showed him the money—which he was never going to get—and he started tossing the explosives into my trunk. I hollered, "Be cool, motherfucker!" He nervously laughed, but I wasn't joking. He was handling the explosives like they were just bricks.

I finally got him somewhat relaxed and laughing. I said, "Hey, man, I'm going to step over here to have a smoke." He followed to join me. When I completed the calculation in my head as to how long it would take the cover team to pounce and separate this guy from the explosives, and fully prepared to jump all over his ass if he took one step back toward that vehicle, I gave the bust signal: "Joey Buttafuoco," woven into whatever I was saying at the moment. I had positioned the bad guy with his back to where the cover team would be coming from and attempted to

---

* Claymores are deadly and designed for maximum personnel casualties. These military-grade mines are command detonated and directional (vs. upwardly exploding) plastic-encased explosives that release about 700 one-eighth-inch-diameter steel balls in a 60-degree radius to a distance of around 110 yards, with an optimum distribution of fragments around the 55-yard range. Also having booby-trap capability, Claymores were heavily used during the Vietnam War.

light his cigarette several times to distract him. *Pow!* Before he could take his first puff, he was face down on the ground in handcuffs. The search warrant recovered the rest of the explosives at the mom's house. It was a good day for the good guys.

The part I left out of this story is that every agent coming out of the academy is looking to bust the big one: a case of M16s stored in Cosmoline, a cache of bombs, or that record drug score. Truth be known, we all thought such mega busts were unicorns, dreamt about but never seen. That day, I caught the unicorn.

CHAPTER 12

. . . .

COLD KNOCKS

A cold knock is when an operator approaches a violator cold, without an introduction. The technique entails finding a violator's weakness of common interest so that the operator can exploit it to get close. You use cold knocks when the target is otherwise unapproachable. You don't have a snitch or any way to get an introduction, so you invent one. This is a slow process and requires good intelligence gathering beforehand.

The violator may own a motorcycle shop or a pub. He or she may regularly frequent bars or hangouts, or street corners. You do your research, and you always measure the risk/reward value of running up on a violator cold. You can't just walk up to a bad guy and say, "Hey, can I buy some drugs?" You have to use finesse. I always liked the approach of literally ignoring them, acting like I couldn't give a fuck about what they had and getting them to come to me with the help of some well-choreographed street theater. Because their greed was always on my side.

At the beginning of the Iron Cross investigation, we had an informant who could introduce me to Lil Rat, but Lil Rat didn't trust the informant all that much, so that was all he could do. The first time I met Lil Rat was at his tattoo parlor. From where I was, on the outside looking in, I knew a guaranteed way to get some alone time with him.

I knew if I asked the boss for three or four hundred dollars for a tattoo, he would laugh me out of his office. We were not allowed to use investigative funds that resulted in any personal gain. These were taxpayers' dollars, and such an expense wouldn't look good in a report. I damn sure wasn't going to pay my own money to advance an investigation, so I hustled. Lo and behold, the local PD Special Investigations Unit boss said they would put up the money.

I milked the process for all it was worth. I was in and out of Lil Rat's shop a dozen times while we discussed designs, and he redrew it several times until I liked it. I also wanted to make sure he knew what he was doing and I wasn't going to get Hep C. I had him draw a four-headed dragon to honor the four ATF agents who died during the Waco raid. Of course, I didn't tell Lil Rat that. After a couple weeks of chatting it up, it was time to get it done. I blocked out time at the end of his day, so no civilians would be coming in and out. I also brought a fifth of whiskey. In hindsight, that was more for me than for him. It wasn't such a brilliant idea to get my tattoo artist drunk.

For the next three hours I sat there doing shots with Lil Rat while getting my free tattoo. He did tell me to slow down on the JD until we were done, because I was bleeding like a stuck pig. We talked about his club, dope, guns, women. I got closer to the president of the club than I could have in three months. When the art was done, he pulled out a spray bottle with a 5 percent alcohol solution in it to apply to my tattoo. He said, "This is gonna sting, brother." He sprayed me, and it did sting. So of course, I said, "Dude, did you even put any alcohol in that, you cheap fucker? I don't wanna catch the herpes or whatever is layin' around this shop."

Lil Rat laughed, pushed some ink bottles aside, and grabbed a spray bottle that had "Asshole" written on it. Before I could ask, he sprayed my still-bleeding tattoo. I came up out of that fucking chair like a rocket. Yep, this was the 100 percent alcohol solution.

From that day forward, I pretty much had unfettered access to the club and easily introduced Bird when he got to town.

. . . .

It gets a little precarious if you're out with your family and a violator approaches you, wanting to sell some dope. This happened many times to most of us—someone knew us from the street or we just looked like someone who might buy dope. Generally, you walk away. Sometimes, you just work the problem. One time my dad was visiting me in Las Vegas, and Bird enlisted him in a cold hit at the Silver Dollar bar.

At first, I was like, "Have you lost your fucking mind, Bird?" It was risky, not to mention we would be violating a buttload of ATF policies. Then when I met the violators at the bar with my dad at the table, I realized *this was perfect*. You'd have to know my pops. Let's just say I was the first and maybe the only cop in my heavily Italian American family.

The deal was these two knuckleheads at the bar wanted to sell us some dope and a couple pistols. We went back to our table and briefed pops on the details. In classic *Godfather* form, we waved the violators over to the table, where my dad, barely looking up, said, "We will take the pistols." Then he looked at me and Bird and said, "But you two know where I stand on that dope shit." We both nodded to my dad in a compliant manner. The two violators damn near kissed his ring.

Bird and I walked them back to the bar and made arrangements to meet the next day. Bird said, "We'll take the dope too. Just don't *ever* tell the old man, or they'll find us all in the desert."

....

The more we found ways to expose their crimes, the more the violators developed new ways not to get caught. Jimm Langley and an agent named Cisco found themselves with a shitload of challenges when they received information about some Miami airport employees accepting pay to help drug dealers skirt security. Although Cisco was well seasoned and had been partnered up with Jimm for a while, working out of the Miami field division, neither he nor Jimm ever had experienced what was about to come. The two agents entered into an elaborate scheme with the violators, who would sneak guns and hand grenades past security. First, the agents would give the arms to the employee to take into the airport. Once the agents went through security, they would meet the violator at a specific terminal. The agents would hand a soda can with five hundred dollars in it to the violator, and the violator would hand them the firearms in a carry-on bag, presumably to carry onboard the aircraft.

Jimm and Cisco had two identical carry-on bags. After a violator handed off the firearms to Jimm, he would go to the restroom, where he and Cisco swapped bags under a stall. Cisco would take the bag containing the firearms and exit the airport, so none of the weapons ever made it onto an airplane.

This was before 9/11 and the formation of the Transportation Security Administration (TSA). Despite the precaution of not boarding an aircraft with the smuggled weapons, when the Federal Aviation Administration (FAA) security apparatus found out what our guys were doing, they blew a gasket. The FAA was not comfortable with us operating within their jurisdiction, and the case was perfected and summarily shut down.

My earlier run-in with one of my old juvenile partners in crime was on my mind when I began working undercover in my home area. I knew the more I immersed myself in the local criminal world, the higher the probability I would be recognized. My father used to run the bar at Nave Lanes bowling alley, which was owned by an influential, wealthy family in Marin County. Several of the Nave brothers had served on the San Rafael city council and on local county commissions. Our families were friends, and the Naves treated my father very well for many years. Whenever I came to the bar to do my homework, I got free bowling games and ate free at the snack bar.

One of the Nave brothers' sons, Paul, was a local boxing celebrity and fought some high-profile fights. Unfortunately for me, he also was a local cocaine dealer who had come directly into my sights. He ran a failing limousine service out of a hangar at the Novato airport. I suspected his business was failing because of his coke habit/dealing. I was working with the Marin County drug task force at the time, and they wanted me to take a cold run at Paul at his limo service. None of the other guys on the task force could do the undercover because they were too well known or just didn't do undercover work. I'd jumped up and said, "I'll do it," at the time, not thinking of the possible ramifications.

I didn't personally know Paul. He was several years older than me, and I presumably was just going to meet one of his employees. After scheduling a meeting with the violator at the hangar, under the pretext of wanting to check out his limos, the surveillance teams got in place and I walked into the hangar. To my surprise, I was greeted by Paul himself. Even though I hadn't met him before, I knew his whole family and recognized him from his pictures in the paper.

Fuck, fuck, fuck.

I said, "Hey, how's it going? I'm supposed to meet somebody here. Tony sent me." He said, "Yeah, that's me. Come on back to my office." In truth, nobody had sent me. I'd been expecting to schmooze an employee to maybe sell me some coke.

As Paul sat down behind his desk, I noticed a sawed-off shotgun leaning against the wall. I'm sure I was supposed to see it. We started talking coke almost immediately, and he wanted to know how much I was looking for. Before answering, I made small talk about renting a limousine and directed the conversation to girls and partying in the limo. I was thinking, "What's wrong with this picture? This is too easy."

When we got back around to the coke, I fed him my usual line: "I'll take all ya have, but I'll settle for a half pound."

He sat up, and I saw the greed light going off in his head. "Really, or are you fuckin' with me?" he wanted to know.

I laughed and said, "No, but I'll take a couple ounces. If it's any good, I'll be back."

In the back of my mind, I was thinking about how I would break this to my dad. This was going to be a personal disaster for his friendship with the Nave family as well as embarrassing to them.

Paul sold me a half ounce right then and there. He wrote his personal cell number on the back of his business card and said, "Go check it out, and if you like it, call me at this number."

I stayed in touch with Paul over several days, and I made several buys while we kept him under constant surveillance, hoping to get to his source. I was a private pilot, and a San Rafael officer named Barbier and I flew the aerial surveillances on this case. I served as the safety pilot during those missions. Each time I entered the office in the hangar, the sawed-off shotgun was in arm's reach.

I kept this all under my hat until it was over. I didn't want to upset my dad, and I damn sure didn't want him to be put in the position of deciding whether to warn his lifelong friends. I knew he never would knowingly put me or any of my fellow agents in danger, but like I said, I was the first cop in this family, and my dad was old-school. There was a reason my ATF friends called him the OG.*

In the end, I ordered up a kilo of coke,† and we arrested and federally charged Paul with the dope and a firearm. In the weeks to come, as I compiled the reports and evidence for the US Attorney's Office, I noticed a seeming lack of interest in prosecuting this case. Back in those days, the San Francisco US Attorney's office was notoriously weak when it came to bringing ATF cases to court. For whatever reason, there appeared to be bad blood and political forces that worked against us. But this seemed like a totally appropriate case for federal prosecution. The limo service was prime for seizure. We were talking a large amount of dope and a Title II weapon, which would add an extra ten years to a federal sentence.

I wanted to know why they weren't interested in prosecuting the case. But what was there to understand? The violator's name was Nave. The family had deep roots in Marin County. I was young and still thought the laws applied to everybody equally. I learned over the years that was not necessarily true. However, in this case, justice ultimately did prevail. The state prosecuted Paul and sentenced him to five or so years in San Quentin State Prison, right there on the bay in the county where we were raised.

He did his time like a man and later returned to Marin to revive his boxing career for a couple of fights. There never was any blowback on my dad or our family. In fact, several of the Naves attended my father's wake.

---

* Original gangster.

† When you were ready to take a violator down, a common practice was to order up the highest amount of dope you could without making the dealer nervous. To state simply, what you are buying dictates the system of measurement. A pound of coke is simpler to weigh than .4536 kilograms.

Usually, cold knocks are initiated by an undercover agent, but not always. Sometimes the violator walks right through the front door. Traveling so close to the underworld on a regular basis exposes agents to some weird and unexplainable circumstances. During the Outlaws investigation, I was sitting in the office one day doing paperwork. Theresa, our investigative assistant, walked in and with a muffled voice said, "Hey, Vince, some guy is on the phone and wants to talk to our 'motorcycle gang expert.'" Steve Kosch, my partner on this caper and my office mate, shot me a look. We'd been partners for a while, so we both just reacted and simultaneously picked up the same desk phone line. Steve covered his mouthpiece with his hand.

The caller asked if I was the biker expert in the ATF office. Criminal organizations had increased their own surveillance and operational security against the cops over the years. I'd be damned before I'd put out any information to an unknown voice on the phone, so I just asked, "How can I help you?"

The guy said he was a member of a "major" biker club in the area and wanted to sit down with me to discuss some things. He'd only do it in person. I told him to call me back in an hour. I needed some serious time to round table this one.

We corralled a bunch of agents and Bob, the boss. Bob already was hyperparanoid about everything we were doing on the case. He had a long history with the Outlaws gang and knew this case was the best bet of crushing them we'd had in years. We theorized that the unknown caller wanted to snitch. We tried to determine who it might be by his voice and mannerisms. We considered this might be a planned assassination attempt. We *all* believed it was an intelligence-gathering attempt by the bikers to get eyes on me.

After much consternation, it was agreed to buy some time, a day or so, and try to work the problem. When he called back, he could sense my suspiciousness and gave the one explanation that settled us down a bit: "Look, I'm an Outlaw, and I'm not playing you. I just want to explore some options, and I'm thinking of leaving the club. I'll be in worse trouble than you if they find out, so I'm trusting you."

We still were skeptical, but I told him I'd meet him, and I'd give him a time, location, and a day, and that he better come alone or I was going to shoot him in the face and everyone with him. I told him when to call me back and to be prepared when he called to then meet me within thirty minutes. We needed to limit the time he/they had to plan, if they were in fact planning something nefarious.

Fast-forward to the meeting. We had an informant inside the club, so we'd been somewhat able to narrow down the possible member who might be reaching out. We had surveillance on all of the members we could find when I made the call. The plan we agreed on was that, at least initially, Kosch would meet him at the restaurant. If one of us was going to be compromised, it would be best if it was him, as I was traveling very close to the club from day to day.

We swapped out our vehicles for ones we didn't care might be compromised. We already were in the restaurant when I made the call, and there were backup agents outside. This deal was so weird that the SAC attended our pre-operational briefing.

When the long-haired, tattooed, greasy, unbathed Outlaw arrived, it was exactly who we had surmised it would be.* Kosch made eye contact and signaled the biker over to his booth. I was three booths away, and

---

* I cannot identify the specific gang member in this story because the Outlaws have long memories, and I'm not in the business of getting snitches killed.

211

he didn't notice me when he walked by. Being a good, no, great cop, Steve casually and discreetly patted him down before letting him sit. They talked for about five minutes, and then Kosch gave me the prearranged signal to come over. We had agreed that Kosch would try to determine what this member's true intent was and then decide if I would come in. I had to trust his read, because I couldn't hear the conversation. I had confirmed via cell phone that the outside guys hadn't seen anything or anyone suspicious.

The gist of the conversation was that the biker wanted to leave the club. He wanted me to exert some federal pressure to line him up with a good job back in his home state and maybe some traveling money to get established in his new life. He immediately followed that with, "But I ain't snitching on my brothers."

I almost came up out of my seat and responded in my not-indoor voice, "Have you hit your fucking head?"

Under the table, Kosch squeezed my thigh in an attempt to chill me out.

When I asked what was in this for me, the biker said that in exchange I would have one less Outlaw to worry about and there would be another productive member of society.

Kosch squeezed my leg so hard I winced.

I said, "Number one, asshole, I don't worry about Outlaws, ever. Number two, I don't give even one fuck if you stay an Outlaw or not. If you do, I'm going to end up sending you to prison anyway. You have obviously confused me with the fucking welfare department. You better hope I never let this shit slip out to your club. They'll kill you just for being a pussy. Don't ever waste my time again."

And with that, Kosch and I got up and walked out.

. . . .

Gundo was the king of cold knocks.

In the 1990s, toward the end of his career with ATF, Gundo transferred back to Missoula, in western Montana, in the same jurisdiction
where he'd been a police deputy decades earlier. He was the lone ATF
agent in a satellite office, and soon after arriving, he was recruited by the
local FBI office to assist them as an informant handler. ATF, and more specifically Gundo, was far better suited to deal with a street-level informant
than the suits over at the FBI office, and they knew it. The FBI wanted to
use this informant to infiltrate the Montana contingency of the Bandidos
Motorcycle Club, one of the big four biker gangs in the United States.

The CI was a gigantic pain in the ass to supervise. Gundo had learned
over the years that these are just the type of people who can be the most
successful in extreme situations and investigations. He quickly found
out—which at this time in his career was *no* surprise—that the highly
structured FBI and the agents on the case had no clue how to accom-
plish the infiltration and had very quickly tired of putting up with this
outspoken and stubborn informant. Gundo told me he felt like a hostage
negotiator between the FBI and the CI.

The plan Gundo sold to the FBI was that they were not going to run
this guy straight at the Bandidos. They would get him into one of the
farm clubs, a less important but affiliated motorcycle club united under
the so-called Bandido Nation. Then the CI would attempt to move up the
food chain. After six or eight months of Gundo handling the CI, the informant became an officer in the Hermanos Motorcycle Club in Kalispell
and was ingratiating himself with members of the Bandidos, who supervised the farm clubs. Although as the informant continued his successful
infiltration, Gundo saw little professional gain for ATF jurisdictional cases

coming out of his continued involvement. It was time for the FBI to sink or swim with their case, and they would have to take back supervision of their CI, who rose within the Bandido chapter and started to meet up with different club chapters in Texas and Colorado. He began uncovering drug trafficking members in the gang. But the FBI's interstate divisional separation ultimately destroyed the continuity of managing the Montana case or the informant.* After years of time and investigative funds had been spent, FBI management halted the investigation with not one arrest or criminal case filed. That was depressing for Gundo because of all the hard work that had been done. They'd been ready to start picking off defendants and uncovering criminal conspiracies, but now it was not meant to be. Or was it?

If the FBI didn't have the stomach to see this through, ATF did. Or at least, Gundo did.

While working the case, Gundo had brought in one of his long-term informants from his days working in Washington State. This CI had worked with Gundo for almost twenty years. Gundo kept thinking about how the Hermanos club had been so easily infiltrated. He wanted to take another run at them with the help of his old informant. The new plan would be to infiltrate locally and stay right there in that part of Montana and start perfecting federal and state criminal cases involving firearms, drugs, and whatever other crimes might arise.

One of Gundo's encounters during this time involved a female drug trafficker in northwest Montana. He had identified many of the players in this conspiracy and was looking to charge one of the minor players and flip them. This is a common practice in long-term cases, in an effort to

---

* Admittedly, these antiquated systems existed with ATF as well. The boss of one field division, when asked to help another field division, invariably would ask, "What's in this for my field division?"

assist in prosecuting the major players and to help identify the source of their illicit drugs—in this case, methamphetamine. Gundo recently had perfected evidence showing her in possession of a firearm, but she lacked any felony convictions to charge her as a felon in possession. Gundo didn't let that slow him down. He confronted the lady with the firearm evidence—"evidence" might be a strong word in this instance, but it was at least information of firearms possession. He then invoked the little-used federal violation involving a known drug user being prohibited from possessing firearms. This tactic was rarely employed because it was hard to prove to a jury when the illegal drugs actually were used in relation to the firearms possession.

Gundo's suspect had been around the block and was not intimidated, so he amped up his tactics. He stated that he wanted to take some hair samples from her head that would be tested for the presence of illegal narcotics in her system. This was total bullshit, but the curveball threw her off her game. She complied, and he obtained the hair samples, which, he told her, would be submitted to the ATF and Montana state forensic laboratories for a relatively new examination process. He hoped his made-up bullshit gave him enough leverage to pressure her into cooperating with his investigation. She declined.

The next two years were spent in northwest Montana, infiltrating the Hermanos gang with the help of Gundo's old CI. Gundo had set up the undercover operation with the assistance of the Montana Narcotics Bureau office in Kalispell. They provided cover/surveillance agents for Gundo's team as well as drug-purchase funds. Many of the cases did not meet the threshold of the US Attorney's Office, but the local district attorney's office gladly would take them on. Many state charges are perfected by ATF UCs.

The closest ATF office was two hundred miles away, so partnering with local narcotics agents was more cost-effective than bringing in a bunch of ATF undercovers. Plus, the local narcotics agents were familiar with the area and criminal players. Gundo did obtain one volunteer from the Helena ATF field office who was willing to work long distance and long hours. Christi Van Werden was a special agent trainee who would have to work with a senior agent until her training period was completed. Gundo would write his investigative activity reports, submit all electronic surveillance tapes, and turn in purchased evidence. Christi would tag all the evidence and place it into custody and keep up on the extensive ATF paperwork. They set up an undercover residence for Gundo's CI in Kalispell, and Gundo would bounce around motel rooms in the area. The state Narcotics Bureau loaned them a couple undercover motorcycles, and they set up their UC identities with backstopping orchestrated out of the Helena ATF field office.

Gundo's prior involvement with the FBI case got him familiar with the Hermanos club, especially the Flathead Crew, named after the surrounding county. He knew that the national president of the Hermanos lived close to Kalispell and originally had been a Flathead chapter member. Now the gang president oversaw all Hermanos chapters located in Montana, Washington, Idaho, and South Dakota. Gundo and the CI made a cold call visit to the president's legitimate business, situated near the picturesque town of Bigfork. They arrived on their undercover motorcycles, and Gundo being Gundo, that visit led to their association with the club.

As they became familiar with the club members, it also became obvious to Gundo that there were no significant identifiable criminal activities taking place within the local chapter. Oftentimes, motorcycle gangs/clubs are made up of all kinds of members. There are sociopaths and psychopaths, but there also are just plain motorcyclists looking for association, and sometimes even God-fearing churchgoers are members (although in my experience, not so much of the latter).* As Gundo and the CI began to meet the other Hermanos, they found themselves in Libby, ninety miles northwest of Kalispell, where a number of the members lived. They rode up to see "Dollar Bill," and about four "brothers" were standing in the driveway of his house. Gundo's focus shifted to one man. "Oh, shit. I know this guy," he thought. He and the gang member had played on the same high school football team. They spent the entire afternoon with this crew, and Gundo's sphincter was slammed shut, worrying that his old acquaintance would identify him by his real name and burn his alias. For the next month, Gundo held his breath, but no questions came out of that meet and greet.

In the mid-2000s, in April, the Hermanos had a spring opener run to Idaho to meet up with other chapters. Riding a motorcycle in the Rocky Mountains that time of year can be dicey. The pack comprised seven Hermanos patched members and Gundo. The informant already had become a prospect (similar to a pledge in a fraternity, but much nastier) but could not make the run. Gundo was considered a "hang around," an accepted associate but not a member. He was riding at the back of the pack with a newer member. As they started into the mountains, it began to snow heavily, and they had another eighty miles to Libby.

When on a run, a club pairs two motorcycles side by side, with the whole pack bunched up together. This is dangerous in good weather but damn near suicidal in snow. Halfway to Libby, the Hermanos member riding next to Gundo lost control of his bike and overcorrected, which

---

* Gundo remembered working undercover to assist an ATF friend on a case in Arizona. The UCs were at a party at a Hells Angels clubhouse that had been the beginning site of a grotesque murder of a female guest of the club. Gundo was standing with other undercover agents, surrounded by Hells Angels, in the same room where this woman had been savagely beaten and later stabbed to death. Right there a Hells Angel nicknamed Lonely Lonnie told how he recently had returned from taking his daughters to Bible camp.

threw him toward Gundo's motorcycle, both going about fifty miles per hour. The bikes collided, but both riders were able to keep their rides upright and slowly come to a stop on the highway. The rest of the crew kept going, unaware that their member had collided with Gundo. The two riders gathered themselves and continued on up the highway to rejoin the pack.

Gundo never said a word to any member about the collision, and as the days went by, he saw a change in how they treated him. The gang members obviously had learned what happened and realized that Gundo knew how to "hold his mud."

Using the street cred of their Hermanos association, Gundo and the CI were able to get close with a midlevel meth dealer in Libby. She liked the CI and thought her association with bikers would give her more security in dealing with her clientele. For Gundo and the CI, the relationship with "Robin" could lead to drug-house security gigs and deliveries. That in turn would produce prosecutable drug and firearms cases.

Just as they were identifying her customers and possible drug source in Washington State, Gundo received a late-night call from the informant. Robin had been found dead in her bathroom from a combination of methamphetamine intoxication and out-of-control diabetes. Gundo hung up the phone and sat wondering, "What the fuck are we gonna do now?" They had just reached the point of a real productive investigation, and it instantly disappeared.

Several days after Robin's death, Gundo was trying to decide if he should close out the case after a year of work. Suddenly, it hit him. They had identified all the dealers associated with Robin in Montana and also had identified several traffickers out of Washington related to her. He just needed to adjust the investigation from a proactive undercover case to a methodical, historical drug-conspiracy case.

Gundo left the informant, still active in the Hermanos, and went looking for evidence to assist in the drug case and any other cases that might pop up. He and his trainee, Christi, started the tedious process of developing the drug-conspiracy case, again identifying low-level members with criminal involvement who could be flipped as witnesses to help develop hard evidence acceptable in court. The state Narcotics Bureau agents helped immensely by dropping a call to Gundo when one of the group got arrested on other charges. Gundo and Christi would go debrief the violator and try to flip them.

Another year rolled by, and they had traced the methamphetamine source to Mexican cartel connections in Yakima, Washington. Earlier in the investigation, Gundo had taken a trophy picture with Hermanos members. The member who took the picture put it in the club's newsletter.

While Christi and Gundo were putting the finishing touches on the criminal case and bringing witnesses to the federal grand jury in Missoula, Gundo received a panicked call from his CI. The national president had been informed by Libby members that a female associate—the same woman Gundo had tried to flip several years earlier—had identified Gundo's picture in the newsletter. Gundo was burned, and that meant his informant was burned too. To add insult to injury, the bitch identified Gundo as a well-known *FBI* agent.

The next week was stressful, trying to get the CI out of Kalispell and moved and hidden. They had to confront the national president about the allegations, and after talking with him, Gundo didn't think the president believed he was working for the cops. But with an eyewitness and the whole hair-sample thing looming out there, Gundo could not take the chance of meeting any of the club members face-to-face again.

All was not lost, by any means. The proactive part of the case was done. They had compiled a drug-conspiracy case with ten suspects in Montana and Washington. They also had made numerous purchases of controlled prescription opiates from various suspects. (This case unfolded toward the beginning of the nationwide opiate crisis.) They had made several gun cases and completed firearms purchases from a Federal Firearms Licensee (FFL) in violation of federal firearms laws. All of the cases were followed by guilty pleas, no trials, and the FFL lost his firearms license. They also uncovered details of three motorcycle thefts in Missoula by the local chapter of the Hermanos.

Not bad for an ex-deputy, huh?

. . . .

One thing you can be sure of: Undercover work is never convenient and never predictable. It interferes with scheduled investigative activities and personal commitments. In the late 1980s, the father of my lifelong friend and next-door neighbor was terminally ill with cancer. I mentioned Jack earlier as the first man to use the term T-Man in relation to me. He was under hospice care. I wanted to be there for my friend Cathy and her family. I intended to leave work early and race to the family home in Petaluma to pay my last respects to Jack.

The phone rang at my desk. It was Randy in Oakland. He was a fairly new agent to ATF, having come from Stockton PD. He was a competent investigator and had a good reputation. He said, "Look, I got a caper you may be interested in. Right up your alley, so to speak."

California Highway Patrol had called Randy after someone lobbed a few grenades at their parked patrol cars. "They never detonated, but they are getting worried that their luck might run out," Randy told me.

I explained that I was busy and asked if he could reach out to one of the other guys.

He said, "I would, dude, but the boss told me to use you."

"Shit," I thought. I wouldn't be going to Petaluma just yet.

I asked if Randy had any suspects. He said, "Kinda." I asked, "What the fuck is a kinda suspect?" He had some leads, he said. "Come over to Oakland and I'll fill you in."

Randy had done his homework. We didn't have enough for a warrant, and any attempt to interview the suspect surely would result in him lawyering up or changing his practices. The suspect was a longtime felon, well acquainted with the system. The only information we had at the time was who he was and where he lived. A jailhouse snitch had suggested to Randy that this guy might have been involved in the attacks, but street talk wasn't evidence. So, our only hope was a chance encounter, tricky because most criminals are inherently suspicious of new faces. The strategy here would be to somehow make him want to get to know me, and it had to appear to be natural and his idea.

We discovered a house under construction at the entrance to the old country road where this guy's trailer was located. Lo and behold, the house was being built for an assistant district attorney. He was more than willing to let us use his construction site for a couple days. Enter Vinny, the plumber. It was slow and tedious at first. A couple guys would come in under cover of darkness with long-range surveillance equipment. Then, in the daytime, whenever this guy went outside for smokes, I would be out front swinging a hammer, looking busy. I'd wave. He'd wave back.

After a few days of not much more than that, I decided to approach his trailer to use his phone or ask for a light or something. Of course, he didn't have a phone. So, I made small talk until he offered me a beer. Of course, I expected, and was not disappointed, when he offered to smoke a joint. I didn't agree, and I didn't disagree. Simulating doing drugs is never a good idea for an undercover. Get caught doing it by the bad guy, and you're toast. If you are being video- or audiotaped, it might not be apparent to a jury that you were simulating. In this case, I was watching the guy intently, and he was so stoned he wasn't paying attention to me. So, I took the joint, made a few puffing sounds, and we were instant friends. I went back to my nonconstruction job. A couple days of this, and *me* buying the beer, and we were best buddies.

Our mutual dislike for the po-po quickly led to him bragging of his criminal escapades. Soon he was telling me how he was gonna "fuck up" some highway patrol cops, and how he had them scared. When he elaborated on his hand grenade–making skills, I acted appropriately impressed. He was pissed because the first couple grenades had failed to find their target. I led him to believe I had an ex-wife (which I did), whom I would like to meet the same fate (which I didn't), but I did not have his expertise. He told me he had to take off but to be back at noon tomorrow, and he would have what I needed.

We hustled to get search warrants. We had twenty-four hours to put together a raid plan and to have Explosive Ordinance Disposal (EOD) on-site. The long, deserted dirt road leading to the violator's trailer made an approach difficult. He also was going to be in possession of explosives. The plan would require me to separate him from the explosives at the moment of execution and to distract him long enough for the arrest team to breach the front door.

At noon the next day, after checking the transmitter and alternate signals, I arrived at the trailer. The violator looked down the road both directions, and then invited me in. Heart pounding but knowing I was minutes away from undercover stardom, I walked into the living room. Scattered everywhere, I could see black powder, fuses, and empty hand grenade hulls—the kind you buy as souvenirs at an Army/Navy surplus store. I felt panic race through my brain: The son of a bitch was smoking a cigarette. To make matters as bad as they could be, he was drilling into the top of a hand grenade body that he already had filled with gunpowder. Black powder is extremely volatile and subject to igniting from heat, shock, or friction.

My heart felt like it was pounding up my throat. All the plans went out the window. I not so ceremoniously muttered the bust signal two or three times. He looked at me as if asking "What?" I gave him a jittery smile and made some silly comment. Then I reached across the coffee table and grabbed the grenade and drill out of his hand, saying something like, "Wow, that's cool."

At that very minute, I heard a loud crash and a bunch of screaming. It was the greatest sound I ever could have imagined. I hit the floor, and the cover team was on the violator like stink on shit. We *all* backed the hell out of there quick. Let EOD go in and blow themselves up. We were just agents.

When the scene settled down, I approached the violator, who was in cuffs, and tried to talk to him, advise him of his rights, et cetera. He just looked up at me, stunned. He thought we were friends and brothers and was shocked that I was a cop. It never bothered me in thirty years, but that sort of betrayal rightly has a tendency to cause conflict in many agents.

I asked Randy, "You got this?" He said, "Yeah, go."

I turned on my pager, and my friend Cathy and my mom and dad had been paging me all morning. I called Cathy, and she just said, "He's gone."

CHAPTER 13

IA

Perhaps you've heard the terms of endearment: rat squad, cheese eaters, headhunters, management hammer, et cetera. Having been a cop for several years before joining ATF, I'll just say I was somewhat versed in dealing with Internal Affairs.* Early in my career with ATF, I heard horror stories, mostly urban legends, about the bureau's IA agents. In fact, several of my early contacts with IA were fair and professional. The division was staffed with seasoned agents who understood the job of being an agent and were able to discern between an innocent mistake and a flagrant policy violation.

That changed over the years. After experiencing some fairly large sexual harassment and discrimination cases/lawsuits as well as internal

---

* I take some pride in the fact that most of my IA investigations related to my off-duty silliness and not serious integrity issues. The same held true for most of the RatSnakes.

corruption, the bureau expanded its IA division. Management created a path for IA investigators to be promoted to Grade-14 agents without having to be a supervisor or doing HQ time. From what I saw, that was all that the "slug" agents in the field needed to hear. Agents who couldn't or wouldn't produce in the field found their dream job with IA: normal hours, a promotion, and no expectation to make cases. Working IA was a voluntary assignment, and the agents were accountable only to HQ. That structure further empowered HQ, and the standards for initiating an Internal Affairs investigation changed. There always was a gray area between what was a management issue and what rose to the level of a true integrity issue warranting an IA investigation. That gray area got grayer.

Those of us in the field felt the climate change. IA could be called in for any reason an SAC desired. Make a complaint about a supervisor, you would be investigated by IA. Piss off your supervisor, IA would come. Make a discrimination or sexual harassment allegation, your ass was going to be a target. We UC agents were wary of IA and their true mission. More often than not, it appeared they reveled in jamming an agent up as opposed to reporting the facts. If you were going to survive a career of UC, you learned how to sidestep management's BS. My boss Ron Mitchell bragged about being 19–1, meaning he had been investigated by IA nineteen times but disciplined only once. That was unbelievable if you knew Uncle Ron.

Right before my Atlanta SRT team deployed to Waco, after the initial shoot-out, a new supervisor transferred in from Miami. I did not know anything about the supervisor except that all my guys in Miami vouched for him. There had been a story about a hard-drinking supervisor in that town who would take his guys out after every operation. One time, after drinking, all the agents left together. Since they all lived north of Miami, they would caravan up the only road leading north. One car, the supervisor's, exited south, but nobody noticed. It was said the supervisor crossed nine bridges and got all the way to Key West before realizing he had gone the wrong way. The funny story made the rounds, and I never thought about it again.

After returning from Waco, after the compound burned down, I reported to my new supervisor: Ron Mitchell. He ultimately took over our SRT team. After one of our first training missions with Ron, he asked, "Do any of you girls drink?" All of our hands went up. We moved to Manuel's Tavern, a favorite cop watering hole in Atlanta. After closing Manuel's, we all went our separate ways.

The next morning, Ron came straggling in around noon. He waved me into his office, shut the door, and filled me in on his evening. He'd left Manuel's and got turned around. He kept driving and driving and didn't realize he was going the wrong way until he crossed Lake Hartwell, about ninety miles from his residence. I lost it. Between gasping and laughing, I said, "It's true." He asked, "What's true?" I said, "You drove all the way to Key West before figuring it out." He said, "Oh, you heard about that."

Everybody loved Ron after that one. Well, except maybe the bosses.

Ron had been an agent in North Florida back during the cocaine wars. There was a bunch of police corruption in those days, and IA was on high alert. One of the favorite tricks used by the bad guys was to make bogus allegations against a cop or an agent. They knew it would bring down a world of hurt on whoever they pointed the finger at. It was sort of payback.

On one such occasion, Ron and several others had been accused of stealing millions of dollars or some shit like that. Hell, it was hard enough to get Ron to pick up a bar tab. A bunch of agents were out drinking and found an IA tracking device on Ron's government vehicle. Apparently, the investigators were dicks, even though months and months of investigation hadn't turned up a hint of corruption by *any* of the agents or cops in this group. The agents were sick of IA busting their balls. They removed the tracking device from Ron's car and placed it on a southbound eighteen-wheeler. IA didn't see the humor.

Needless to say, Ron became a dear friend of mine, and he was my son's sponsor for his Confirmation ceremony.

....

There were undeniable perks that came with being a RatSnake—such as the right kind of attention from the opposite sex. What was the point of being a super-secret agent if you couldn't tell anyone?

One of our single guys was in a bar in Miami, chatting up a young lady and getting nowhere. Well, Casanova—his real name, no shit—decided to play his trump card and tell her who he was and the dangerous shit he did for a living. We all played that card at one time or another. Hell, how do you think I got such a beautiful wife?

Casanova threw his best stuff at her, but she left without giving him her number. What she *did* do was look up another telephone number: the number to ATF headquarters in Washington, DC. This presumably innocuous socialite was highly offended that this young UC would tell all of our nation's secrets to someone he had just met in a bar. In fact, he hadn't given up any secrets beyond his identity and maybe embellishing a few war stories. Nonetheless, he got his ass chapped and a formal reprimand.

Nic, on the other hand, and that is *not* his real name, did pretty much the opposite: he blamed the game. Alone one night, he ordered up an escort, a.k.a. a hooker. The problem, from his perspective, was that he ordered a redhead, and when there was a knock at the door, they had sent a brunette. He felt that entitled him not to pay the lady—and not to pay her by showing her a badge and a gun. The next knock at the door was from the local PD, who summarily arrested him for theft of services. Nic hadn't been with the bureau long enough to be traumatized, but he got enough doctors to say he was, and he kept his job. Although he never was allowed in the field again.

Dino narrowly avoided a career-ending IA investigation. I say "career-ending" not because it warranted a termination but because his supervisor at the time was a huge pussy who gave him no support. As if it couldn't get any worse, the first-line supervisor disliked UC types and made it his mission to fuck with them at every turn. Dino gave him the opportunity, and the boss took it.

Dino left a post-operation celebration at a local tavern and made a wrong turn on the way home. He strayed into another lane, which caught a Georgia state trooper's attention. These situations could go either way. The trooper could have used his discretion and afforded Dino professional courtesy—which none of us ever expected but surely appreciated—or he could go by the book.

The trooper decided to go by the book due to Dino's level of intoxication. If there is humor to be found in this scenario, it is what did *not* go in the trooper's report. When the trooper advised Dino that he was going to arrest him, Dino had the brilliant idea to try and haul ass.

FACT #1: Dino already had identified himself.

FACT #2: Dino is like five foot nothing and was drunk, and the trooper was around six foot five and sober.

The way Dino described it made me laugh so hard I cried. Apparently, when Dino turned and took one step toward his escape, the trooper grabbed him by the collar. Dino remembers trying to run with both feet off the ground like in a Wile E. Coyote/Road Runner cartoon.

Dino dealt with the consequences of his mistake, and I'm happy to say that he eventually rose from the ashes in a big way.

I knew when agreeing to write this book that I eventually would have to get around to Casper. Ah, Casper. The biggest fucking asshole career criminal I ever met. Casper was a snitch who apparently had performed well for Jay Bird over a year's time in Arizona. He supposedly had made a bunch of introductions for Bird as well as some buys. In my earliest days as a cop, the detectives at Athens PD always told me never to use a forger as a snitch, because a forger's sole purpose in life is to lie. That stuck with me throughout my years at ATF, and Casper was a convicted forger extraordinaire. However, he also came endorsed by my best friend, and I needed a snitch for a motorcycle gang case, and Casper needed work.

Casper was a problem from the perspective that he wasn't working off a beef. He was a hired gun, doing it for money and excitement, so we couldn't hold going back to jail over his head. Strike one was when he arrived in Georgia with some trailer-trash chick in tow, purportedly his girlfriend. When a UC is working with a snitch, there is enough risk of compromise without the extra baggage of another party. We decided we'd try it. We could always cut him and her out and put 'em back on a bus if they got unmanageable.

Strike two followed closely. Another chick from back home showed up, this one purportedly Casper's ex-girlfriend. We made it clear that we were paying him and him only, but we were none too happy about this shit. As the case progressed, it became clear that Casper and his road whores were fucking around on the side. First, I caught him with pot. I documented it, read him the riot act, and moved on.

I was on loan to Macon for this case, and as it expanded, I needed help. I thought who better than the guy who sent this shitbird to me. When I ran it by Uncle Ron, he put his head in his hands and said, "Fuck me, no wonder I drink." But Ron was an agents' boss, and he greased the wheels to get Jay out there. The day I took Jay to pick up his UC motor-cycle, we rolled into the ATF parking lot in Atlanta so Bird could check in with the bosses. Ron was walking out to his car, and we both gunned our bikes and came sliding up to him sideways. He stared at us for a few seconds, and then said, "I knew this was a bad idea."

By the time Bird got on the ground in Macon, most of us—the case agent, Dave Brown; the supervisor, Bart McIntyre; and the cops we were working with—had had enough of Casper's bullshit and were ready to send him and girlfriends number one and number two packing. But we hoped that Jay could reign them in. Well, he couldn't, and we found out that Casper had been stealing welfare and government checks and cashing them. He was done.

We gave them each traveling money and put all three of their asses on a bus back to Arizona. We managed their exit as gingerly as we could and blamed it on the bosses no longer wanting to pay for an informant. By this point, Bird and I were deeply embedded in this motorcycle gang, and the last thing we needed was for Casper to fuck us up.

Within a day or two of Casper leaving town, Uncle Ron called and said, "Find a way to step away from the violators for a couple days. I need to see both of you in Atlanta, ASAP." When we asked why, Ron uncharacteristically said, "I mean yesterfuckingday."

This could not be good. We laid down a temporary story about going to protect a dope shipment and hauled ass to Atlanta, where Ron called us into his office and said, "Fellas, get ready to get butt fucked."

We were shocked, wondering what we supposedly did. The short answer was that—according to Casper and his bitch girlfriends—Bird and I allegedly had committed more heinous acts than Bonnie and Clyde and Al Capone combined. Casper had never left town. Instead, he walked into the local FBI office with a laundry list of shit we supposedly perpetrated.

Before we could even begin to respond, Ron said, "Calm the fuck down. I know you guys didn't do any of that shit, but because they went to the FBI we are going to have to bend over backwards to make sure no one can say we ever covered shit up. You know the drill, boys. Go smoke a cigarette and let's take a ride over to Internal Affairs."

The IA boss in Atlanta apprised us in the most general terms of some of the allegations made by Casper. Then he ordered us not to go back to Macon or to engage the bad guys even telephonically. We said, "You ain't our boss, and you ain't the SAC." But Ron said, "That's coming from the boss."

We were fuming. Being yanked away from the case in this manner presented a slew of issues. Time, man-hours, and money would be wasted. Our biggest concern was having our cover blown for no good reason. We begged the SAC to let us put an exit strategy together. "Give us two days," we said. The bikers were expecting us back, and we wanted to create an emergency that would justify us leaving town for a while. If we left and never showed up again, they might just forget about us. Best-case scenario, the FBI and IA would clear us quickly, knowing it was all bullshit anyway, and we could show up again and continue the case. Although that wasn't all that realistic, because we now had to assume that Casper had compromised us.

I am embarrassed to say that what followed was nothing more than a witch hunt. The FBI conducted their part professionally, but ATF IA was headhunting from the get-go. They wired up one of the whores and had her call me. She was asking me what I should do or say, pretending like she was in Arizona and not with Casper. IA got a great recording of me saying, "The only thing you can do, tell the truth." (Click, the line went dead.) They did the same thing to Bird. We didn't know at the time that IA was trying to use Casper and his girls to set us up. Since we'd been ordered not to be in contact with these assholes, we both reported the calls to IA and were kind of surprised when they just blew it off.

IA verbally said: "We have statements from some of the agents suggesting you guys did some of that shit."

I knew they didn't have any statements, because we didn't fucking do it. Most of the allegations could have been proven or disproven by a rookie cop. But apparently the goal wasn't the truth; it was to finally fry me and/or Jay. There was an element in ATF leadership that would have been totally happy never doing another UC operation and basically held the attitude that all UC operators were dirty. Sad to say, but true.

After conducting what could only be described as an attempt to railroad Bird and me, it finally came down to our individual interviews with IA. This was their chance to catch us lying after they had built their case against us. It didn't matter if we were innocent of all of the allegations. If they could prove one lie was told by us, that was it. Do not pass Go. You're fired. And rightfully so in an investigation conducted with integrity.

My interview was with Fred Drew, whom I consider the absolute lowest-life IA agent, hell, the lowest-life *agent* ever. I knew as soon as I walked into his office that it was not going to go well. He was there alone. IA, and in fact most field agents, never conduct a serious interview by themselves. You never want to get into a "he said, she said" scenario with a suspect.

The second flag went up when I asked him if, at the end, I could have a copy of the taped interview and he replied something to the effect of, "Oh, I don't need to record this." I knew then that I'd better go slow and pay close attention, because this was going to be an attempted lynching.

He went through the allegations, and I just said, "Good God, nothing about sex with animals in that folder?" Casper and team had alleged everything else. The part that seriously changed me forever was that Drew asked me to disprove certain allegations that, as I later learned, IA/FBI already had proven to be false. The interview went on for four or five hours. Somewhere in the middle of my answering a question, he blurted out, "Will you take a polygraph?"

I stopped talking, shocked that he had cut me off with that. He turned and gazed out the window, not looking me in the eyes, and asked again. "Will you take a polygraph?"

Without hesitation, I said, "Absolutely, as soon as you poly those three fucking convicts and any one of them passes."

Unknown to Jay and me at the time was that IA already had polygraphed Casper and the two criminal chicks, and all three failed. Throw in the fact that all three were felons and drug addicts, and you'd think IA would have been a little more neutral.

After an interview is completed, it is customary for IA to ask that you reduce your answers to written form. They want to lock you in to your statements. In my case, I was insistent that I write a statement. There was no way I was going to let this guy portray my answers however he wanted. It took me three hours to type my statement. It was stressful, and Drew's demeanor was hostile. He stood behind me the whole time I was writing. He tossed out suggestions for how to phrase some of my answers. In the middle of my typing, he said, "Make sure you say that you refused to take a polygraph." I spun around in my chair, and he meandered away. He said my failure to take a polygraph would be seen as a sign of guilt. That is not only untrue, but it's highly unethical to intimidate a witness like that.

After I finished writing my statement, which included pointing out the abusive nature of this IA agent, he refused to accept it. I was thinking to myself: "I bet you do." I simply said, "Take it, or don't. I am going to have your secretary date and time stamp it, and it will be available for the reviewers if they want it."

I will let you in on a little secret. If he had refused to include my statement in the report, he would have been fired.

At the conclusion of the IA investigation, Jay and I were issued clearance letters. Our records were clean. Normally, that would have been a good day. In my case, I was told to report to the ASAC's office. Ralph was a do-nothing agent and a scared-of-his-own-shadow supervisor and a kiss-ass headquarters ladder climber. He apparently detested undercover agents and everyone like us. From what I saw, the main accomplishment of his career was streamlining our paperwork flow. So I reported to his office as ordered, where he sat behind his desk in his usual monogrammed dress shirt and cuff links. He didn't bother to stand up or shake my hand. He just said, "Sit down."

I could see the red IA file on his desk. Every agent is entitled to a copy of the investigative file when it is complete. Ralph slid the receipt for the file across the desk to me. After I signed the receipt, he slid the file over to me. He was holding my clearance letter in his hand.

"If even one of these allegations were true, I was going to bury your ass," he told me, and then he sort of flung the letter at me.

I have never wanted to reach across a desk and throat punch anybody's ass so bad in my entire life.

The day before, another agent I knew, Bruce, had warned me what to expect. Bruce said, "Look, when you go in there, just tune him out. If he pisses you off, just think to yourself: 'You may have all the power over me, but if I wanted to, I could kick your fucking ass right now.'"

There in his office, I looked at Ralph for a long minute, and Bruce's words came to mind. All of a sudden, Ralph was irrelevant. I calmly said, "I knew we had your support all the way, boss."*

In the end, the case was scrapped. Because we were not allowed a few days to lay down an exit story to the bad guys, it would have been impossible to reintegrate and explain our absence. Like an agent named Bill Eastman always told me, "Sometimes the dragon wins."

---

* I'll just say there was poetic justice for Ralph in the end.

I have seen a lot of IA dodges in my day, but Jimm Langley has to hold the record. There have been FBI Ten Most Wanted fugitives who went underground for shorter periods than Jimm. To appreciate the sheer cunning involved, we have to go back to the beginning of this story.

Jimm and Cisco had been working like dogs in Florida, and they decided to take a night off. They knew of a tiny bar with good music, cheap drinks, and redneck girls. Admittedly, it was sort of a biker hangout, but even ATF agents are allowed to go out socially. They were off duty and not in government vehicles. As the night went on, the lady bartender took a shine to Jimm, and there was mutual flirting. What Jimm didn't know was that the huge, nasty-looking biker sitting at the end of the bar was the bartender's boyfriend.

At some point, the biker got tired of Jimm's advances on his girlfriend and decided to make an issue of it. He approached Jimm, and they squared off, chest to chest. Jimm had every intention of backing down and offering to buy the guy a beer. Just then, not knowing exactly what was happening, Cisco stepped in and badged the guy, hoping he would stand down. Instead, the biker knocked the badge out of Cisco's hand.

There are very few things in this life that can't be negotiated, and physically disrespecting a cop's badge is one of them. No cop on this planet would ever let a non-cop touch or handle his badge, and Jimm unloaded on the guy.

Jimm is a pretty big boy, and shit got broken, and the cops got called. The biker hauled ass, and Jimm and Cisco sat and drank their beers, waiting for the cops. The cops came and met with the manager and the two agents. There was about one hundred dollars' worth of damage, and Jimm and Cisco paid it on the spot. The manager was happy, and the cops were happy. But since the police were now officially involved, they followed policy and called Jimm and Cisco's boss. The boss thought nothing of it, but to be on the safe side, he told the agents to report the incident to IA the next day. That turned out to be a bad decision that nobody could see coming.

Because this was viewed by everybody involved as a nothing deal, Jimm called Carlos S., who at this time was in IA. He told Carlos, "Hey, there's nothing to this. Why don't you take the case and come down on a road trip." Unfortunately, the case got assigned to none other than Fred Drew—yes, the same IA agent who had interviewed me in the Casper debacle. While all of this was going on, Jimm suffered a severe back injury when a steel filing cabinet fell on him. He was placed on temporary disability.

Drew's investigation didn't prove anything beyond a bar fight. That should have maybe gotten Jimm a week or two on the beach. Instead, the head of IA, Richard Hankinson, decided that Jimm and Cisco should be terminated. Jimm was close with the SAC in Miami, who had been keeping him in the loop. Since Jimm was on disability, he wasn't required to come to the office or report anything beyond his medical condition. Facing a possible termination fight, Jimm hauled ass. He moved out of town and never answered his phone. The bureau cannot begin a disciplinary action until the agent has been served. They couldn't serve him if they couldn't find him.

This went on for almost four years, during which time Box was the only one who had direct contact with Jimm. A few other RatSnakes may or may not have had contact, but IA would never know if we had. As the action moved forward against Cisco, Jimm contacted the SAC and took all the blame. He even offered to resign to save Cisco's job.

With so much time having passed, and the central bosses having been moved or transferred out of their positions, the SAC broke the news to

Jimm that he'd been able to get the termination proposal dropped. "They have decided to recommend a two-week suspension," he told Jimm.

Two weeks on the beach was doable, and Jimm came home. After returning to his duties, he remained in Miami until he was transferred to the ATF Academy. If there was an IA Hall of Fame, Jimm Langley's RatSnake jersey would be retired.

. . . .

One more Jimm story.

When Charlie Fuller took over the UC program at the academy, he began taking the show on the road. At the request of any specific local jurisdiction, ATF would take the training to them. It was more cost-effective for the sponsoring agency, because more of their officers could attend locally instead of going all the way to Brunswick. After Charlie retired, Jimm and Box expanded the road shows.

I only made it to one or maybe two of those traveling academies, mostly because every time they planned one, I was in the middle of a case and couldn't break away. Later, there was a change in ATF leadership at the academy, and let's just say they weren't Vince friendly.*

One particular school was held in the Carolinas, and God was looking out for me, because it was one of the ones I missed. It was not uncommon for the locals at the training to show the instructors the area nightlife and/or hold a big barbeque or some other event to thank them. On this particular trip, the students scheduled an excursion to a high-end gentleman's club, a.k.a. titty bar. The club required patrons to sign in as a guest. Jimm

---

* Some of the new bosses came into the academy with the mentality that they were going to clean up the place. They didn't want to continue with the old cadre, who weren't coat-and-tie guys. I guess they preferred to ignore the fact or had no clue about how many lives we collectively saved over the years.

and Box, who were practically always in role, signed in as Billy Hoover and Ronnie Carter.

> FACT #1: You are taking a chance when you sign the names of the bureau's fucking director and deputy director.
>
> FACT #2: It wasn't likely that anyone but Jimm and Box would ever know.
>
> FACT #3: Uh, wrong, Two Dogs.

A dispute erupted in the club, not of Box or Jimm's initiation, but it spilled out into the parking lot. The patron on the other end of the dispute swung on one of the agents. In response, one of them leveled the dude. Security and the cops came. The cops got the story and ran the guy off. Simple bar fight, no big deal. Disaster narrowly avoided. Or so they thought.

Sadly, the patron had a preexisting medical anomaly, and he went home and died a day or two later. As you can imagine, there was a huge investigation. The fight and subsequent death comprised tragic but unrelated events, and Box and Jimm were cleared of any wrongdoing regarding the death.

During the death investigation, IA swarmed all over the case. When they pulled the sign-in sheet at the club and saw Ronny and Billy's names, the shit hit the fan. Not that either of these two knuckleheads, meaning Jimm and Box, were ever on track to get a Gallatin Award,* but that caper ensured they *never* would receive it.

---

* The Gallatin is awarded by the US Treasury Department to agents who serve their entire career without any suspensions.

CHAPTER 14

....

5150s

In November 1943, as World War II raged on, the US military dispatched Marine and other ground combat troops via boats to the Gilbert Islands, roughly halfway between Hawaii and Papua New Guinea. The location of this loose chain of atolls and coral islands was deemed strategic to the United States' larger plan to neutralize Japanese bases in the central Pacific. The Marines arriving at the Gilbert Islands in low tides and approaching the open beach had no cover against the vigorous defense launched by Japanese troops. The worst of the fighting occurred at Tarawa Atoll, where a bloody seventy-six-hour battle took the lives of more than five thousand courageous American, Japanese, and Korean troops.

As a Marine, I often wondered what motivated those young men to continue to charge into the fray while watching their fellow soldiers being cut down by the hundreds before ever making it to the beach. Were they crazy? It is not natural for human beings to wade into certain death. My point is that one man's crazy is another man's call to duty. Like the Marines at Tarawa, RatSnakes might seem crazy through a different lens.

In order for law enforcement in the state of California to hold someone involuntarily due to perceived mental instabilities, the individual must be designated "5150" per California's Welfare and Institutions Code. But in a RatSnakes world, you walk through the door *because* you are 5150. I suspect there is something in our psyche or DNA that makes us want to do this job that could be considered crazy. Certainly, my personality drew me to the danger, the excitement, and the adrenaline. My mother always said of me: "Vinny, when you're bored, you start breaking things."*

To be clear, I am not bragging about the events I'm going to tell about in this chapter, nor am I justifying them. I'm merely sharing them. On the one hand, I recount some of these stories with appropriate embarrassment and remorse. On the other hand, I don't ask for forgiveness, but maybe just some good old-fashioned understanding. We were asked or, at the bare minimum, encouraged to go to places and be with people that no average person would agree to visit or associate with. We were asked to voluntarily go into environments that held a high probability of violence and to enter those places alone. Manuals full of orders, policies, and directives could not and did not address the real, day-to-day challenges of

---

* I have seen our crew do some crazy shit for a laugh or entertainment. A guy named Yott once jumped from a two-story window, severely damaging his ankle, in order not to miss a ride to the bar. I watched Milton break one of those old, hard-plastic telephones over Yott's head during an innocent argument. Jimm filled our rental house hot tub and swimming pool with so many soapsuds that we couldn't use them for three days. Then he did it again. I was called upon to talk Fitz off a second-story balcony because one of our group had antagonized him to the point that he was going to try to leap from there into the pool—which I was reasonably certain his fat ass wasn't going to make. I got so pissed off at everyone taunting him, and his refusal to come off the balcony, that I ended my intervention with: "Then jump, you stupid motherfucker." The only reason we weren't scooping up his body parts was because one of the female agents offered to show him her tits if he'd come down. That worked.

doing undercover work. Just as landing a speeding jet onto an aircraft carrier would scare the shit out of most of us, jet pilots settle into a comfort zone. This is the only explanation I have for what you are about to read.

. . . .

Bird and I were ferrying a couple of drunk HQ suits back to their condo on St. Simons Island. These two guys, JD and TC, were bosses sent from Washington to oversee the training at the academy. They were button-down-oxford types but agents nonetheless, and personal friends, and they liked to go drinking with us UC guys. Problem was, they couldn't get out of headquarters mode and had spent the whole night belittling field ops, undercover operators, and street agents. By the time we headed back to the island, Bird and I had heard enough about how we didn't see the "big picture" of the importance of HQ.

Bird was driving. He looked into the back seat and said, "For the rest of this ride, how about you two shut the fuck up."

Well, of course they didn't because headquarters guys knew everything. Just ask them. As we were on the bridge passing over the intracoastal waterway, one of them said something stupid *again*. My pistol was on the seat. I grabbed it and held it up and said, "Last chance to shut the fuck up." I was just teasing, but then Bird started to say, "I dare—"

I didn't let him get the words out of his mouth before I emptied the magazine out the window into the water below. When my weapon went empty, Bird looked at me in disbelief and then smiled. The two guys in the back seat went Casper-the-fucking-Ghost white. We drove the last couple miles in silence. The only sound in the car was the ringing in our ears.* We rolled into the condo parking lot and exited in our different directions. The only time I heard of the incident being mentioned was years later,

---

* If you never have shot a gun inside an enclosed space, my advice is *don't*!

when Bird was telling the story to a bunch of cops and TC begged him not to.

. . . .

Generally speaking, the words "gun" and "play" don't belong in the same sentence. To the average citizen and probably even most cops, a gun is like a snake waiting to bite. As special agents, we had it pounded into our heads that guns always must be respected and treated with extreme caution. Deadly force is not a laughing matter and is treated by law enforcement as perhaps the most daunting of our duties. That being said, you already have it down that many seasoned ATF agents who deal in firearms daily are less sensitive to the presence of and use of guns. For RatSnakes, having loaded guns pointed at you by bad guys becomes all too commonplace and even, well, boring. I found out early in my police career that RatSnakes aren't the only ones unimpressed by guns.

I responded to a burglary alarm and was thrilled to find that the burglar was still inside. However, as I observed him exiting a window about ten feet away, I realized that between us was a ten-foot cyclone fence with razor wire at the top. I was carrying a standard police-issue Remington 870 shotgun. It was clear I wasn't going to scale that fence and lay hands on the violator, so I did the only thing I could think of. I leveled my shotgun at his head, racked a round in the chamber, and screamed, "Freeze, motherfucker!"

If you ever have heard the sound of a shotgun being racked, you know it is distinctive and ominous.

The violator snapped his head around, looked at me for a microsecond, and then took off like a rocket. He knew, and I knew, that I wasn't going to shoot him. Lesson learned. Don't ever bluff, because your bluff will be called. I slumped, unloaded the shotgun, and hoped nobody would ever hear about it.

Years later, as an ATF agent, I had a particularly dangerous CI during a joint case with the FBI. We were targeting one of the most violent street gangs operating in Atlanta. Said informant was becoming somewhat of a control problem and had been in the system long enough to become a jailhouse lawyer. I truly don't recall what prompted me to go "bad cop" on him, but it was some sort of physical threat or confrontation, which isn't unusual with snitches. We were way too far along in this case, and we had too much invested in this snitch to allow him to go sideways. So, when he said or did whatever it was that I no longer was willing to tolerate, I reached under my jacket and unsnapped my holster. My FBI counterpart hadn't yet arrived at our meeting, and the CI and I were alone and secluded away from the public outside a vacant industrial warehouse, where he wouldn't be seen with us.

When he saw me unsnap my holster, he immediately bowed up and said something to the effect of, "I know that you're not even allowed to take your gun out of your fucking holster. You don't scare me."

I snatched my 9 mm pistol out of the holster and cranked off a round right next to his head, hoping to give the appearance that I had lost my fucking mind. In reality, I had chosen a safe backstop of piled-up wood, leaning against the abandoned building behind him. He grabbed his ears and dropped down to the ground, cussing up a storm. I imagine being that close to the discharge did sting his hearing pretty good.

My FBI counterpart arrived for our usual debriefing and planning session. He saw that the CI was somewhat unfocused and asked him, "What's wrong?" The informant looked at me and blurted out, "Nothing." The FBI agent looked at me, and I just smiled. He didn't ask, and I didn't tell.

. . . .

I found myself alone with yet another troublesome informant. This one previously had been convicted of a quadruple murder. He weighed quite a bit over three hundred pounds and was pretty drunk, as well as agitated by some shit my DEA counterparts had pulled on him regarding money we owed him. He didn't like or want to deal with DEA anyway. He felt I knew what I was doing and wouldn't get him killed. But this night it was us/me (cops) against him (murdering, pissed-off gangster). Things escalated quickly because I could not afford to lose my authority as the controlling agent, but clearly, we were about to come to blows. It was pretty obvious that I would get the short end of that deal. His fists were like ham hocks, and he had that "I don't give a fuck if I go back to prison" look on his face.

Without the obligatory unsnapping of my holster as a warning, I pulled my pistol and blew out the driver's-side rear tire on his car. Then I pressed the hot gun barrel to his forehead and calmly said, "The next one goes into your head."

He took a huge step back, threw his hands up, and muttered, "All right, all right."

After a few more tense minutes allowing things to calm down, I peeled off a couple hundred dollar bills out of my own money and assured him I'd straighten out the DEA guys. Would I have shot him if things had continued to go south after I blew out his tire? He believed I would, and that's all I will say on the matter.

. . . .

If we are going to talk crazy, let's talk really, really crazy.

Jimm Langley's boss asked him to help a struggling agent with a biker case. After a year, the case hadn't produced any actionable intelligence or evidence. Jimm was just back from working another extended biker case in Texas but said he would try to jump-start this Florida case.

After being a hang around for approximately three months, Jimm got an opportunity to take it to the next level. The club he was riding with went to another club's open party. When they all got ready to leave, Jimm's battery was dead. Most Harleys require you to take the seat off to get to the battery. The delay while Jimm broke out his tool kit and jumper cables pissed off the club members. It was cold out, and he was holding them up from making the forty-mile ride back to their clubhouse. It only took about fifteen minutes to make the repair, but the other bikers were "motherfucker"-ing him pretty hard for the inconvenience. Once they were ready to roll, and after Jimm had apologized as much as he was going to, the club president approached Jimm and his ATF UC partner with an offer: "If you ride those bikes all the way back to the clubhouse naked, you'll have your patch within thirty days."

Becoming patched members would gain Jimm and his partner unfettered access to the criminal inner workings of the club. The partner declined. He didn't want to get caught and get in trouble with ATF. Or maybe it was just too cold and too far to ride.

Jimm, on the other hand, asked, "Can I at least wear my boots?"

The president nodded that he could, and within a minute Jimm was standing in the parking lot butt naked except for his boots. He made the forty-mile trek without incident.

When Jimm arrived at the clubhouse, he got his clothes back but noticed the ASP baton* he carried as his weapon of choice had been misplaced or stolen on the trip. He was pissed and protested to his fellow bikers. The club vice president told him to come by the next day and they would make it right regarding the missing nightstick. The next day, Jimm was presented with a stolen pistol as a replacement for his lost ASP. The case was now headed in the right direction.

Jimm didn't forget the president's promise to patch him into the club,

---

* A telescoping baton favored for its carrying ease and psychological impact.

but he also never mentioned it. He patiently waited the thirty days, knowing he would leverage the promise at some point. The month passed, and Jimm was called to the clubhouse for an undisclosed reason. To be summoned by the gang boss always was a nerve-racking situation for a UC. Jimm walked in to see that all the officers of the club were present. The president began to explain that they had taken a vote and that they would patch Jimm in three more months. This was decision time for Jimm and a pivotal moment in the case, not to mention that he hadn't forgotten freezing his balls off for forty miles. He made a last-minute Hail Mary pass. It could only go one of two ways.

He snatched off his prospect vest* and threw it at the officers. As he turned to walk away he said, "I ain't riding with brothers who have no honor."

As Jimm reached the door, the president called him back. "We were only fucking with you," he said, and tossed Jimm his member patch.

No matter what side of the crazy fence you sit on, Jimm's bike stunt was batshit nuts. If the bosses had found out, he would have faced serious time on the beach and possibly termination. However, the ultimate prosecution of the case was successful, with numerous club members pleading guilty to drug and firearms charges. Since they all pleaded out, Jimm was spared having to recount his Lady Godiva–like motorcycle ride that fall Florida night.

. . . .

During the first half of my career, the Bureau of ATF still was under the oversight of the Secretary of Treasury and the US Department of Treasury. After the attacks of 9/11 and the subsequent restructuring of the federal government law enforcement apparatus, ATF was placed under

---

* Usually a leather vest or jacket with a sewn-on rocker designating the wearer as a prospective member.

the US Attorney General and the Department of Justice as the Bureau of Alcohol, Tobacco, Firearms and *Explosives*. Whether main Treasury or main Justice, there were very strict rules about the discharge of firearms. Any discharge of a firearm was highly discouraged unless the agent was involved in a life-threatening encounter. All discharges of duty firearms not on an official shooting range, intentional or otherwise, were to be reported immediately.

One of those occasions that a rule or two may or may not have been ignored was on a hot, shitty, hungover day in the Las Vegas desert where, without backup, Bird and I were out with ten or twelve militia members under the guise of being taught antigovernment tactics. The "colonel," as he demanded to be called, slowly walked past some Hogan's Alley– type targets the militiamen had set up against the rocks for the occasion.* Slowly and methodically, he shot each target while describing the course to us in a very condescending manner. He hit about half his shots and had real shitty tactical technique.

Bird went first, playing the young militia recruit. He walked the course, passively shooting, acting very unskilled, and thanked the colonel for his guidance. Bird's performance was a calculated act to build up the boss of this militia and ultimately gain his confidence and be allowed to join the group. We had intel that this particular group was capable and possessed the resources to attack government installations.

When Jay was done, the colonel said something like, "Don't worry, son. You'll get better."

It was very hot in the damn Nevada desert. I didn't want to be there. I'd been away from home for months. I had been out gambling and drinking until about three hours before this so-called training session. So, when my

---

* Hogan's Alley is the FBI Academy's original live-fire range, set up to look like a normal city street to add to realism during training. Targets would pop up with pictures of either bad guys or innocents, setting up shoot/don't shoot scenarios.

turn came to eat shit, I wasn't hungry. I tactically loaded my pistol, made sure I had extra mags, and when the colonel said "Go," I went full-out balls to the walls. I blazed past those targets doing speed tactical reloads. I had kill shots on every target, and when I came to the last target, a coyote popped up out of a cave and I shot him dead too. I holstered and shouted, "Clear!" and then yelled back at the colonel, "How'd I do?"

Translation: "Fuck you, *Colonel.*"

He stood there, slack-jawed.

Bird leaned against a car, smoking a cigarette, half smiling, half pissed. The militia group called a side meeting and said for Bird to join the pow-wow. I was not invited. Later that evening, he told me they had said, "Bird, you gotta rein Vinny in. He acts a little crazy." Bird bought me a drink and said, "Dude, stop scaring the bad guys." We laughed.

CHAPTER 15

···

HOLLYWOOD ON CRACK

Hollywood ain't got shit on us. In the movies, the bad guys' responses are known in advance. In undercover work, nothing truly can be known ahead of time. I have used the term "pretending" when talking about UC roles. Undercover work is acting at its best, and it is damn hard. Things happen without warning, and you'd better be able to disguise your fear, anger, or disdain.

Movie actors do numerous takes to get it right. Undercover agents get one per scene.

TAKE 1: UP AGAINST THE KLAN

While at that massive KKK rally at Stone Mountain with Futvoye and those guys, I had to muster all of my acting skills.* At one point, we were sitting on the back of our pickup truck, waiting to meet up with a violator. He came walking up with his young child. This guy's son was about ten years old. When he introduced the boy, the dad said, "Tell them who you are, son."

The kid spouted some memorized line, something to the effect of: "I'm a white American, and I hate Jews and niggers."

I was floored. I had two sons close to his age. As I sit here recalling, I can say with total certainty that if it had been my case, I would have shut it down right then and there and spent the next hour giving that Klan father the beating of his life. Instead, it was incumbent on me to stay in role and finish the job.

As soon as I could, I went home and hugged my kids.

TAKE 2: THE EMISSARIES

Feeding off your partner in a UC environment isn't something you can be taught. It's on-the-job training and survival of the fittest. If you do UC with one partner long enough, it's almost like a marriage. You know what the other person is thinking before they say it. You finish their sentences, and you fill in their silences. Most importantly, you both know what *not* to do and when not to do it.

---

* I first ran into the Klan back in my days as a city cop. While I was off duty, they had approached my vehicle while attempting to slide their hateful literature through my truck window. As a kid growing up in California, I'd never seen them all hooded up, and they scared the shit out of me.

On one such occasion, I was thankful Bird was my partner because we had that kind of simpatico relationship. While infiltrating Lil Rat's outlaw motorcycle gang, he wanted us to go raise some hell at a competitor's tattoo parlor. The competitor apparently was talking shit about Lil Rat around town. Bird and I immediately recognized this as a test. We used the ruse of stopping to gas up our bikes to steal a few minutes away to get a plan together. We already had seen a couple club members trying to do surveillance on us, no doubt reporting back to Lil Rat on how well we followed his orders. Whatever we were going to do at the rival tattoo parlor had to appear legit from a distance.*

In five minutes, Bird and I threw together a plan, more like a very loose theory. As we rolled into the parking lot of the rival tattoo artist's shop, we had eyes on the two guys following us. They parked slightly down the street. I remember thinking: "They can't hear us, so it only needs to *look* good."

The shop was closed and the lights were dimmed, but the guy's truck was there and we could see movement inside.

Jay said, "I'm gonna hang back over here."

Over here was just a few feet away, behind a pillar for cover if this went badly. I walked up and pounded loudly on the door. That mostly was for our friends down the street. I saw the guy inside stand up and stagger a few steps, looking toward the front door. Through the window glass we both could see that he had picked up a shotgun.

I whispered to Bird, "Just be cool."

The guy inside flung the door open. The first thing out the door was the barrel of a 12-gauge shotgun. I had my hand very close to my pistol,

---

* Remember, we could *act* crazy and give the illusion of committing crimes, but we couldn't actually commit crimes. We couldn't commit an act of violence against a citizen without cause. Exceptions exist but in very limited scenarios and only with the approval of the Department of Justice and the US Attorney's office.

but as the barrel of his gun touched my forehead, I could see that his finger wasn't on the trigger.

Generally speaking, in the law enforcement community, when the bad guys' guns come out, the good guys' guns come out too. Cops are conditioned to this response when confronted with lethal force, a knife, or a gun. But in the UC world, the bad guys' weapons being drawn sometimes signals success for the operation.

I calmly said, "I hope you don't think you're the first person to ever point a gun at me, but if you don't want to be the last, you better lower that motherfucker most ricky-tick."

He started to say something, which is exactly what I wanted. Under a peak stress situation, unless you have muscle memory—usually acquired by training a specific motor skill over and over—your brain takes time to process the simplest action. In other words, this guy wasn't good enough to talk and shoot at the same time. I also could tell he was way more scared of me than I was of him. I took comfort that if I was wrong, and he shot me, Bird already had drawn a bead on his head, and even Bird couldn't miss from that far away.

We had a pact that if some violator ever shot one of us when we were on a deal, he/they would never see the inside of a courtroom. I'm glad neither of us had to live up to that pact.

While this guy was trying to respond to my brazen comment, with my left hand I snatched the shotgun out of his now sweaty hand and simultaneously beaned him upside his head pretty fucking hard with my motorcycle helmet, which was in my right hand. He went down like Smokin' Joe Frazier.

It was an extremely calculated act on my part. He had a gun to my head. Legally, Jay or I would have been completely justified shooting him dead right there.

The guy had fallen backward into the shop. Bird and I scurried inside, locked the door, and pulled the shades. Now our friends down the street couldn't see or hear shit. We chilled the guy out, never giving ourselves up as cops. He said he had heard talk on the street and figured some guys from the club were gonna come fuck him up. We acted as emissaries and told him we'd come to smooth over the riff and that I only hit him because of the whole shotgun thing. He bought it, apologized, and thanked us for working to rectify the dispute.

We left, and when we walked out, as expected, our friends down the street had left. A couple hours later, Lil Rat called us and wanted us to meet him at the bar. He was a cheap fucker, so when we walked in and he right off paid for our drinks, we knew he knew what had gone down.

Well, at least he thought he did.

We documented the entire episode in our reports so the US attorney wouldn't be blindsided if it ever came up in court. He was fine with it. He actually considered pursuing charges for assault on a federal agent against the rival tattoo artist when the case wrapped up. But absent blood or broken bones, I always shied away from that charge. Claiming foul after the fact kinda made me feel like a pussy.

TAKE 3: BABYFACE

Carr, a.k.a. Babyface, was one of the most sought-after UCs in the country. He had balls as big as a fifty-five-gallon drum. He was calm, thoughtful, and got along with everybody. Basically, the opposite of me. We always said of him: "The only thing we don't like about Carr is that we can't find anything not to like about him."

Babyface would tell you that the greatest achievement of his career was working a long-term OMO case and never riding a motorcycle, not even once. And they patched him.

Like me, Babyface had grown up in Marin County. We became friends and worked together anytime we got the chance. On one such occasion, he came to help on a job in San Francisco. Carr and I got together for a few cocktails the night he came to town, but we didn't talk much about the deal. During the briefing, everybody was given their assignments, normally read aloud to the group. Carr was the primary UC on this one. He was going to meet up with some Mexican gangbangers and buy a couple guns and some dope. As ATF had advanced its UC protocols over the years, a hostage negotiator was included on the scene of every deal in case the worst-case scenario played out. So when it came to me, the supervisor read out my assignment as the on-scene hostage negotiator.

Carr said, "Oh, fuck no. If they take me hostage, don't let Vince talk to them. They will surely torture me."

I'm happy to say nobody got tortured. In fact, my services as a negotiator weren't needed that day and the buy went as planned.*

TAKE 4: NOT GUILTY, YOUR HONOR

The notion of undercover work invokes glamorized images—often advanced by books and movies—as a glitzy, fraught-with-peril infiltration of Mafia-like criminal organizations. While danger can arise in any UC situation, in reality, there are varying levels and degrees of undercover work. One of my first undercover assignments was to enter a bar with another agent and sit at the bar as close to the primary undercover agent

---

* Another agent, Koz, worked primarily with Carr. They did some phenomenal infiltrations that have made national headlines. Koz is one of the foremost authorities on OMO investigation in the country. I cannot elaborate more on his contributions, as he is still in the field, although his infiltration of the Mongols Motorcycle Club was highlighted in the acclaimed television show *Gangland Undercover*.

as we could get. The primary UC was meeting with a methamphetamine cook and negotiating for a large amount of drugs. We were there as countersurveillance in case the violator wasn't alone and also to function as cover in case the deal went bad. We had to blend in. So, we drank on government funds until our UC left safely, and then we surveilled the violator away.

Even some agents don't give much thought to the fact that there are many instances where they are undercover without formally intending to be. For example, many witnesses and victims in high-crime areas don't want to be seen talking to the po-po, so law enforcement agents might dress and act to blend in. In some situations, meeting with an informant while in uniform or even a coat and tie could be fatal. Commonplace surveillances include an undercover element. Staging for a planned raid or a search and arrest warrant often has a UC component. You wouldn't want to sit down the street attracting all kinds of attention while preparing to crash in somebody's door.

But sometimes being too good at blending in is a bad thing.

After executing about ten search and arrest warrants on the Outlaws Motorcycle Club chapter in Atlanta, Georgia, hours later I had to appear in court at the defendants' initial appearance. The way it worked is that the marshals would keep the prisoners in their holding cells until they were called to court. The arresting agent then would collect the prisoners from lockup and walk them into court. Our operation had kicked off around 4 AM, and our entire field division, local police, and US Marshals were tied up all day gathering and logging evidence and transporting prisoners. I had to break away and race to the federal courthouse in Atlanta for the hearings.

I stood before the judge with four of the violators, who clearly had not bathed in days. They looked like they'd just come off the set of a biker movie, wearing their fucking colors (vests with the gang's logo embroidered on the back). The judge called the courtroom to order and explained the proceedings. He then looked directly at me, the only one *not* in shackles, and asked if I would like to enter a plea.

I guess I was looking a little rough that day. Oh well. Street theater at its best. Or worst.

TAKE 5: ONE NIGHT IN MACON

Operational security always is a priority during undercover operations. This includes making operations "need to know." Assuring cover teams blend in and don't compromise the UCs. Having identities appropriately backstopped. Mastering appearances and dialogue. Sometimes this even means keeping local law enforcement in the dark.

While Bird and I were working the Iron Cross Motorcycle Club investigation in Macon, due to OPSEC concerns only the top brass and the Special Investigations Unit knew we were operating in the area. We just had completed a meth buy from one of the club's associates at a local bar and were returning to our UC pad to secure and document the evidence. It was around 2 AM, and we were screaming down the highway on our bikes. I had an ounce of methamphetamine in one boot, my pistol in the other, and, as I soon learned, a burned-out taillight.

Predictably, the red lights of a police cruiser lit us up. I began to pull over and Bird continued down the road. I remember thinking, "You fuckin' bastard."

Deciding I'd just take the speeding ticket and deal with it later, I produced my UC driver's license and insurance.

The officer who pulled me over, one Sgt. Boney, was not aware of my identity or my mission, and I needed it to stay that way. The decision to come out of role is based solely on the undercover's judgment. It's up to the UC to consider many factors, including public safety, compromising the investigation, officer safety, and other pertinent aspects of the investigation. In this case, there was some intelligence that a small group of local cops were sympathetic to the Iron Cross gang. Our agreed-upon tactic for this case was to stay in role at all times.

Looking the way I looked, driving a beat-up Harley at one hundred miles an hour, caused the sarge to be a bit suspicious. Rather than write the ticket and send me on my way, he decided to pronc me out on the side of the highway at gunpoint. In all fairness, I would have done the same thing. He was alone in a one-man unit. Jay had pulled over a ways down the road and was watching this unfold.

Sgt. Boney first patted me down for his safety, luckily missing the firearm and dope in my boots. He then had me stand and place my hands on the hood of his car and continued to do his job, i.e., interrogate me: Where are you coming from? Who were you with? What are you doing out so late? Is that your buddy pulled over down the road?

Wanting to end this contact without further drama, I respectfully answered the sarge's questions. However, after about twenty minutes standing in the cold and having complied completely, I got irritated and blurted out, "Are we just gonna stand here all night, or are you gonna write me a ticket and let me go home?"

That pissed him off big-time. He stepped up to where his face was inches from mine and in his best Southern bubba voice said, "Boy, I'm driving this ship, and you'll stand here until I say you don't. Understand, boy?"

"Yes, sir."

"Good. Now I want to search your bike. Do I have permission to search your bike?"

That's where it kind of went south. I had nothing illicit in my saddlebags or anywhere else on my bike, but now I, too, was pissed.

I said, "Yes, sir . . . if you have a warrant."

The sarge said, "Okay, smart-ass, I'm calling a dog."

"Call two if you want," I told him. "There ain't nothing there."

He did.

Unknown to me, by this time Bird had contacted the lieutenant in charge of the Special Investigations squad we were working with. Shortly after the detection dog arrived, the sarge waved off the K-9 handler and told me to sit in the front seat of his patrol car. Apparently, the lieutenant had called the police chief, who in turn radioed the sergeant and identified me as law enforcement. *Not cool.* But the choice was out of my hands at that point. I sat in Sgt. Boney's cruiser and listened to his lecture, which basically was his attempt to justify being such an asshole. I acknowledged his hard work.* Then I was on my way.

TAKE 6: THE RICHMOND JOB

For some, being asked to be the undercover agent on a case is their worst nightmare. For others, *not* being asked is considered a slight. As I've said, early in my career, I took every shitty gig that came down the pike, partly because I was building my reputation in the bureau and partly because they never offered me the good gigs. One of our agents had a snitch who was offered up by the California Department of Corrections for us to use. That should have been my first clue to steer clear. ATF worked closely with Corrections' Special Services Unit. SSU agents *all* were senior prison guards, and their purpose in life (besides IA investigations) was to target the most violent of the parolees and revoke their parole and send them

---

* We never were able to confirm through our investigation that there were any dirty local cops.

back to prison as quickly as possible. Snitches fell out of the trees to keep from going back.

This case involved an armed robber SSU had targeted to go back to prison. The robber did what they all did: he offered up a friend as a tradeoff. First, this snitch couldn't be trusted. He was a convict. He easily could have compromised me. So, we decided to do a little street theater. The task force arranged for me and the informant to meet. But in this case, he wasn't advised that I was a cop. Instead, he was told that I was a bad guy looking for dope and guns. (An informant utilized in this fashion is referred to as an "unwitting" informant.) We met up, had some beers; he was good with me and made the call.

The only way the target violator would agree to meet me was if I went to his house in Richmond in the company of the unwitting informant. Richmond is located north of San Francisco and right across the bay from San Quentin—literally, across the bridge from the prison gates. Because of this, many parolees land right there in the so-called Iron Triangle, i.e., Central Richmond. The city has the reputation of being one of the most violent cities in California.

The deal was set. The plan was for me and the unwitting to go into the violator's house and buy the dope and a stolen gun. We would leave, roll back across the Richmond–San Rafael Bridge to Marin County, ironically in eyeshot of San Quentin prison. Once in Marin, a marked California Highway Patrol unit would pull me over and ultimately arrest both me and the unwitting.

We got to the house, did the intros, and chatted with the violator, who took a liking to me. He offered me a beer, and I took it. After we did the deal for the dope and gun, I looked at the unwitting and said, "Let's bounce. I've got shit to do."

The violator asked the unwitting what he was going to do after I ran him back to Marin. "Just party," was the answer. The violator jumped up, put on his jacket, and told the unwitting: "I'll go with yah."

What I didn't know was that the violator didn't have a car and wanted to ride with us. The op plan called for me and one bad guy in the car. I could hardly tell the guy I just did business with that he couldn't ride with us. To be honest, I remember not knowing what I should do.

ATF undercovers are the best because we have the best agents in the field covering us. Before I had to figure this one out, my pager went off with a 10-4, letting me know that my cover team, led by Joe Stafford, was adjusting the plan on the fly. So I got in my G-ride and headed to the toll bridge with the violator sitting in the back seat and the "informant" in the front.

Plans change; shit happens. The violator now sitting directly behind me in the car was a two-time convicted murderer. He was armed. Now the question became how would this violator respond as things proceeded? I had to try to control events inside the vehicle until we all were out of the car and in custody. My heart was pounding as we approached the tollbooth. I was shit talking, trying to distract these guys so they wouldn't notice that every other tollbooth lane had one of the cover cars going through at exactly the same time as us. Of course, the guys in the car with me had no idea there were cops in the eight unmarked vehicles flanking us. But when you are undercover, your brain sometimes will fuck with you. I was on high alert until we passed through the toll.

As soon as we exited the bridge, looking straight at the highway sign that read "San Quentin Next Exit," a highway patrol car hit its lights. Immediately, panic set in on the violators. The guy in back was screaming, "I got dope on me!"

I told him just to chill, that I probably was speeding.

Talk about absolute trust. I had to believe that Joe Stafford had accurately described me and completely briefed the highway patrol officer. If not, I might get shot as a bad guy. Unknown even to me, because of the unexpected passenger's criminal records, the cover team had ratcheted up the planned traffic stop to a felony vehicle stop. The CHP's loudspeaker boomed at us. The officer followed felony-stop protocols and ordered us out of the vehicle one at a time. We all were arrested as planned without incident.

Before complying with the order to exit the car, the backseat violator looked straight at the unwitting, whom he had known for years and done time with, and said, "I knew you were a fucking snitch."

Not me, not the new guy, whom he had met just an hour earlier. Now that's playin' a role, baby.

CHAPTER 16

....

DYS*FUNK*SIONAL

Undercover operators are trained to know when to say "when," but it's not always that easy. Going in and out of role too often can blur the lines. Imagine being in a room full of Hells Angels, with women flashing their tits all night. Cussing, drinking, shooting off guns just for the hell of it. Then, after a couple hours sleep, you get up at home to make your kids breakfast. While you are having your first cup of coffee and chatting it up with your kids, your pager goes off, and you have to shoot a quick call to one of the violators.

You step away from your children to make the call, which goes something like this:

UC: Hey, motherfucker, it's 7 AM. What's your fuckin' problem?

VIOLATOR: Bitch, you said call as soon as I got your speed, and I got your speed. Meet me in an hour.

The violator hangs up, and you walk back to the breakfast table to finish getting your kids ready for school. Your wife walks into the kitchen.

WIFE: I need you to take the kids to school.

UC: Can't do it, babe.

WIFE: Why not?

UC: I got a deal to do in an hour.

And so, it goes. Day after day, week after week. Never knowing for sure where you belong and what really matters.

The RatSnakes really do put the *funk* in dysfunctional. I look back and wonder, how did this group even happen? I never have been closer to any group of people with the possible exception of my Marines. If one of my ex-wives said it, they all said it: "You love them more than me." I have no comment. What I will say is that when my mom and then my dad died within seven months of each other, each and every RatSnake offered to come help me and attend their funerals. Jay came to my dad's funeral—out of respect and because my dad loved Bird. I often thought my dad loved him more than me.

Earlier, when Mom passed, Bird was the first one there. The morning of her funeral was sort of a zoo, trying to get the kids and stepkids ready and all. I also was taking care of my ailing dad, so I appreciated the help. Well, most of the help.

My dad had a stout daily regimen of medicines he had to take. I kept them in one of those containers marked "Sunday–Saturday, Day and Night," so he could help keep up with it. First thing in the morning, I gave Dad his medicines, so I wouldn't forget. Being the ever-helpful sort of adopted son, Bird also gave Dad his medicines right before we went out the door. Unfortunately, they were his fucking nighttime medicines, which included Ambien to help him sleep. We got out of the funeral and walked over to the hall for the reception. I remember thinking, "Man, Dad isn't taking this very well." It wasn't until later that I figured out what happened.

Over those couple days, we had sat up fairly late with Darren and his wife, Deanna, and numerous other members of the Core, drinking and telling Mom stories. Her trust paperwork happened to be lying on the table, and Bird absentmindedly leafed through it. Suddenly, he busted out laughing uncontrollably. My dad asked, "What the fuck's wrong with you?"

Unbeknownst to me, Bird was named alternate executor if I had predeceased my mom. Really, Mom? Bird?

Then again, I shouldn't have been surprised. In the early days we didn't have cell phones, but the government office had the Federal Telecommunications System (FTS) that allowed us to make toll-free calls anywhere in the country. Early one Sunday morning, Bird and I decided to sneak into the Macon ATF office to call home and talk to our wives and kids and drop off some paperwork. When I say early, I mean 0500 early. This was a risky endeavor while working UC. The last thing we needed was to try to talk our way out of being seen walking into an ATF office or a police department.

Bird and I were sitting about ten feet apart, facing each other as we talked to our respective spouses on the phone. Unknown to Bird, I had hung up with my wife and called my mom in California. When Bird hung up his phone, he signaled to let him say hi. I waved him off, but he persisted. I put the call on hold and said, "Go ahead, motherfucker."

Bird picked up the phone, intending to flirt with my then wife, and said, "You know how bad I want to lick your thighs? I've always thought you were hot."

In a nanosecond, he started spitting out apology after apology to my mom. He was red as a fire truck.

On that same day every year thereafter, my mother would call Jay's cell phone and say, "What are you wearing, Bird?"

It never got old. Ever.

....

Our families adapted to our chosen profession, or they didn't. Not all of the parents and spouses enjoyed or participated in our foolishness on all levels. Many of my peers never discussed their cases with their spouses. They didn't want them to worry, or it was just that one touchy subject that kept the UC away from home. Some of our spouses assimilated to our core group; others tolerated our group but were just as happy not to engage socially. They were never looked down upon; we knew how fucked up we were. Ours was a quirky group that stood out in a crowd socially, which made some spouses uncomfortable.* Many RatSnakes kept their professional and private live completely separate. That was not me. What you saw was what you got. Everybody in my personal circle knew exactly what I was about.

That's a long intro to make the point that our family members didn't pick this life; we did. My first wife married a clean-cut police officer who wore a crisp uniform and a shiny badge. She ended up with a husband who looked like a thug, and it was challenging just to go out to dinner. Operators leave parents, wives, husbands, and children every day, sometimes for extended undercover operations. I once had to leave my dad after he traveled three thousand miles to see me and his grandkids. When the UCs don their capes and go off to save the world, somebody has to

---

* At one of our reunions, Fitz thought he was going to be funny. He walked around the houseboat naked, day and night, against our collective objections. Somebody's wife was sleeping on a couch, and Fitz tried to take a picture of himself standing right next to her, still naked. She opened her eyes, sat up, and kicked him square in the balls. She made her point, and he gave her a wide berth from then on.

stay at home to bathe the children, pay the mortgage, get to work, and spend long nights alone.

While I was living a very unconventional life, I insisted that my wife and kids continue with a traditional family environment. I was blind to the fact that my high-octane, chaotic life consumed theirs. I overcompensated because I wanted a different life for my family. As a result, I was unrealistic in demanding perfection from them.

That fact is that UCs missed their baby's first words, children's sporting events, recitals, birthdays—all the valued things that supposedly we were fighting to protect. On more occasions than I like to remember, I had to tell my kids, "I can't be there. Please take pictures." I missed wedding anniversaries. I missed my son's very last high school football game. We UCs carried a special kind of guilt, knowing that these sacrifices by our families sometimes caused resentment, loneliness, and could tank a marriage. Imagine time after time, looking at your spouse and saying, "I gotta go." They know you don't *gotta* go. You choose to go.

The payoff for the family? No glory, no shiny uniform and badge. No police car parked in the driveway. No bragging at the neighborhood get-together. They couldn't discuss their husband or wife's cases or heroic accomplishments. Instead, they made excuses for their spouse's appearance and demeanor.

One time in particular stood out for me. On one long-term undercover, Jay and I were able to cut away for a few days and go home. Jay couldn't fly home, so he came home with me. At the time, I lived in a cliquish, suburban neighborhood with a country club. Jay and I left our area of operation and rode our motorcycles to my house. It was early on a Sunday morning. We looked like we had just left a biker clubhouse, because we had. The Harleys we were using for the case were loud.

We rolled up, and several of my neighbors were outside in their yards. We stepped off our bikes, took off our helmets, and waved and greeted my neighbors. Everyone ignored our greeting and rapidly went back into their houses. Jay looked at me and asked, "What the fuck?" I didn't know what to say. My wife and kids came out and greeted us, but then my wife said, "Could you guys hide the bikes in the garage and come inside?"

There was no doubt that being an undercover, having the walk and having the talk, could blow up in your face, because not everybody knew you were a good guy. Joe Stafford and Larry Williams stopped at a tavern on the way home in San Rafael, California. After a couple hours, another group of hard-looking guys came in. Over the years, I've been told about seven different versions from all who were involved. Here is the best I can glean.

Drunken words were exchanged, it spilled out into the street, and a knockdown, drag-out brawl ensued. It got bloody, guns were produced on *both* sides, and a shot was fired, which luckily didn't hit its target. Then the badges came out, on *both* fucking sides. Turned out, a group of narcs from up north had picked the same watering hole. Imagine looking like any of us and trying to de-escalate a situation while trying to convince anybody you were a cop.

Joe found Larry the next morning at his house, in his bathtub, missing several teeth. That night would be a tough one to explain all around.

I've mentioned the phenomenon of the lines blurring and what we UCs described as personality fragmentation. Bottom line, UC men and women often blew off steam at a far more elevated rate than might be considered normal. Can you imagine one of the ladies in your neighborhood flashing her tits at a gathering? I can. Would you smash your husband's head with a frying pan if he and his friends whipped out their dicks to compare sizes because of a dare?

I have said all along that everything about my world from day one has been dysfunctional. That is not an excuse but hopefully some sort of explanation for some of what I've shared. I cannot just blame the cop business or undercover work for my personal dysfunctions. I got them honestly. Hell, when my first marriage was faltering, my mother called Bird and tried to blame it on him leading me astray. That might be the funniest thing I've ever heard. Before Bird met me, he barely drank and never smoked or cussed.

His response to my mom when she confronted him—I think she was attempting to ground us from hanging out anymore: "Fuck that, Mrs. Cefalu. He was already fucked up when I met him."

Case in point. I had gotten a Honda 90 when I was eleven or twelve years old. One day, I was outside playing, and my mom was taking a nap. My dad was bored and decided that he would go have a few cocktails at the bowling alley where he bartended. He thought riding my street-legal enduro motorcycle might be a good idea. I don't believe before that very moment that my father had ever ridden a motorcycle, so it probably was a really bad idea.

Mom woke up and started cooking dinner. She asked where Dad was, but neither of us noticed that my bike was gone. When Dad was late for dinner, her first call was to the bar at the bowling alley. It was only ten minutes away on the back roads, and they said he had just left. (They *always* said he had just left.) Within about fifteen minutes, Mom and I heard the sounds of a motorcycle engine, spitting and sputtering like it was about to die. We ran out to the driveway to see my dad, bloody from head to toe.

One of the handlebars was broken, and the bike was barely running. Mom asked, "What the hell happened to you?" He said, "You're not going to believe it, honey, but I was jumped by a bunch of Hells Angels." Mom turned and stomped away. My dad laughed and said to me, "Don't worry, buddy. I'll get it fixed."

The true story was that while coming back from the bar, shit-faced, he hit a gravel patch and went down hard. So, Bird was probably right about not being the sole bad influence in my life. As a kid, I already was used to it. Hell, half the days while Mom worked, I went to my dad's bar, and that's where I did my homework.

. . . .

Operators weren't the sole source of dysfunction in the bureau. The agency itself had some idiosyncratic and outdated perspectives and practices. It has been said that back in our early days, ATF was a "good ol' boy" network, meaning the highest-level positions within the agency were held by old white guys. That was true to a large extent. Keep in mind that the bureau was formed as a standalone agency less than ten years after President Lyndon B. Johnson signed significant civil rights legislation. As I've said, the agency originally was manned by former Treasury special agents. At that time, there weren't a lot of black Treasury agents. Hiring quotas were just starting to be enforced, and the vast majority of our agents were from or assigned to the South, so we'll just leave it that ATF was not the most diverse agency in its early days.

With new firearms jurisdiction and overlapping narcotics responsibilities, it made sense to recruit agents who were African American, Latino, Asian, et cetera. The original Treasury Enforcement Agent (TEA) test was so math-intensive that it was difficult to get enough qualified applicants, black, white, or otherwise. Shit, I made 70.2 on the test, which required a score of 70 to pass. I had graduated college just a year before I got hired. You'd think my math skills would have been better than that.

The government's Schedule A hiring authority allowed some applicants to initially forego the TEA test. If you had a special skill the bureau needed, ATF could waive the TEA test for up to three years. Foreign-language skills, technology skills, and such were covered under Schedule A hiring. Schedule A also was interpreted as relevant to the ability of black applicants to perform undercover work in environments where white agents traditionally could not. This was lowering the bar and a basically impotent waiver. Remember that ATF could not and would not require agents to work undercover. But the hiring practice accomplished getting an abundance of minority new hires, which was the true goal.

Just like our country was slow to adjust to the civil rights movement and the changing of discriminatory policies across the land, so was ATF slow to embrace change. When he was my group supervisor in Atlanta, "Uncle" Ron Mitchell used to tell me stories. Once while assigned to the Macon, Georgia, field office in the early 1970s, he had a new-hire trainee who was black and who had not yet been to the academy. One day the boss walked in and said, "Mitchell, the big boss called down from Atlanta and said he needs a nigger for an undercover."*

Ron reminded the boss that the young black agent hadn't been to the academy yet, and by policy he couldn't do undercover work. The boss said something like, "I was talkin' about you, Mitchell. Get your ass up to Atlanta, ASAP.

In fact, that young agent rose to be one of the first black supervisors in ATF.

Fast-forward to when I was in the bureau, in the 1980s, and sitting in Uncle Ron's office one day. Ron got a call from his former trainee, now a supervisor. Ron put him on speakerphone and introduced me over the telephone. The supervisor was just making a social call and started off by saying, "Can you believe they made me the head nigger in charge up here?" Ron said, "How long you been the head nigger in charge?" The supervisor said, "I been a nigger my whole life, but I only been the boss for a month."

---

* Before you start running me personally up the racist flagpole, these stories are shared to give an unvarnished look behind the scenes. In 1972, I was thirteen years old.

We all cracked the hell up. This was a far contrast to the ATF that I and others first walked into.

The Schedule A hiring process had created a lingering rift. Some white agents who had to pass the TEA test were resentful. Some early minority hires clearly suffered abuse. Tensions rose to a boiling point. As I've mentioned, ATF was embroiled in litigation when I signed on, and the racial division was palpable in the workplace. There were several individual discrimination suits pending. Those early lawsuits resulted in a class-action lawsuit against the bureau that wouldn't be settled for years.

Because undercover wasn't a required duty, some involved in the lawsuit argued that they were tasked to carry an inordinate amount of UC work, which I thought was total bullshit. Nonetheless, it became a rallying cry, and some of the senior and supervisory agents poisoned the new hires against "being slaves to the Man." Many black agents didn't buy into that narrative and loved UC work. Some of the black agents worked circles around the white guys doing UC.

Unfortunately, the Schedule A situation resulted in some agents using this absolute defense for not doing a UC operation: "I don't feel comfortable in that role." That was a legitimate out for black, white, female, and any other agents. But when some of the black agents noticeably would not accommodate a white agent's request to do a UC, it was pretty obvious what was occurring. What made all of this so destructive was that, for the most part, we were friends and comrades. Those were hard times, and we got through them. All the while, I don't believe I ever denied another agent my skills or support for an investigation. I adhered to the Marine Corps' philosophy regarding race: We all were Marine Green. When I joined the bureau, the only color I cared about was ATF Blue.

Our agents were the brightest and most straightforward in the government, bar none. That personality coupled with this job could foster a certain complacency or callousness toward danger. One day in Sacramento, such a mindset led to an unexpected tragedy that cost two of our agents their lives. Mark* was one of the best operators and one of the coolest, most calm and collected agents in the bureau. I thought very highly of him. Some of the facts of what happened remain in dispute to this day.

Mark shared an office with his trainee. The trainee was struggling with the entry-level pay and not being able to reunite with his young wife. This was a common complaint for new agents in the California offices. We actually had several quit and return to their old jobs back home. The new agent was constantly lamenting his circumstances, and Mark apparently was tired of his whining.

Mark took out his pistol and made some comment, clearly mocking and out of frustration, to the effect of, "Well, why don't you just kill yourself?"

At some point during this exchange, the gun went off accidentally and killed the young agent. I know Mark, and I trusted him many times with my life. I believe his version of the story. He has a family and is as low-key as anyone I know.

During the ensuing investigation, there were conflicts in the story regarding exactly how the gun had fired. The trainee's family insisted on a prosecution. Mark was convicted and served a few years in a work camp.

Like I said, two lives were lost that day. It happened in an instant, and but for the grace of God, that could have been any one of us.

---

*   Not the flashily dressed Mark of the marijuana fields.

One night I got a phone call. Anthony had killed himself, in the office. Another good friend of mine had been present at the time. I remember liking Anthony from day one. He had been assigned to attend advanced undercover school, coincidentally the one I was teaching. He took the job seriously. He had a very easy-going personality and a great smile and attitude. He wanted to excel at UC work, and he did. He worked out of the Los Angeles field division, which had a large group of seasoned UC operators. He was obviously trained well in the field.

I hung up the phone with tears in my eyes. I didn't need to be told the details to know why Anthony had pulled the trigger on himself. He was one of the several undercovers who worked the Waco Branch Davidian investigation. He had posed as a UPS delivery driver after it was reported by UPS that a box had broken open on a previous delivery and was found to contain hand grenade bodies. As with most significant undercover operations, the strategy involving Anthony had been round tabled by agents, bosses, and trainers alike. It was agreed upon as a reasonable attempt to get close to David Koresh, who later would share that he'd been suspicious of the ponytailed UPS driver. As mentioned, after the standoff, the subsequent independent Treasury report—or the Blue Book report, as we called it—hadn't faulted the undercover operators but rather some of the assumptions in the overall strategy. Anthony, however, took this as an assignment of guilt and in his mind took responsibility for the failed raid and the subsequent deaths of our agents. Rather than seeing himself as a courageous hero, he took the blame.

I wish I could say Anthony was my only friend damaged that rainy day in Waco.

Every agent who walks into an undercover operation starts out excited. They know all the bad shit that can happen, but most of us block it out and hope it doesn't happen. I'm certain that is the way my friend Robert

Rodriguez approached his involvement when agreeing to be an under-cover during the David Koresh/Branch Davidian investigation. He did everything right, but his life would end up in turmoil for years to come.

Part of the plan was for Robert to take on the role of a student at the local technical college. As such, he and several other ATF UCs rented a house directly across the road from the Branch Davidian compound. This allowed ATF to have real-time surveillance and collect intelligence on the comings and goings of the cult members. It also allowed Robert to approach the Davidians in a neighborly fashion with hopes that he could infiltrate the group and get eyes on their firearms and explosive viola-tions. So far, so good. Robert was able to ingratiate himself with Koresh and got valuable intelligence from inside the Mount Carmel compound. He later told me that he despised Koresh and could barely stand being around him. Robert was a seasoned guy, so he was able to control his personal feelings.

The Blue Book report later called into question using Robert in lieu of an agent who was younger and closer to college age. I'll just call bull-shit. Appearance is a very small part of undercover if you have game. The report went on to disclose that Koresh had shown some indicators that he didn't completely trust Robert. Let's be clear here. When a madman is planning an apocalypse with a mass murder/suicide ending, he probably is fairly paranoid. If it sounds like I am defending Robert, it is because I am. Although Koresh may have had some suspicions, it did not stop him from allowing Robert to come around and interact with the group. Robert did his job and provided extremely useful evidence and intelligence related to the activities of the Branch Davidians.

On February 28, 1993, with hundreds of ATF agents (staged out of public view) prepared to serve the largest search warrant in American law enforcement history, Robert was asked to do the unthinkable. The senior bosses, who were going to give the "execute" command to initiate the raid, wanted Robert to go back into the Davidian house one more time to get one last look inside. This was barely an hour before ATF would launch the raid. Robert had concerns about whether he could get out in time. I have my personal opinion about why that shouldn't have been asked of Robert, but I wasn't there. I wouldn't arrive for twenty-two more days. Being a good agent and wanting to do all he could do to ensure the safety of his fellow agents, Robert agreed. As has been reported publicly, including testimony before the US Congress, things were about to go to shit for Robert and everybody involved in the investigation.

After entering the compound, as he had dozens of times before, Robert engaged Koresh, who was holding a Bible. A Branch Davidian member, who was also a mail carrier, came in and called David aside. Koresh returned, shaking and visibly anxious, and made some cryptic comments to Robert. The gist was: "ATF is coming."

Koresh had been warned by the mail carrier, who was loyal to Koresh. Minutes earlier, a reporter had unwittingly tipped off the mail carrier by asking where the compound was. Robert nervously excused himself, wanting to warn his fellow agents that they had been compromised. He later told how the walk outside to his truck and the drive back to the UC house, a mere two hundred yards away, felt like the longest trip of his life. He fully expected to be shot in the back.

Upon entering the UC house, he immediately and aggressively relayed the compromise to the agents and senior bosses, who were in the house waiting to give the go-ahead for the raid. Robert adamantly insisted that the operation be aborted. This fact later would be disputed by the bosses present. After the tragic deadly raid, the highest bureau officials denied that Robert had made it clear that the ATF plan was compromised. Other field agents validated Robert's story, but that did not stop ATF upper management from claiming that they "didn't know we were compromised." The falsehood enraged the field agents, and dozens stepped up and spoke to the media. This was when I as well as many others lost faith and trust in our leadership. None of the shot callers really were held accountable for what ensued, and some were later promoted.

The Waco raid drew virtually every SRT team into the fray. Three teams were involved in the initial raid, and those of us on the other teams were called upon during the standoff and subsequent trials. Since the standoff was continuing, and we did not know how long we would be in Waco and on the perimeter, I cut all my hair off and morphed into tactical operator mode. My team remained on the ground through the fire and initial crime scene investigation. When I returned to Atlanta, I was burned out. I stepped away from undercover work and just worked cases for the next year or so, trying to process what I had just been involved in. I wondered if Waco would be the straw that broke ATF's back.

CHAPTER 17

THE COST OF DOING AMERICA'S BUSINESS

Bambi went to a guy to buy some heroin one night, just like any other night. When she met the guy at the door, they started chatting and one of the violators there asked the main violator, "Who's this?" The main violator was stoned and couldn't remember. He said, "Tell the man your name, baby."

Bambi said at that moment it felt like somebody stuck a hot poker through her brain.

"Who am I supposed to be right now?" she wondered. "Am I Bambi, am I Shelly, or am I Michelle? What am I supposed to buy from this guy? Crack? Heroin? Guns?"

This was in the 1990s, and we were all grinding on cases and supporting each other's cases. Bambi had been working so many buys that she literally forgot who she was. Buying a gun one day, crack another, heroin the next, a murder for hire the next—it was all running together. Bam told me she muttered some bullshit, made the deal as fast as she could, and got the fuck out of Dodge. She was scared at what had happened, and it was time for a vacation.

Our bodies are designed to function under peak stress for short periods of time. So generally, the body's physical response of producing dopamine and adrenaline, for example, is a healthy reaction to a threat or danger. But if our bodies produce too much of these naturally created chemicals, we build up a tolerance. In other words, our bodies can be conditioned to have to produce more and more of the substances that allow us to continue functioning under intense mental and emotional strain. It's not unlike the way heroin junkies build up a tolerance and need more dope to get the same high. Bambi and the rest of us were constantly running at red-line capacity. The physical damage alone wore on UCs and could be devastating.

We all know that the mind can be a fragile thing, and there's no doubt that some agents endured significant and debilitating trauma that prevented them from continuing or returning to UC work. But we RatSnakes did not like UC work used as a catchall excuse for disregarding job responsibilities or otherwise fucking up. One of our female agents chalked up three DUIs, two of which were in government vehicles. According to her, it was not alcoholism that caused her problems, it was her undercover exposure. Another UC operator, a supervisor, responded to a fire scene drunk off his ass and in a government vehicle. Yep, it was the UC work.

We felt that the tendency by some to make UC work a scapegoat for gross misconduct or personal problems gave management the I-told-you-so card. In the late 1980s and '90s, several of us fell prey to management attacks, I believe as a direct result of being career UCs and not because we did anything specific to warrant a beatdown. ATF's management structure was heading the way of the FBI, and the newer bosses didn't seem to like RatSnakes tainting new hires in their own images. White, clean-cut men and women ruled the day. They often could not understand the RatSnakes because most of them were not in the field long enough to begin to relate.

I have been a Catholic and a Christian all of my life. I've raised my children with those beliefs. Some of what I have written may have caused you to cringe. I'm guessing you have questioned some of the RatSnakes' methods and many of our actions. Please know that each and every one of the agents praised in this book have given their all so that others will not have to confront evil face-to-face. Many of these agents did so at great personal expense. Many of us were in our twenties when we entered the UC world. In the early days, there were no hard and fast rules beyond being the good guy and not breaking the laws you enforce.

My personal method of trying to stay grounded was and is by faith in God. I attended Mass on Sundays, sometimes even when on operations. I needed to be reminded that I was one of the good guys. I remember early on being confused about the proposition of using deadly force against another human being. I turned to the church and "Three Our Fathers Jack" for guidance. Father Jack came from a family of seven siblings. Four were cops and three were priests. I met him when I was a young patrol officer in Athens. He eventually helped me find the clarity I needed.

Father Jack held confessions only on Saturdays between 4 and 5 PM. If I was working, I'd call out for ten minutes to go do my confession. Once, while I was in the middle of my confession—conducted with the priest and confessor on either side of a privacy screen—my police radio broke squelch. Father Jack just said, "Please continue, Vince." I laughed. No matter what my confession was, he always gave me a penance of three Our Fathers, a.k.a. the Lord's Prayer. When I asked why, he said, "It's just easier to remember."

I believe we ultimately will be judged by God. We RatSnakes already have been judged by those we have served, those we served with, and those who had the advantage of knowing what we didn't know at the time we were asked to do something. Some of us will be judged more harshly than others, I'm sure.

I don't intend to simplify anyone else's job, but at the end of the day a sanitation worker knows he must pick up the trash. A firefighter knows his or her job is to put out fires. A UC's job is essentially defined by mythical duties: seek out evil, dwell among it, and don't be consumed by it. What does that really mean? In the final analysis, I'm not certain I even know. What I do know is that for nearly three decades, I watched brave men and women do their best to execute a job where "gray area" doesn't begin to cover it. For their troubles they have been shot, spit on, pissed on, run over, investigated, and attacked by the agency they served. They have been cut out from the glory, transferred for their own safety, and often seen as a necessary evil. Yet they kept going out into the dirtiest parts of our country. After a successful case, they didn't get to stand in front of a camera or be heralded in front of their family or friends. They were used and then put back in a cage, so to speak, or sometimes discarded altogether.

We all had been warned in the academy what sort of life we were entering. The instructors made it abundantly clear that we were not valued and were always one case away from being discarded if things got shitty. Great pep talk, Charlie and Pat. They told us that in discussions with superiors, we would be referred to simply as "undercover agents," meaning that aspect of our work was believed to be all we brought to the table. Sure enough, there is one such reference I will never forget. Our deputy director was visiting the field offices in Atlanta. When he got to my office, I was pretty excited to meet the big man. Instead, the first words out of my SAC's mouth were, "Mr. Director, meet one of our UC agents." My heart sank. It was all true.

UCs often want to be the quarterback on a case, thereby adding to their responsibilities. As noted earlier, I was trained that, generally speaking, the UC shouldn't also be the case agent. The case agent really should have the quarterback position, and if the case is going to involve undercover work, there's lots to do. Open and maintain the paper flow of the investigation. Ensure that the proper approvals are granted and then extended when needed. Account for all funds being used. Manage and acquire manpower. Oversee and run all aspects of surveillances, UC operations, and security. Ultimately, it falls on the case agent to manage the prosecutorial efforts when the case is done. The UC should be laser focused on gathering intel/ evidence in a lawful manner and not preoccupied with anything else. It does happen that a UC sometimes acts as his/her own case agent, but those are usually one-or-two-days gigs. In-and-out buys, and done. In any case, as a UC, you definitely want a case agent and a supervisor who have significant UC experience, since they are the shot callers on scene.

A lack of coordinated effort and lack of UC tactics severely hampered a case that popped up while I was assigned to Stockton, California. A detective I knew and had worked with while teaching criminal justice at University of the Pacific called me aside one night. He had a case he thought I might be interested in, so I agreed to meet him the next day. From the beginning, I knew this case was a disaster waiting to happen, but shit, we didn't turn down hard cases. I wish I had. In short, it had public corruption (which is really FBI jurisdiction), dope, dirty cops, Hells Angels, and an institutional vendetta against one of the targets by the cops presenting the case to me/ATF. The FBI already had declined the case before the PD brought it to ATF. *That* should have been a clue. Historically, the FBI would jump on about any case to keep it out of ATF hands.

As we formed an ad hoc task force, the power struggles started out of the gate. Our—meaning ATF's—position was the *only* position the task force was allowed to have: ATF case, ATF rules. The task force was split down the middle. Half were super happy ATF was there; the other half resented us coming in. Once we got a commitment (which they would later violate) from the local leadership that ATF would steer this train, we put together a plan. The divided allegiances made it hard. As the case agent, I opted for an infiltration. A UC operation would require a time and asset commitment. The other side wanted to go straight to a wiretap. But this was now my circus, so my monkeys. I began scouring the field for potential UCs who weren't tied up on another case, who could commit the time, and who had the experience. I could not actively participate in this UC operation because of my years of contact with the Hells Angels. I was too well known to them. After reaching out far and wide, I sealed the deal with a UC named Brett. He'd come on when I was in Atlanta, and I'd had a hand in training him. I trusted him. Wanting a female backup for Brett, my supervisor and I vetted a few women for a potential girlfriend role. We decided on DD, a battle-hardened agent who had previous experience in the biker world. She was not optimum for that reason, but after round tabling it with her supervisor, we agreed there probably would not be any overlap from the previous case. This turned out to be a point of contention that the *other* side would later use, erroneously, to scrap the case and go back to the FBI.

As our UCs made great strides getting close to the bad guys, the other faction on the task force began to undermine me and my side. Every day, the word "wiretap" was mentioned. After I'd explained the Federal Rules of Criminal Procedure about a hundred times, the assigned US attorney even made the two-hour trip up from Fresno to meet the task force and explain why a wiretap wasn't appropriate and why we shouldn't/couldn't do it. In plain terms, federal rules state that you must exhaust every other investigative technique before the Department of Justice will sign off on a federal wiretap. Wiretaps are viewed as the most extreme intrusion on an American citizen's rights. Trust me when I say that the other side wasn't dissuaded.

During this time, I had little to no help from ATF in the way of manpower. I had two undercovers from out of town, and support was waning on the local PD side of the house. The undercovers were in limbo. Were we continuing? Did we need to establish a UC residence and more permanent backstopping? My supervisor didn't have a lot of street experience. Before taking the job, he was assigned as a tactical operations officer, meaning one of our electronics geeks. He then moved through a couple office positions before being made a supervisor. From what I saw, he appeared scared of his own shadow when it came to no-shit street work. By the time he was confronted by the local PD bosses regarding the division and animosity between the two sides of the task force, he basically punted and threw me under the bus. At the SAC's direction, he called me one night to say that I was going to be replaced as the lead by someone with much more experience, but I would stay on to direct the case.

My response was along the lines of: "Fuck you. That's bullshit and you know it."

His response was basically: "Yeah, I know, but the SAC said if you don't go along, he will transfer your ass to North Dakota, and he means it."

I said, "And you're gonna lay down and take that shit?"

"Nothing I can do. He's the SAC. You're on your own."

I thought: "Now he isn't just a bad supervisor, he's a pussy too." I ended up being right.

. . . .

In 2005, after a great deal of soul-searching, I reluctantly blew the whistle on corruption within ATF. Specifically, I spoke out against illegal wiretapping in the racketeering case (*US v. Holloway, et al.*, 2009) described above. I wasn't a crusader. But there were so many abuses being perpetrated by certain individuals within the bureau that I couldn't bury my head in the sand. I did initially report the abuses to the San Francisco field division management staff. That ultimately expanded to HQ senior managers, who wanted to shut me up.

My whistle-blowing and complaints to the US Office of Special Counsel were the subject of numerous television and radio interviews. By 2007, I was removed from fieldwork and relegated to a desk job, essentially paid my salary to do next to nothing. No, let me clarify. I was paid full salary and benefits for doing exactly nothing. In 2010, I was featured on a CNN three-part exposé about internal corruption and retaliation, and the floodgates opened. My allegations became small fish compared to some of the reports I was receiving from across the country. My phone rang off the hook with calls of support as well as other agents seeking guidance for how to proceed with their own tales of corruption and mismanagement. In 2012, I was commissioned to write an article for *Townhall* magazine's February issue, in which I discussed ATF corruption relating to the by then infamous Fast and Furious operation.* In October 2012, I unceremoniously was served with termination papers in the parking lot of a Denny's restaurant near Lake Tahoe, California. I filed a whistle-blower reprisal and retaliation lawsuit against ATF.

Jay Dobyns also had filed significant allegations through the Office of Inspector General.

All of this prompted me to set up a website dedicated to cleaning up corruption inside ATF. In 2009, I launched CleanUpATF.org (CUATF),

---

* See excerpt from "Diary of an ATF Whistleblower." *Townhall*, January 30, 2012. https://townhall.com/tipsheet/elisabethmeinecke/2012/01/30/diary-of-an-atf -whistleblower-and-the-corruption-that-led-to-fast-and-furious-n684826

providing a forum for agents and other personnel to voice their grievances and concerns. ATF management's response was quick and predictable. Management launched retaliation against many agents who spoke out. Our acting director Kenneth Melson had *all* ATF computers blocked from accessing CUATF, and the website was heavily monitored by the Department of Justice. I also learned that the bureau sought guidance from main Justice as to whether ATF could take legal action to shut the site down.

CleanUpATF.org offered agents a venue to seek advice and to make their allegations public, with hopes that Congress would take notice. Congress did notice. Thanks to Senator Charles Grassley (Republican from Iowa) and Chairman Darrell Issa (Republican representative from California's 49th District), several congressional inquiries into ATF activities were started.

"Gunwalking" is cop speak for the concept of allowing criminal suspects to "walk" off with guns without police interdiction. This controversial practice became a hot spot of the growing scandal. In 2006, ATF launched Project Gunrunner, an initiative aimed at curtailing US-Mexico cross-border gun and drug trafficking and violence. An offshoot of Project Gunrunner was Operation Fast and Furious, centered in Arizona, by which ATF allowed more than two thousand weapons, including hundreds of AK-47s and .50-caliber rifles, to illegally enter Mexico as part of a sting operation targeting Mexican drug cartels. It later came out that ATF was not able to track most of these guns, and the Mexican government had not been fully apprised of the case. After Border Patrol Agent Brian Terry was gunned down in December 2010 in Arizona, just north of the Mexican border, ATF insiders started anonymously voicing their concerns about Fast and Furious, including posting on CUATF. Many believed that Brian Terry had been killed by foreign nationals illegally in the country and armed with AK-47 rifles thought to be trafficked by Fast and Furious suspects who had not been arrested by ATF.*

Meanwhile, Darren Gil, my old partner from San Francisco, had risen higher than any of our group. He was named the country attaché for the US embassy in Mexico. Early on, in an attempt to help with my lawsuit with ATF, he offered me a job on his overseas team. All I could think of was defending my actions and my honor, and I declined. That single decision was probably the best one I ever have made. In the months and years to follow, headquarters fuckery would challenge Darren to pick between breaking the oath he took and facing career destruction. He was ordered to defer his decisions regarding guns flowing into Mexico and was advised that SAC William Newell of ATF's Phoenix field division would have managerial oversight. Darren eventually lost his job as attaché. We later understood why: Operation Fast and Furious was in full swing and its proponents didn't want Darren muddying the waters.

The problem for Darren was, of course, that Agent Terry had been killed by a gun we/ATF could have intercepted. Darren and I struggled over long telephone conversations to find a reasonable explanation for those guns turning up in Mexico. Neither of us wanted to believe the rumors about the bureau allowing gunwalking across the border. As stories about Operation Fast and Furious popped up on my website, I began conferring with the House and Senate Oversight and Judiciary committees. The scales tipped around March of 2011 when an ATF agent posted on the site under the username Desert Rat. That post opened a Pandora's box. Desert Rat stated that ATF knowingly allowed firearms to cross the US border—guns that ended up in the hands of Mexican narcoterrorists.

---

* There was widespread news coverage of the fallout from Operation Fast and Furious. For example, see Sharyl Attkisson, "A primer on the 'Fast and Furious' scandal." *CBS News*, February 12, 2013. https://www.cbsnews.com/news/a-primer-on-the-fast-and-furious-scandal/

The shit hit the fan, and the media had a heyday. As the main guy in charge of CUATF, journalists, lawyers, and congressional aides wanted to talk to me. In turn I brokered introductions of agents to these people and encouraged the agents to tell their stories. It was a very scary time.

When Arizona-based ATF Agent John Dodson went public on the network news in March 2011, speaking out about Fast and Furious, Darren knew the cross-border gunwalking rumors were true. He'd been kept in the dark about the operation and didn't like it. That same month, Director Melson announced a panel was being formed to review firearms trafficking strategies used by field division managers and special agents. A month later, the House Oversight Committee issued a subpoena for ATF documents. US Attorney General Eric Holder testified that he had only heard of Fast and Furious over recent weeks. He rejected Republican calls for his resignation and ultimately was cited with contempt for failing to turn over documents relating to the failed operation.

One by one, agents and supervisors stepped up and testified before Congress about the gunwalking debacle. When requested, Darren decided to testify and became a voice against the disastrous operation. That was the kiss of death for his career with ATF. He was summoned back to Washington, DC. He called me the night he received word from Director Melson's minions that he had eight days to relocate stateside. That was unheard of but consistent with the corrupt behavior of the bosses running the agency at that time.

In August 2011, the Department of Justice removed Melson as acting director of ATF and assigned him to the Office of Legal Policy. He retired in September 2012.*

I was contacted by the Terry family, who appreciated the sunlight we

---

* For a summary of the congressional case, see "Operation Fast and Furious Fast Facts." *CNN Library*, September 18, 2017. https://www.cnn.com/2013/08/27 /world/americas/operation-fast-and-furious-fast-facts/index.html

were lending to the murder of their loved one. There was little comfort for the fact that our worst fears had come to pass. ATF's ridiculous plan had cost a fellow law enforcement officer his life.

. . . .

I've had years to reflect on whether I made the right choice to speak out against the agency I served and loved. I wouldn't have done anything differently. I took an oath to defend this country's Constitution against all enemies, foreign *and* domestic. I've tried to be fair in my account of what happened. The events discussed above do not reflect on the field agents but on a broken system. I am hopeful but not convinced that the Bureau of ATF will endure and regain its former greatness.

In 2010, Darren Gil made the decision to retire. He and his wife headed for a coastal area. He went on to finish his PhD and now teaches criminal justice and international affairs.

Bird retired, still mired in a lawsuit the government refused to settle. He won his case, but ATF appealed. The presiding judge was so disgusted by the government's conduct toward Jay that he ordered a Special Master to investigate corrupt actions by Department of Justice officials. Unfortunately for Jay, before the investigation could be conducted under the judge's watchful eye, the judge passed away and so did the Special Master's investigation.

Jay came away from his time in ATF banged up and bitter, no doubt. Our conversations these days are less and less about ATF. Honestly, it is hard to find a RatSnake who hasn't suffered some form of retribution at the hands of ATF management. But to a man, or a woman, they will say that if they had it to do all over again, they would.

In my twenty-seven years of service to ATF, I had compiled eleven Special Act or Service Awards and dozens of letters of commendation. I was awarded Special Agent of the Quarter for two consecutive quarters and received the second-highest evaluation possible for twenty consecutive years.* My greatest achievement from a personal standpoint was a 100 percent conviction rate on every case I brought to court during my tenure.

After I reported corruption within my field division and within the bureau, I was transferred six times, suspended three times, and reprimanded three times. There were two failed attempts to terminate me over the course of my lawsuit. Fortunately for me, my allegations were reviewed by the Office of Special Counsel, which ultimately defended me in concert with private counsel. It is extremely significant that the OSC took on my case. The government was fighting the government on this one. My lawsuit dragged on for approximately eight years, spanning two US presidents, five attorneys general, and three ATF directors. It consumed taxpayer resources to the tune of thousands of man-hours and millions of dollars. I hold the retaliatory approach of ATF leadership responsible. The most depressing part was that one of the judges involved in my lawsuit advised me to abandon hope for accountability. She said that almost never happens. She was a wise judge.

I never left my house for even one of the transfers. Four of my last six years in the bureau were spent sitting in a ten-by-ten-foot office with no duties other than to sit in that office. My last two years were spent at my residence in Lake Tahoe, California, still with no duties, but receiving full pay and benefits. If any of that leisure time sounds great, please remember that I was a RatSnake, built for speed and the deep desire to actively serve my country. Those years of forced downtime were tortuous.

My old "friend" Steve M. had jumped on the Hate Vince bandwagon without ever bothering to directly ask me why I'd spoken out to begin with. In my opinion, he deceived and lied and did the agency's dirty work.

---

* Well, you know me. I got that one penalty day at the beach for sending the off-color joke over the email system.

I resented this showboat having any say-so over my career, especially since I and many others thought he'd been a train wreck in the field.* ATF just kept promoting him. One of the last times we clashed was when he was the SAC in San Francisco, and he went after my job, using the guise of an on-the-job injury I'd suffered as a reason to transfer me to a non-agent position in DC, expecting me to quit or retire. He manipulated the system through the ASAC to effect that reassignment. After deposing the ATF bosses in my whistle-blower lawsuit, the government attorney came back after lunch and said that Steve had consented to settle the case and place me back in the field. My attorney and I agreed, only to find out it was merely a stalling tactic and Steve, not for the first time, went back on his word.

In October 2014, ATF settled my lawsuit out of court. I received a significant monetary settlement, my fucking Denny's parking lot termination notice was rescinded, and my official record was cleared. I formally retired that same year. Although prevailing in the grueling lawsuit was a huge victory, I am more gratified knowing that by speaking out perhaps I helped change the world, if only for a minute. This was not how I planned to leave the bureau, but it was what God had planned for me. I learned a long time ago that it is not a perfect world.

I am not bitter. I am proud.

---

* Steve M. loved to show off a braided ponytail he had worn decades earlier and kept on his credenza. I took every chance when he was with somebody in his office to point out that this probably was an OSHA violation. Steve's self-serving style and agent disputes while he was in charge of the San Francisco field division got him a trip back to HQ where he would retire from ATF in obscurity.

CHAPTER 18

··

A SPECIAL PLACE
IN HEAVEN

When people say, "Wow, you're a hero," my response is, "No, not really, but I worked with a bunch." For my part, I tried really hard each and every day as an ATF undercover operator to always take the high ground and never to use my skills for evil—even if that meant a guilty party went free. I tried as best I could to play by the rules. The thing I am most proud of is being allowed to travel with and work beside some of the greats in the business.

The RatSnakes I had the honor to work with don't seek fame, although some have been catapulted into it. We don't need a thank-you. Most of us would say, "No, thank *you*." It was our privilege to serve. We were paid well and received intangible rewards. It's not everywhere in the world that a young punk gets another chance to make good. Or that a woman steps into a predominantly man's world and garners the same respect. Or that a Cajun from Louisiana, a redneck from Montana, or a kid from Puerto Rico are selected to protect presidents and world leaders.

I've talked about the drawbacks to the life we chose, but not all was a dark sacrifice. We had a lot of fun and fucked up a lot of bad individuals. Most of us came out the other side better people for having been RatSnakes. I can tell my sons about the loyalty and dedication of the men and women I served with in the Marines, but that time in my life preceded theirs. When I was a RatSnake, my boys got front-row seats to the love, loyalty, and bravery of the people you have read about in these pages. Those who came before will disagree, and those who come after will disagree, but we, *the* RatSnakes, lived the golden days of ATF.

These people and this job gave me a reason to get up every day. No matter how dark my life has been at times, no matter how beaten and broken I've felt, the RatSnakes have been there for me. We will keep the memories of our group alive as long as we are alive. The walls of the ATF Academy carry some of our pictures, and some of the stories about us will be passed on to future generations of agents. Our history is further immortalized on the walls, ceilings, and urinals of Pam's #1 cop bar and will be there until Pam's is no more. As the bureau continues into a new era, of course, there will be agents and covert operators, but there never will be anything approaching the RatSnakes.

. . . .

Gundo would be the first to go. He had the fleeting moment when he entered management as a first-line supervisor but had the good sense to backtrack. He has since retired with his supercool wife, Kitty, in the Pacific Northwest and also takes care of his ailing mother. He had a couple minor health scares but remains connected to the group and makes our reunions often. Gundo was and is the quiet warrior and yet the same carefree, fun-loving guy we rode with all those years. He still rides his Harley but nowadays with his clothes on. Exposing himself to great peril, he stood up for Bird and me during our lawsuits against ATF. As an operator, he volunteered for every shit detail to come down the pike, and I never saw him without a smile on his face. He taught me much.

Dino is the epitome of the phoenix. A soldier, an officer, both an Army Airborne and honor graduate. A federal prison guard who survived a riot and, finally, a RatSnake. You've read of Dino's successes and a couple failures. Yet Dino didn't just survive, he thrived.

I have joked and made some disparaging remarks about ATF management. I hope that I also have conveyed my great respect and pride in our leadership when they got it right. They certainly got it right when they gave Dino a second chance. I am proud that one of our own rose to executive levels within the bureau. Dino held several ASAC positions and served as an assistant attaché to ATF's Mexico mission. He never forgot where he came from and stays engaged to this day with the Core. He was not afraid to stand toe-to-toe with the bad guys, and he was equally aggressive when standing up to management.

Dino recently retired from the bureau. He and MA live in suburban Atlanta, Georgia, where they are both in the same city for the first time in many years. He spends his time doing consulting work and going to Atlanta Braves games. He and I last saw each other at Bambi's fiftieth birthday party (a.k.a. a gathering of the Kiss My Ass Club, because Bam became eligible to retire that day). We spoke recently, as I was finishing this book, and had plans to see each other at the next RatSnakes reunion.

Bambi clearly is one of the most extraordinary operators in the bureau. She never told another agent no. She never told the bureau no. Because of her devotion and dedication to her chosen profession, despite having several good relationships over the years, she never married or had children. She is still with ATF, although we all hope that she soon joins us in retirement, because she has paid her dues. Despite the challenges of the job over the years, she never lost her big, sweet smile. She has at last found her person. He has two children whom Bambi adores and is helping to raise. He's a great guy, and the RatSnakes have embraced him. Bambi's father, a no-shit American war hero, recently passed away. I never met him, but I know how proud he must have been of his baby girl. Yah did good, Michelle.

I have to give a shout-out to Neta Rice, executive director of the ATF Association of Retirees (ATFAR). Her silver-haired husband, John Rice, ran my ATF Academy class, and he did so with an iron fist. John was an agent's agent and a legend in ATF and our arson program. John passed years ago, and Neta remained at the ATF Academy until she retired. During that time, she took each and every one of us RatSnakes under her protective wing. Having lived the life, she understood and took pity on this young, crazy bunch and did her best to protect us from ourselves. Most of us stay in touch with her to this day.

Charlie has survived over twenty years in retirement and by all accounts is loving life in the Southeast. From time to time, he posts pictures of his houseboat and his classic car. After leaving ATF, he took his lifelong skills and experience and built the most unique and successful private advanced undercover training business in the country. He often calls upon RatSnakes to teach and enhance his program. Charlie has remained loyal to the core of agents he trained, and we cross paths on occasion, the last time being at Box's retirement party. He suffered the tragic loss of his wife but has since remarried the new love of his life. I often wonder if he knows what high regard we hold him in and how many lives he probably saved.

Patrick Kelly, again, may you eternally rest in peace. Shortly after our reunion to celebrate Patty's life, he passed away due to cancer. He left behind his wife, Gina, who stays in our lives and prayers to this day. I saw Pat a few years back for his seventy-fifth birthday party. Care to guess where the party was held? Charlie rented a limousine for us to ride in to the gathering. All the old, crusty and the new, young, wet-behind-the-ears RatSnakes attended. It was a walk down memory lane with a handful of heroes who by this time had been featured on *60 Minutes*, *20/20*, the History Channel, and National Geographic. A couple were *New York Times* best-selling authors. A few were TV and movie stars. At the end of the day, I guess that's not so surprising: they were RatSnakes.

Jimm—the first guy I met in federal law enforcement and with whom I am in touch to this day—finally pulled the pin and retired to the southeastern United States with his wife, Nina. Jimm had risen to legendary status during the widely acclaimed Warlocks infiltration case. He later got a chance for a change of scenery and moved his young family to FLETC and joined Box running the undercover program. He always was a standout agent. A month before his retirement, Jimm called me from a surveillance he was on to bounce some ideas off me. He was by himself, overlooking a target location where he would make one last cold knock. Less than two months away from putting all of this behind him, he was still risking his ass to make that one last buy to get one more illegal weapon off the streets.

Jimm helped me throughout my life, personally and professionally, including assisting throughout my dispute with ATF. Loyal to the end, he has nearly talked me into leaving Lake Tahoe and taking up with him and many other retired ATF agents in the Southeast.

Toward the end, Box paid the price for being vocal about the treatment some of us RatSnakes were receiving at the end of our careers. It cost him a fairly cushy job as the spokesman for ATF in Tampa. Fortunately, he still had friends at the top and found a soft landing as a polygraph examiner. In fact, he was the only Spanish-speaking polygrapher in the field. Box retired in 2016, and he and Carmen, now also retired, left Miami but not Florida. Box continued doing polygraph examinations for other agencies for a period of time after retiring from ATF. He now is completely retired and by all accounts just having fun with his sexy baby mama. Rarely a day goes by that either Box or Carmen aren't sending pics of their grandbabies. He is the main coordinator of our RatSnakes reunions.

If you want to know more about Jay Dobyns nowadays, just turn on the TV. He is a featured guest on talk radio and television specials surrounding his time in biker hell. His *New York Times* best seller *No Angel* is being adapted into a feature film. His latest book, *Catching Hell*, was released in 2018. He consulted on and also acted in the 2018 Gerard Butler film *Den of Thieves*. Bird also coaches youth football and continues to inspire young athletes in his home state of Arizona.

Jay and I previously collaborated on projects featuring the RatSnakes and undercover operations. Bird has kind of changed lanes and signed on with a group of veterans and first responders who provide training and services to those banged up psychologically from their careers. Jay and I crashed like two trains running head-on in a tunnel. What brought that on is between Jay and me, and as far as I'm concerned, it will remain that way.

Milton had seen a lot and done a lot, and he grew weary of undercover work, the demands of the field, and the wear and tear on his well-being. He ultimately stepped into a first-line supervisor position. By all accounts, he was the guy you wanted to work for, although, sadly, he slowly stepped farther and farther away from some of the RatSnakes. None of us will forget his presence for decades or his damn low-country boil. I was a better agent for having known and worked with him. We still talk from time to time, and he is enjoying his retirement. Hopefully, we will meet again soon, but if not, I knew a hero and nobody can take that away from me.

On February 28, 1993, a fragile cease-fire had been secured between ATF and the Waco Branch Davidians. ATF had to tend to our dead and wounded. Milton and three other agents had to holster their weapons and proceed to the inner courtyard of the compound to rescue team leader

Kenneth King, who was badly wounded. At each window they passed, there were taunts and threats from the Branch Davidians, who had weapons pointed at the agents. The four agents secured Ken and loaded him onto a ladder because no stretchers were available. Then they had to walk back past those same windows and then down the long driveway to safety. They could have been executed at any point, but they weren't leaving without our wounded agent. For me, that level of heroism in battle represented the very best of ATF.*

. . . .

As I come to the end of this book, I wonder if I have done the RatSnakes justice. I wonder whether I have conveyed the courage, the honor, the integrity, and the sacrifices they made for their fellow Americans. I have spent the last few months at my computer, sometimes in awe, sometimes laughing my ass off. I got to recall the joy I felt going to work every day with these people. Knowing they would be the ones to come crashing through a door or tearing down a wall to save me if things broke bad. These were their stories, not mine. I just felt compelled to tell them.

---

* Word is that Milton may in fact attend our next RatSnakes reunion. That would be awesome.

....

SMOKIN' AND JOKIN'

What the hell. Here are a few more stories for the road.

THE RED CARPET, THE CAUSEWAY,
AND THAT ANNOYING CIA GUY

One UC academy class was particularly long, and the students performed well. They worked through every problem and advanced the UC scenario for the next day. Because they did so well, we thought we should celebrate, and it was off to Pam's #1. We didn't need a reason to celebrate. Advanced UC school was a rite of passage of sorts. Agents could establish relationships that would advance their street cred and make a name for themselves. I'm certain that many of the shenanigans were directed at fitting in. Don't get me wrong, this was a group of overachievers who worked the scenarios like the pros they were. But they also were a bunch of high-octane agents thrown in with a bunch of high-octane instructors. It was a perfect storm.

It was getting late at Pam's, and Darren and I had to make it across the causeway to Brunswick without getting arrested. He was driving, and if I haven't mentioned it before now, Darren had a thing about speed. So, there we were at 3 AM on the main drag, heading toward the F. J. Torras Causeway at about ninety miles per hour, and not for any reason other than Darren liked it.

I spotted a chick hitchhiking on the side of the road and hollered, "Let's give her a ride." Darren slammed on the brakes and came sliding sideways up to the hitchhiker. I should note that at this time I was divorced. Not that being divorced made picking up a hooker at 3 AM okay. More precarious for us was that a Georgia state trooper had seen it all go down. When he pulled us over, I had somebody on my lap who shouldn't have been, Darren had a gun on him he shouldn't have had, and we were both drunk.

The trooper had no sense of humor and did not care what kind of badges anybody had. He said, "Really, a hundred miles per hour?" Darren replied, "My speedometer only said ninety, sir."

The trooper had Darren in cuffs at the back of the vehicle and was in the process of telling me to "shut the fuck up," when, in a desperate Hail Mary pass, I asked that he not contact our supervisory instructors.

The trooper decided that would be the perfect punishment and would save him a buttload of paperwork. He demanded my supervisor's telephone number, and I hesitantly gave it to him. At least, I pretended to hesitate.

Within ten minutes, Box and Jimm rolled up. They got out of their car and came over and started chewing on Darren's and my asses, threatening every punishment possible. They put on quite the show. This satisfied the trooper, and he uncuffed Darren and turned us over to our bosses. The trooper had no way to know that we all had left the same bar thirty minutes earlier.

Not lost in the irony of this entire debacle is that by this time, the great Pat Kelly had retired from ATF. One of his first postretirement jobs was as chief of the FLETC police. The base has its own federal police force that provides security for the center as well as protecting the well-being of students and employees. Believe it or not, crimes have occurred right on the facility, and I'm not talking about just misdemeanors. There have been reports of drug use, sexual assaults, thefts, and other crimes at FLETC over the years. Granted, they are few and far between, but every now and then a questionable hire slips through the cracks. Although Pat chose not to stay in that position very long, I can't help but believe that our collective foolishness didn't help the cause. That is purely my opinion. Not every UC class that graced St. Simons Island was as raucous as this one.

In fact, we couldn't leave the center after this class graduated without at least one more incident, now could we? The story goes that in the final days of class, there was a verbal confrontation with a student from the CIA's uniform division. The argument allegedly escalated to one or two of the females from our class threatening to throw the CIA employee off of his balcony. He went crying to the base police.

Several of the students happened to be returning to the center after this incident. Several of them may or may not have been involved. So, when their vehicle approached the gate and they were asked for their IDs, in true UC fashion, they all provided fake IDs. The problem was they were riding in the exact same vehicle described by the pussy CIA guy. When interviewed by IA, they were able to explain it away by saying they were just practicing their UC techniques. Box and Jimm backed 'em up.

ONE OF THESE THINGS IS NOT LIKE THE OTHERS

After a night of drinking off base from FLETC, a couple of us were standing in the parking lot, shooting the shit at 2:30 AM. My companion, we'll call him "Box," was one of the permanent instructors at the ATF Academy. "Box" casually popped his trunk open. Whatever he was doing didn't catch my attention until I saw that in his trunk he had about thirty red-handled training pistols, all in holsters. The red handle designated the guns as inert, unable to fire, welded shut, and easily identifiable to police and civilians. "Box" was babbling about whatever, probably trying to distract me. Even in my highly intoxicated state, I noticed that one pistol on top of the pile did *not* have a red handle and was not in a holster. Even though the instructor was a career-long friend of mine, I immediately registered danger. He was reaching for the black-handled pistol, and I couldn't react. My brain was forming the words, but my drunk mouth wouldn't let them come out.

Within two seconds, he jerked the pistol out of the trunk and fired one shot, right between my feet. I felt a sting on my right calf. I froze. I looked at him in shock as he tossed the gun back in the trunk, closed the lid, and began to enter the driver's side of the vehicle.

I mumbled, "I think you fucking shot me, bro."

Without a word, he started the car, slipped it into drive, and sped off.

I looked down and could see the bullet impacted in the blacktop. I looked at my leg. No blood. It probably was just some frag that hit my leg. I hollered after the disappearing vehicle: "Fuck you, motherfucker! That shit ain't funny!"

I then realized I'd better haul ass so I didn't have to explain to the local cops what happened. Truth be known, it was funny as hell. At least, we thought so.

SPECIAL SPOUSES

Being the significant other of a no-shit UC operator requires a special kind of crazy. My third wife—I know, the jokes write themselves—quickly learned what she was up against. Shortly after Robyn and I began dating, the RatSnakes got together at my house in Lawrenceville, Georgia. Robyn was just dropping by to get the key to my pool so she and her kids could use it later when we were all gone. She was met by an agent named Fitz, butt-ass naked, throwing a football in my front yard with another member of the crew. Being drop-dead gorgeous, Robyn was like a magnet to a drunk-ass Fitz.

It was just really bad timing on her part. I hadn't had an opportunity to ease her into the fold. After explaining to Robyn that Fitz played football for the Dallas Cowboys, which he didn't, and how he loved kids, which he didn't, I handed her my key and said, "Run." She did.

A year later, our second annual Core reunion happened in Panama City, Florida. I invited Robyn to come along—and then for several weeks warned her not to. This would be her second exposure to the RatSnakes. We drove all day and got to the rental house late and exhausted. Box showed us our room, and we just wanted to crash and then jump into the fray the next morning. I knew that was never going fly, but I tried. Five minutes after I'd closed, locked, and then barricaded the bedroom door, which kind of freaked Robyn out, all hell broke loose.

I thought the pounding would bring the door right out of the frame. Four or five voices were screaming: "Oh, *fuuuck* no, Cefalu. Get out here, you pussy. We got Jack. Wake the fuck up!"

I didn't even try to ignore them, as it would just encourage them. I just said to put some clothes on quickly, and then I opened the door. Milton fell through the doorway, followed by Gundo, Fitz, and Box, who had ratted us out. After hugs and kisses were exchanged by the guys, they all wanted to plant a sloppy welcome-aboard kiss on Robyn. Welcome to the RatSnakes, baby. I looked over my shoulder at her as I left the room and said, "I warned you." I walked out to the pool where everybody else was gathered, laughing.

The next time I saw Robyn, she was being dragged across the yard toward the pool, hanging on to her favorite pair of Victoria's Secret panties, with one of the RatSnakes holding on to the other end of the lingerie. By the time they got to the pool, the panties were stretched to a size sixty-four. I heard Robyn say, "You can have 'em now, fucker, but you owe me new panties."

There was nothing else to do but marry her.

RANDY'S PANTS

Admittedly, this may be my all-time favorite experience. Remember ex-cop Randy? On this day, there was a plan for Randy to go to a violator's house, buy an illegal machine gun, and leave. He already had met with and bought drugs from this particular violator, so we weren't too worried. A bad guy usually won't risk pulling a rip-off in his own house. But because the violator picked the location, we had a substantial cover team using both long-range still photography as well as video of the outside of the house for evidentiary purposes. In hindsight, I wish we hadn't video recorded this one, and so does Randy.

The violator's meth-driven paranoia kicked in that day. Randy walked up onto the porch and knocked on the door. The bad guy opened the door just a crack, and we heard over the wire, "Man, are you a cop?" Randy said, "What the fuck, man. Let me in." The violator said, "You wearin' a wire?"

This question was met with a classic Randy play. Right there in front of God and everybody, in a neighborhood at high noon, Randy unbuckled his belt, unbuttoned his shirt, and dropped trou. I mean around his ankles, underwear and all. In a nanosecond, the violator ripped open the door and was yelling at Randy, "Jesus, man. All right, all right, come in."

A textbook buy went down that day—well, it was textbook until Randy's dick was seen waving in the wind. The video had to be turned over to the defense, who made enough noise that ATF had to give Randy a few days on the beach. The violator went to prison.

. . . .

RatSnakes forever. Forever RatSnakes.

—**Vincent A. Cefalu**

GLOSSARY

The following terms and acronyms are commonly used in law enforcement and undercover work.

TERMS OF THE TRADE

Assistant Special Agent in Charge (ASAC): *Slang:* ASACK. The second-highest-ranking official in an ATF field division. Some of the larger field divisions have two ASACs.

Briefing: Prior to any undercover operation, all involved law enforcement personnel gather to receive a comprehensive overview of the case and the planned operation. Briefing content includes times, dates, pictures of undercover agents and violators, contingency plans, individual and team assignments, and weaponry.

Bust Signal: A predetermined verbal or visual signal used by an undercover agent to communicate distress or trouble or to initiate an arrest.

Buy Bust: An undercover operation intended to culminate in the immediate arrest of the violator(s).

Buy Walk: An undercover operation intended to purchase contraband and then let the violator(s) leave. This tactic is used to continue buying contraband or to allow the agent(s) to perfect the case before arrests are made.

Confidential Informant: *Slang:* CI, informant, snitch, rat. A person willing to provide information on a criminal friend or associate or a group of such. CIs sometimes make undercover purchases and wear wires. CIs may make introductions to violators and vouch for undercover agents. CIs sometimes work for money. Some try to "work off" existing charges. Others are just concerned citizens or wannabe cops.

Debriefing: After every operation, the same parties originally briefed will reconvene to identify what worked well and what didn't work so well. Reporting and evidence assignments as well as corrections to future operations often occur during debriefings.

Field Division: Formerly called "districts," a divisional section of ATF organized geographically. At the time of this writing, ATF had twenty-six field divisions. Depending on size and population, a field division might encompass one state (such as the Atlanta Field Division, which oversees Georgia), part of a state (Florida is split between the Miami and Tampa Field Divisions), or multiple states (the San Francisco Field Division oversees Northern California and Nevada).

Field Office or Group: The specific squad or unit responsible for a designated area within a field division.

Group Supervisor: *Slang:* Group Supe. The first-line supervisor for squads located in the same city as the field division. The Group Supervisor designation is used to avoid confusion; a Group Supervisor is the equivalent of a Resident Agent in Charge. For example, first-line supervisors in the city of Atlanta are called Group Supervisors; in Macon and Savannah they carry the title Resident Agent in Charge.

Headquarters: *Slang:* HQ, Puzzle Palace. Refers to ATF headquarters located at 99 New York Avenue, NE, Washington, DC 20226.

Operator: Often used interchangeably with "agent." SWAT and SRT team members refer to themselves as operators. Undercover agents are also referred to as operators.

Organized Crime Drug Enforcement Task Force (OCDETF): A multiagency task force originally formed by then Vice President George H. W. Bush to besiege the cocaine cowboys primarily in South Florida. These task forces were later expanded to large cities.

Panic Button: *Slang:* "Oh, shit" button. A small battery-operated pressure switch that when depressed sends out a unique squelching sound over police radios to signal distress.

Props: Items used to enhance an undercover appearance. Anything can be used as a prop to give a violator a reason to believe an agent is a bad guy. Something as simple as a set of drug scales on a kitchen table can be a prop. The term can also refer to guns ATF uses to show violators. There are other, more elaborate props that intentionally are not discussed in this book.

Resident Agent in Charge (RAC): *Slang:* Rack. First-line supervisor serving outside an ATF field division's primary city.

Special Agent in Charge (SAC): *Slang:* SACK. The top boss in each ATF field division.

Street Theater: A planned or choreographed set of events to convince violators that the undercover agent is a legitimate bad guy.

Undercover: *Slang:* UC, operator, RatSnake. An undercover agent. The term also refers to an undercover operation.

Wire: A transmitter usually worn secretly on the person or placed at a particular location. For the purposes of this book, the term specifically refers to the Kel kit.

COMMONLY USED ACRONYMS

AO: Area of Operation

ASAC: Assistant Special Agent in Charge. *See above.*

ATF (also BATFE): Bureau of Alcohol, Tobacco, Firearms and Explosives

ATFAR: ATF Association of Retirees

ATTU: Alcohol Tobacco Tax Unit of the IRS

CI: Confidential Informant. *See above.*

CIA: Central Intelligence Agency

DEA: Drug Enforcement Administration

EOD: Explosive Ordinance Disposal

ETB: Explosive Technology Branch of the ATF

FAA: Federal Aviation Administration

FBI: Federal Bureau of Investigation

FFL: Federal Firearms Licensee

FINCIN: Financial Crimes Network

FLETC: Federal Law Enforcement Training Center

FMTT: Fuck Me to Tears*

FNG: Fucking New Guy†

FTS: Federal Telecommunications System

IA: Internal Affairs

IED: Improvised Explosive Device

ILEA: International Law Enforcement Academy

IRS: Internal Revenue Service

NCIC: National Crime Information Center of the FBI

OCDETF: Organized Crime Drug Enforcement Task Force. *See above.*

OIG: Office of Inspector General

---

* Not an officially sanctioned term.

† Also not an officially sanctioned term.

OMO: Outlaw Motorcycle Organization

OPSEC: Operational Security

PC: Probable Cause

PD: Police Department

RAC: Resident Agent in Charge. *See above.*

RICO Act: Racketeer Influenced and Corrupt Organizations Act

ROI: Report of Investigation

SA: Special Agent

SAC: Special Agent in Charge. *See above.*

SRT: Special Response Team(s)

SWAT: Special Weapons and Tactics

TEA: Treasury Enforcement Agent test

TECS: Treasury Enforcement Communications System

TOO: Tactical Operations Officer

TSA: Transportation Security Administration

USSS: United States Secret Service

ACKNOWLEDGMENTS

Thank you for taking the time to read this far. Don't be a slacker now. Hell, you may just be mentioned in my acknowledgments.

I first want to thank Beth Davey, my agent, and Kevin Lake for encouraging this project. Thank you to Glenn and the whole staff at BenBella Books for taking a chance on me, a virtual unknown. You could have picked anybody. (Of course, because of your good judgment, you're gonna get even richer than you already are.) Karen Lacey, you got me in the door. Laurel Leigh, the stars aligned for me and this book when you agreed to edit my book. In my humble opinion, you took a good book and turned it into a great book.

To all my ATF brothers and sisters, thanks for letting me be part of a great team. What can I say about the RatSnakes? This book is for you, about you, and because of you. You ARE my family.

To my kids, thank you for giving me a reason to push harder every day.

Mom and Dad, there is nothing I can say that would equal your unconditional love and devotion. I miss you.

To Hanna Boys Center and all of the juvenile justice professionals for never giving up on me. To the Athens Police Department and all of the officers, detectives, and staff who raised me in this business and taught me that being a cop is about being a guardian of our communities and not just a cool ass job. To Lou and Mac, Joe, Larry, Bill, Joyce, Uncle Ron, Bob, and all those who taught me how to be a special agent and a UC operator, thank you. To all my partners, Bird, Darren, Bob, Steve, Butch, I love you guys. Thanks for keeping me alive and probably out of jail.

Chuck Mote, you saved my ass. To Gary and the boys at Polk Springs, thank you for taking me in. To Mary Lynn, you will always be the boss of me.

And finally, to all of you who have purchased this book, thank you from the bottom of my heart.

ABOUT THE AUTHOR

VINCENT A. CEFALU was born and raised in the San Francisco Bay Area. After leaving to join the United States Marine Corps, he served six years overseas and stateside. Upon receiving his honorable discharge from the Marines, he hired on with the Athens-Clarke County Police Department where he served as a patrolman for almost four years.

Upon completion of his bachelor's degree in criminal justice, he was hired by the United States Customs Service and assigned to Key West, Florida, where he spent almost two years chasing smugglers. Cefalu ultimately found a home with ATF as a special agent. He went on to complete his master's degree and served in many capacities with ATF before retiring in 2014. He has two sons and three stepchildren, a daughter and two sons.

He spends his days teaching, riding his Harley, drinking, having fun. He offers up his free time to local senior citizens and law enforcement charities. This is Cefalu's first book, though not his first published work.